Visual Basic® 6 Database Programming For Dummies®

Cheat Sheet

T0254532

Microsoft Jet Database Engine Types

Data Type	Size	Description
BINARY	1 byte per character (as large as you need)	You can store *any* kind of data as a binary type. The database engine does nothing to it, so what you put in is precisely what you get back out, bit for bit.
BIT	1 byte	True or False (1 or 0) only.
BYTE	1 byte	An integer value between 0 and 255.
COUNTER	4 bytes	Used for AutoNumbered fields (also called AutoIncremental fields — see Chapter 2) where the Jet engine provides a unique identification number for each record added to a table.
CURRENCY	8 bytes	A scaled integer between -922,337,203,685,477.5808 and 922,337,203,685,477.5807.
DATETIME	8 bytes	A date or time value between the years 100 and 9999.
GUID	128 bits	A unique identification number generated for use with remote procedure calls.
SINGLE	4 bytes	A single-precision floating-point value with a range of -3.402823E38 to -1.401298E-45 for negative values, 1.401298E-45 to 3.402823E38 for positive values, and 0.
DOUBLE	8 bytes	A double-precision floating-point value with a range of -1.79769313486232E308 to -4.94065645841247E-324 for negative values, 4.94065645841247E-324 to 1.79769313486232E308 for positive values, and 0. Both the DATETIME and COUNTER data types are DOUBLEs.
SHORT	2 bytes	A short integer (between -32,768 and 32,767).
LONG	4 bytes	A long integer (between -2,147,483,648 and 2,147,483,647).
LONGTEXT (Memo)	1 byte per character. Zero to a maximum of 1.2 gigabytes.	This is sometimes called a *Memo* data type.
LONGBINARY	Expands as needed from 0 to a maximum of 1.2 gigabytes.	Employed with OLE objects.
TEXT	1 byte per character	Between 0 and 255 characters.

FOR DUMMIES
BESTSELLING BOOK SERIES

Visual Basic® 6 Database Programming For Dummies®

Cheat Sheet

Shortcut Keys for the Visual Basic Editor

To Do This	Press These Shortcut Keys
Display the GoTo Line dialog box	Ctrl+G
Move to the bottom of the current window	Ctrl+Page Down
Move to the top of the current window	Ctrl+Page Up
Move left one word	Ctrl+←
Move right one word	Ctrl+→
Move left one character	←
Move right one character	→
Move up one line	↑
Move down one line	↓
Move to the start of the current line or the start of the text on that line	Home
Move to the end of the current line	End
Move to the beginning of the document	Ctrl+Home
Move to the end of the document	Ctrl+End
Move to the next pane in the current window	F6
Move to the previous pane	Shift+F6
Move the insertion cursor to the beginning of the page	Page Up
Move the insertion cursor to the end of the page	Page Down
Scroll up one line	Ctrl+↑
Scroll down one line	Ctrl+↓

The Five LockTypes in ADO

LockType	Constant	Description
Read-only	adLockReadOnly	No editing allowed (the default)
Pessimistic	adLockPessimistic	Locks records at once during editing
Optimistic	adLockOptimistic	Locks records only when you use the Update command
	AdLockBatchOptimistic	Defers all updates until you complete the batch update

The Four ADO Cursor Types

Cursor Type	Constant
Forward-only (usually the default)	adOpenForwardOnly
Keyset-driven	adOpenKeyset
Dynamic	adOpenDynamic
Static	adOpenStatic

For Dummies: Bestselling Book Series for Beginners

Visual Basic® 6
Database Programming

FOR

DUMMIES®

Visual Basic® 6 Database Programming FOR DUMMIES®

by Richard Mansfield

WILEY

Wiley Publishing, Inc.

Visual Basic® 6 Database Programming For Dummies®

Published by
Wiley Publishing, Inc.
111 River Street
Hoboken, NJ 07030
www.wiley.com

Copyright © 1999 Wiley Publishing, Inc., Indianapolis, Indiana

Published simultaneously in Canada

For general information on our other products and services or to obtain technical support, please contact our Customer Care Department within the U.S. at 800-762-2974, outside the U.S. at 317-572-3993, or fax 317-572-4002.

Wiley also publishes its books in a variety of electronic formats. Some content that appears in print may not be available in electronic books.

Library of Congress Cataloging-in-Publication Data:

Library of Congress Catalog Card No.: 99-65862

ISBN: 0-7645-0625-0

10 9 8 7 6 5 4
1B/SQ/QU/QU/IN

About the Author

Richard Mansfield has written 22 computer books, four of which became bestsellers: *Machine Language for Beginners*, *The Second Book of Machine Language*, *The Visual Guide to Visual Basic*, and *The Visual Basic Power Toolkit* (with Evangelos Petroutsos).

He used to write two columns and frequent articles in computer magazines, but for the past ten years he has focused full-time on writing books. Overall, his books have sold more than 500,000 copies worldwide and have been translated into nine languages.

But that's not the whole story. He's startlingly sedentary, preferring to sit and read, write, or program his computers instead of move around. Cooking is a favorite hobby, and a serious workout by his standards. The old adage holds true for him: When he feels the urge to exercise, he lies down until it passes.

He understands that extensive — indeed marathon — sitting goes against the current American pursuits of running, lite food, fast mall-walking, leaping about in aerobics groups, age-defying, and other forms of bodily denial and self-discipline.

He's hoping for the best, nevertheless, and so far, so good.

Dedication

This book is dedicated to my brother, John.

Author's Acknowledgments

First, I'd like to thank my acquisitions editor, Debra Williams Cauley, for her thoughtful suggestions and balanced overview. More than once, she offered invaluable advice.

When I consider the suggestions offered during author review by the editor of this book, John Pont, and the technical editor, Nickolas Landry, the one word that comes to mind is *exacting*.

Sometimes, you get a thoroughgoing project editor, and sometimes, a thoroughgoing technical editor. Rarely do you get two such editors on the same book. Although they certainly put me to the test with their detailed feedback on my manuscript, I think the result justifies all our efforts. In the end, this book is stronger, tighter, and has greater technical depth thanks to their substantial input. Their persistent striving for excellence benefits all involved with the book, not least the readers. I hope you agree.

And throughout the entire process of preparing this book for publication, neither of these fine people became, in the medical sense of the word, frenetic. As far as I know.

Publisher's Acknowledgments

We're proud of this book; please send us your comments through our online registration form located at www.dummies.com/register/.

Some of the people who helped bring this book to market include the following:

Acquisitions, Editorial, and Media Development

Project Editor: John W. Pont

Acquisitions Editor: Debra Williams Cauley

Technical Editor: Nickolas Landry, MCSD

Editorial Manager: Mary C. Corder

Editorial Assistants: Beth Parlon, Alison Walthall

Production

Project Coordinator: Regina Snyder

Layout and Graphics: Brian Drumm, Kate Jenkins, Clint Lahnen, Barry Offringa, Tracy Oliver, Jill Piscitelli, Doug Rolleson, Brent Savage, Jacque Schneider, Michael A. Sullivan, Maggie Ubertini, Dan Whetstine, Erin Zeltner

Proofreaders: Christine Pingleton, Marianne Santy, Rebecca Senninger, Ethel M. Winslow

Special Help
Jodi Jensen, Stephanie Koutek, James Russell, Suzanne Thomas, Korina Wilbert

---

Publishing and Editorial for Technology Dummies
Richard Swadley, Vice President and Executive Group Publisher
Andy Cummings, Vice President and Publisher
Mary C. Corder, Editorial Director

Publishing for Consumer Dummies
Diane Graves Steele, Vice President and Publisher
Joyce Pepple, Acquisitions Director

Composition Services
Gerry Fahey, Vice President of Production Services
Debbie Stailey, Director of Composition Services

Contents at a Glance

Cartoons at a Glance

By Rich Tennant

page 9

page 347

page 87

page 35

page 217

page 303

page 163

page 123

Cartoon Information:
Fax: 978-546-7747
E-Mail: richtennant@the5thwave.com
World Wide Web: www.the5thwave.com

Table of Contents

Introduction

* *

Welcome to the world of database programming in Visual Basic 6. Microsoft has put many of its best cutting-edge tools into this powerhouse package. And this book shows you how to use these great tools.

Visual Basic 6 is both powerful and diverse. If you want to do almost *anything* with database programming, you can do it with Visual Basic. But, best of all, many of Visual Basic's features are designed to be easy to use. The tools include hundreds of efficiencies, step-through wizards, and shortcuts. For example, even if you have no experience at all in adding a database to an application, you can find out how to do just that in about five minutes. (Seriously! See Chapter 3.)

Of course, other tasks are not as rapidly accomplished. Otherwise, this book would be five pages long, and people wouldn't be paid much for database programming.

Want to connect a Web page to a database? Want to design a brand-new database? Those jobs do take longer. How much longer depends on what you want the Web site to do or how complex your database is. But if you can click a mouse, write ordinary Visual Basic programming, and follow straightforward directions, you can do the job. This book shows you how to create effective Windows database applications and Web pages with database connections.

About This Book

My main job in *Visual Basic 6 Database Programming For Dummies* is to show you the best way to accomplish the various jobs that, collectively, contribute to successful database programming in VB. If a task requires programming, I show you, step-by-step, how to write that programming. In other cases, I tell you when there's a simpler, better way to accomplish a job. Otherwise, you could spend days hand-programming something that's already been built — something you can create by clicking a simple menu option, adding a prebuilt component, or using a template. Because Visual Basic 6 is so huge, you can easily overlook the many shortcuts it contains. I've been on the betas for VB for about ten years now, and I was on the VB 6 technical beta for nearly a year during its development. I've also written several books on Visual Basic. All modesty aside, I do know Visual Basic well.

Unlike some other books about Visual Basic database programming (they must remain nameless), this book is written in plain, clear English. You can find sophisticated tasks made easy: The book is filled with step-by-step examples that you can follow, even if you've never written a line of database programming or designed anything.

Visual Basic does require some brains and practice to master, but you can handle it. To make this book as valuable for you as possible without writing a six-volume life's work on all of Visual Basic's database-related features and functions, I geared this book toward familiarizing you with the most useful tools. You use them to create either Windows or Web database applications. There are dozens of ways to get a job done in VB, but there's always one way that's best — most sturdy, most effective, and, often, most efficiently programmed.

How to Use This Book

This book obviously can't cover every feature of all the Visual Basic applications. Instead, as you try the many step-by-step examples in this book, you'll become familiar with the most useful features of Visual Basic database programming and many of the shortcuts and time-saving tricks — some that can take years to discover on your own.

Whether you want to create stunning Web sites or impressive Windows applications, this book tells you how to get where you want to go with applications that use databases. It's estimated that 80 percent of VB programs written today *do* involve databases — so if you haven't programmed with databases before, you're likely to find yourself working with them pretty soon.

The following are just a few of the goals that you can achieve with this book:

- ✔ Build professional-looking, effective database programs.
- ✔ See how to move Windows applications to an intranet or the Internet (and be smart enough to know when to use wizards to help).
- ✔ Make the transition from Microsoft's traditional DAO (Data Access Objects) to the new ADO (ActiveX Data Objects) technologies.
- ✔ Understand how to best use the many database features built into Visual Basic 6.
- ✔ Kill bugs in Windows applications or Web sites.
- ✔ Get the most out of VB's Data Environment Designer.
- ✔ Know how to use SQL, the database query language.

Many people think that programming is hard to do. And that database programming is even harder. It doesn't have to be. In fact, some common database jobs have already been written into VB, so you don't have to do the programming at all. If you're smart, you don't re-invent the wheel. Sometimes, all you need to know is *where* in VB to find the components, wizards, templates, and other prebuilt solutions. Then, drop them into your application. And when you do want to program, Visual Basic often makes the job both easy and very enjoyable.

This book tells you if a particular wheel has already been invented. It also shows you how to save time by using or modifying existing templates to fit your needs instead of building new solutions from scratch. But if you're doing something totally original (congratulations!), this book gives you many step-by-step recipes for creating database applications from the ground up.

Foolish Assumptions

In writing this book, I had to make a few assumptions about you, dear reader. I assume that you know how to use Visual Basic's editor and understand Visual Basic programming in general. I also assume that you don't know much about database programming. Perhaps most importantly, I assume that you don't want lots of extraneous details — you just want to get the database programming job done.

How This Book Is Organized

The overall goal of *Visual Basic 6 Database Programming For Dummies* is to provide an understandable reference for the Visual Basic programmer. This book will be accessible to developers and programmers with little or no database programming experience.

The book is divided into eight parts, with several chapters in each part. But just because the book is organized doesn't mean you have to be. You don't have to read the book in sequence from Chapter 1 to the end, just like you don't have to read a cookbook in sequence.

If you want to create a report, go right to Chapter 6. You're not expected to know what's in Chapter 4 before you can get results in Chapter 6. Similarly, within each chapter, you can scan the headings and jump right to the section covering the task that you want to accomplish. No need to read each chapter from start to finish. I've been careful to make all the examples as self-contained as possible. And each of them works, too — they've been thoroughly tested.

The following sections give you a brief description of each of the book's eight main parts.

Part I: The Basics of Databases

This part of the book demonstrates the elements of databases and database management. You find out what's available in Visual Basic 6's generous suite of database programming tools. You see how to use Visual Basic's specialized tools to make most any database-related job easier.

Part II: Making a Connection

Part II covers the tools and techniques necessary to connect a component, Web page, or Windows application to a database. You find out all about the VB Data Control and see how to use the Data Environment Designer.

Part III: Contacting the User

Part III explores how to display data to users (like bosses who ask for reports). Visual Basic offers you good assistance when the time comes to display data in an organized, helpful report. You also see how to construct a sturdy and intuitive user interface for the front end of your database application.

Part IV: Building a New Database

Sometimes, you have to start from the ground up, and this part demonstrates how to design and build a database from scratch. You find out how to use the Visual Data Manager to build a brand-new database and modify existing databases. You also experiment with various approaches to indexing and data validation. Finally, you see how to create custom data-bound ActiveX UserControls.

Part V: The Internet Connection

Part V covers the various ways to use databases with a Web site, including both Active Server Pages and IIS applications. You also find out how to employ the ActiveX Document Migration Wizard to port existing traditional (Windows) programming to Web pages — painlessly.

Part VI: Hands-On Programming

Part VI is all about programming — writing and testing source code. You see how to use tried-and-true database programming strategies. You discover how to make the important transition from the older DAO technology to the newer ADO and OLE DB technologies. You focus on the various alternative database techniques that Microsoft offers to see what's best for each particular programming job. Finally, Chapter 17 zeros in on the most common database programming errors — how to trap them and what to do to fix the critters when you *do* trap them.

Part VII: Working with Queries

Part VII demonstrates the many ways you can retrieve sets of records from databases using SQL, the standard database query language. You see how to employ VB's useful Query Designer tool to design and test new queries. You also find out all about creating *joins* — relationships between data from different tables, how to use functions to calculate with retrieved data, and how to use *action queries* to modify the structure or dynamically change the data in a database.

Part VIII: The Part of Tens

Part VIII includes a chapter that describes the features of ten outstanding third-party add-ons you can use to extend Visual Basic's capabilities. And Chapter 21, "Ten Topics that Don't Fit Elsewhere in the Book (But Are Important)," covers such information as the best Web sites for staying current with database-programming issues, using the API Viewer, and how to customize the Visual Basic IDE (Integrated Development Environment) by writing your own "third-party" wizards. (Yes, there is a Wizard of Wizards that helps you design your own wizard.)

Conventions Used in This Book

This book is filled with step-by-step lists that function like recipes to help you cook up a finished product. Each step starts off with a **boldface** sentence or two telling you what *you* should do. Directly after the bold step, you may see a sentence or two, not in boldface, telling you what happens as a result of the bold action — a menu opens, a dialog box pops up, a wizard appears, you win the lottery, whatever.

A primary convention used in this book is that I've tried to make the step-by-step examples as general as possible, but at the same time make them specific, too. Sounds impossible, and it wasn't easy. The idea is to give you a specific example that you can follow while also giving you a series of steps that you can apply directly to your own projects.

In most of the examples, I use the BIBLIO.MDB sample database that comes with VB 6. For instance, a listbox is filled with particular records from BIBLIO, or you type some data, and it's stored as a new record in BIBLIO, and then you read the record back and see it on-screen.

However, you might be working on a job and want to use my step-by-step examples with *your* database programming. To accomplish these dual goals, I often say something like this: "Type in the file path to the database you want to open." (This enables you to plug the database of your choice into the example.) However, right after that statement, I'll also say something like this: "But if you're following my example, type **C:\Program Files\VB98\BIBLIO.MDB** (or the path to BIBLIO.MDB in your hard drive)." This way, you can simply follow the precise example I'm illustrating, if you prefer.

Also, note that a special symbol shows you how to navigate menus. For example, when you see "Choose File⇨New Program," you should click the File menu and then click the New Program option in the File menu.

When you need to deal with programming code, you see it in a listing that looks like this:

```
Sub Form_Load()
```

And if I mention a piece of programming within a regular paragraph of text, I use a special typeface, like this: Sub Form_Load().

Every line of code that you see in this book is also available for downloading from the Dummies Web site at www.dummies.com/resources/programming. Take advantage of this handy electronic version of the code by downloading it from the Web site so you can then just copy and paste source code instead of typing it by hand. Saves time, and avoids pesky typos.

What You Need to Get Started

To use this book to the fullest, you need only one thing: a copy of Visual Basic 6. Visual Basic is sold in three versions: Learning, Professional, and Enterprise. This book assumes that you have the Professional Version or the Enterprise Version (which includes the Professional Version but adds some features). This book does not, though, *require* the Enterprise Version.

Icons Used in This Book

Notice the eye-catching little icons in the margins of this book. They're next to certain paragraphs to emphasize that special information appears. Here are the icons and their meanings:

The Tip icon points you to shortcuts and insights that save you time and trouble.

I use the Technical Stuff icon to highlight nerdy technical discussions that you can skip if you want to.

A Warning icon aims to steer you away from dangerous situations.

The Remember icon suggests that you not forget an important piece of information.

Where to Go from Here

Where you turn next depends on what you need. If you want the lowdown on Visual Basic's database-related tools, as well as some important database terms and concepts, turn to Part I. If you're looking for the answer to a specific problem, check the index or the table of contents and then turn directly to the appropriate section.

Part I
The Basics of Databases

The 5th Wave

Real Programmers don't like to be bothered when they're working.

In this part . . .

Understanding, and doing, database programming doesn't have to be a tough job. If you've tried before and were baffled by it, or you're trying it for the first time, you've chosen the right language (Visual Basic) and the right book (this one).

Been confused by blizzards of acronyms (ADO, RDO, UDA, DAO, OLE, BAM-BAM)? Been turned off by books that make most everything hard to understand? Been to bewildering classes in school? Part I of this book wafts you gently into the world of database programming and ensures that you have a good, solid understanding of what databases are, how they work, and what you can do with them.

In Visual Basic 6, Microsoft has assembled tools that are highly effective and, in most cases, very easy to understand and use. (I tell you which tools are *not* useful and should be avoided. I also demonstrate how to use the majority that *are* useful.)

So, turn on your favorite music, get something to munch on, fire up Visual Basic, and start having some fun. (The big secret that programmers try to keep from bosses is that creating computer programs with Visual Basic can be lots of fun.)

Chapter 1

The Big Picture: Visual Basic's Database Features

In This Chapter

▶ Sampling Visual Basic's most important database features

▶ Connecting an application to a database in less than five minutes

*V*isual Basic 6 includes many tools to help you create, revise, manage, and otherwise deal with databases efficiently. This book shows you how easy it is to use those tools, and this chapter introduces the main tools. At the end of this chapter, you find a quick example. It should prove to you beyond any doubt that in choosing Visual Basic to do your database programming, you made a very wise choice, indeed. You connect an application to a database in 17 swift steps.

This chapter does *not* attempt, though, to give you all the main ideas — the terms and concepts — of database programming. Chapter 2 attempts that. So if you come across a word or two, or a concept, that's unclear in this chapter, take a look at Chapter 2 or this book's index for additional explanation and examples.

Checking Out the Database Tools in Visual Basic 6

Visual Basic 5 and earlier versions had some database facilities. But a lot was missing, too. You often had to open Access or some other database development tool to accomplish some common database programming tasks, such as designing and testing a SQL query. (Here's an example of a SQL query: `SELECT TOP 5 PERCENT * FROM tblSales`. This query means "Give me the upper five percent of sales." For a detailed description of SQL, see Chapters 18 and 19.)

Now, with VB 6, you can count on finding most everything you need right there in Visual Basic. Here are some of the highlights — the powerful database features you find in Visual Basic 6:

- **ADO (ActiveX Data Objects):** The main element of Microsoft's new *universal database access* (UDA) strategy. It's *universal* because it's eventually supposed to extract data from e-mail files, ordinary text (TXT) files, and other non-traditional data sources.

- **The ADO Data Control:** A VB control that employs the new ADO database technology. Eventually, the ADO Data Control will replace the DAO Data Control that's been on the VB Toolbox for years now.

  For extensive examples of ADO, DAO, and other Microsoft database technologies, see Chapters 14 through 16.

- **The Data View window:** A great tool when you want to manipulate the structure of a database. (The *structure* of a database is its internal organization — what categories it's divided into. It's similar to the structure of a CD collection. If you are a seriously neat person, you may arrange the CDs into various categories, somewhat analogous to the *tables* used to organize data in a database. See Chapter 2 for explanations of the major database terms.) With the Data View window, you can create and modify database diagrams, tables, views, stored procedures, or triggers. (The Data View window even permits you to drag a table and drop it into the Query Designer for instant database connection. What could be easier?)

- **The Query Designer:** A quick way to define and test SQL queries by using drop-down lists, check boxes, and other shortcuts. If you want, you can save the queries in your database, speeding up execution. Figure 1-1 shows the Query Designer, along with the Data View window.

- **The DataRepeater Control:** A container that repeats custom controls. In other words, you define a custom set of components (for example, six TextBoxes plus six Labels to display records that contain six fields). This set of components is your UserControl. Then, you place this UserControl on the DataRepeater, which enables users to scroll through a huge, ListBox-like group of these UserControls. It's one good way to display multiple records in an easy-to-navigate format, as shown in Figure 1-2.

- **The DataReport Designer:** A great new utility for those who have to create reports, this surprisingly easy-to-use tool generates reports of sufficient complexity for many tasks. In addition to showing your reports on-screen or printing them, you can even send the resulting reports to HTML files (.HTM) for display in Web pages.

- **The Data Environment Designer:** A kind of all-purpose pipeline for connecting a VB project to a database. A similar tool, the UserConnection Designer, was available in previous versions of VB. The Data Environment Designer offers everything the UserConnection Designer did, but goes beyond it. For example, the Data Environment Designer permits drag and drop: You can simply drag a table from the Data

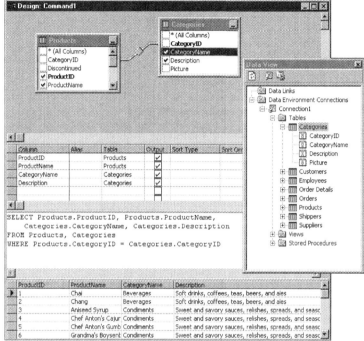

Figure 1-1:
Use the
Query
Designer
together
with the
Data View
window to
define and
test SQL
queries the
easy way.

Environment Designer (see Chapter 4) and drop it onto a VB form. Automatically, the form fills with the right amount of Labels and TextBoxes to show the data. Each TextBox is also automatically bound to your DataEnvironment (and thus to a database).

The Data Environment Designer also permits multiple data connections. It can handle new OLE DB data sources (along with the older ODBC sources), it can be directly bound to controls, and you can manipulate it via programming. You can find lots of examples that show off this great tool in Chapter 4.

✔ **The ActiveX Document Migration Wizard:** A tool that makes quick, semi-automatic work of translating any of your oldie (but goodie) VB applications and utilities so you can plug them into Web pages. As we all somehow sense, the *Windows* metaphor for computing is not-so-gradually being replaced by a *browser* metaphor: Forward and Back buttons, Favorites and History lists, pages divided into frames, and all the other elements of a browser. If you're asked to add some functionality to a Web site, the ActiveX Document Migration Wizard is one of the fastest ways to get that job done (see Chapter 11).

✔ **The WebClass Designer (choose File⇨New Project and then select IIS Application):** A designer that helps you create programming that runs on a server and can considerably beef up your Web pages. With IIS (Internet Information Server) applications, you can use classes,

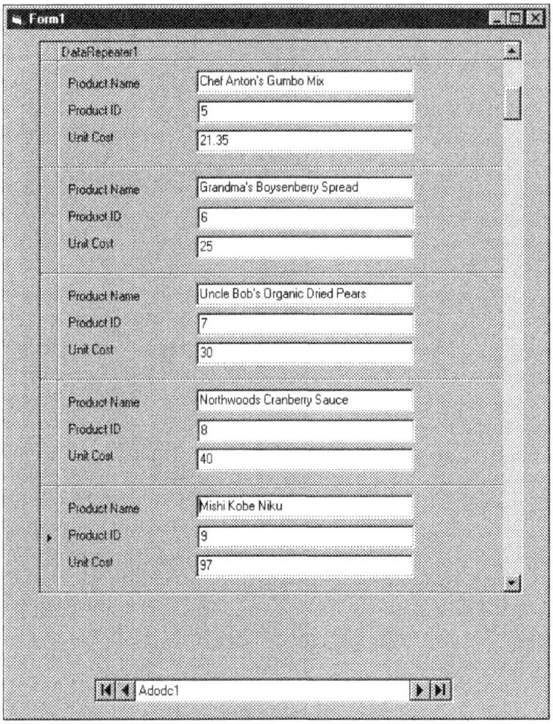

Figure 1-2:
The Data-
Repeater
offers the
user a
scrollable
stack of
multiple
records.

compiled VB code, and ActiveX components. You can exploit the IIS object model, gaining extra control over the contents and behavior of Web pages you send to visitors.

The WebClass technique is superior to writing script for several reasons. For one thing, your coding is not mixed right in with the HTML, so you can keep it from prying eyes. The code is further concealed because it is compiled and it never leaves your server anyway. IIS applications also employ the ASP (Active Server Pages) object model, but VB automatically generates the necessary wrappers for you. Yet another victory of a VB Designer over the tedium of having to write all the programming by hand. See Chapter 13 for all the details about this designer.

✔ **The Visual Data Manager:** A tool that makes designing a new database, or manipulating an existing one, quite easy. You simply choose Add-Ins➪ Visual Data Manager, and you're a few steps away from defining the organization of your database. You can't define relationships in the Visual Data Manager or add other complexities, but you can get a good start and then later, if you decide to, add programming code or use Access to make further adjustments. (See Chapter 18 for details on relationships in database programming.)

Get Your Hands On This: Five Minutes Tops

The preceding section describes the main database-related features of Visual Basic, but this chapter wouldn't be complete without a hands-on example you can try. This book is filled with step-by-step examples showing you how to make good use of all the tools and technologies I describe in the preceding section. And the following example demonstrates how *easy* VB often makes tasks that would otherwise take days of learning and programming.

So sample this example and prove to yourself that VB is often the shortest distance between problem and solution.

In all likelihood, no faster way exists in any programming language to connect a database to an application than to use one of Visual Basic's Data Controls. To see how fast (five minutes tops) you can get data out of a database and piped into an application so the user can see it on-screen, follow these steps:

1. **Start Visual Basic by clicking its icon on your desktop.**

   Depending on how you've specified VB's startup options, you may or may not see the New Project dialog box. If you don't see this dialog box, choose File⇨New Project.

2. **Double-click Standard EXE in the New Project dialog box.**

   A typical Visual Basic project template appears, with a blank Form1 as the starting point for your work.

3. **Double-click the Data Control icon in the Toolbox.**

   A Data Control appears on Form1.

   The VB Data Control is a component on the VB Toolbox that makes it a snap to open a connection to a database (without having to write any programming). Chapter 3 offers examples that show how you work with this useful component.

   If the VB Toolbox is not visible, choose View⇨Toolbox.

4. **Double-click the DatabaseName property in the Properties window.**

   The DatabaseName dialog box appears, showing the VB folder. By default, Microsoft Access-style databases (they have an .MDB extension) are listed. An .MDB file is one kind of database, and it's the style you use in this example.

If the Properties window isn't visible, press F4. Also, you should see two sample databases in your VB folder (BIBLIO.MDB and NWIND.MDB). If you don't see these files, you might have the Data Control's Connect property set to some other database type. The solution is to close the dialog box, select Access for the Connect property in the Properties window, and then repeat Step 4. The Connect property defines the *type* of database you want to use the Data Control with. There are various types of databases, just as there are various types of graphics files. Each type organizes data differently, so VB needs to know which kind of database you're using.

5. **Double-click BIBLIO.MDB in the dialog box.**

The dialog box closes, and the DatabaseName property is set to point to BIBLIO.MDB. You have connected your Data Control to the BIBLIO.MDB database. You can't just "open" a database the way you open a graphics file. It's not that simple. Between your VB application and the database stands a *database engine* (a set of tools, rules, and behaviors). In this example, you are connecting to the database through the Microsoft Jet engine, which is used by both VB and Access. For details on database connections and engines, see Chapter 5.

If you still don't see BIBLIO.MDB in the dialog box, locate it by clicking the Windows Start button and then choosing Find⇨Files or Folders. If you *still* can't find it, rerun Visual Basic's setup program and agree to install all templates and samples. The BIBLIO.MDB sample database is used extensively in this book, and it's on your VB CD.

6. **Stretch the Data Control so it's about 2 inches wide and position it at the bottom of Form1, as shown in Figure 1-3.**

7. **Double-click the TextBox icon on the Toolbox.**

VB adds a TextBox to the form.

8. **Stretch the TextBox so it's about the same size as the Data Control and position it near the top of Form1.**

Figure 1-3:
You, the happy programmer, can use a Data Control to connect your VB application to a database in no time.

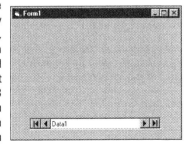

9. **Click the TextBox on the form.**

   The TextBox is selected (and stretch tabs — tiny blue boxes — appear around it). The Properties window displays the TextBox properties. (If the Properties window isn't visible, press F4.)

10. **Attach the TextBox to the Data Control by double-clicking the TextBox's Datasource property in the Properties window.**

    The Datasource property changes to Data1, the name of the Data Control.

11. **Click the Data Control.**

    The Data Control's properties appear in the Properties window.

12. **Click the RecordSource property in the Properties window.**

13. **Click the drop-down arrow icon next to the RecordSource property.**

    A drop-down list appears, displaying all the tables available in the Biblio database that you're connected to, as you can see in Figure 1-4. (A *table* is the largest category in a database. For example, a database for a CD collection might be divided into these tables: Pop, Rock, Industrial, Metal, Rap, and Techno.)

14. **Click the Authors table to select it.**

    The recordset you chose now becomes the set of records that are displayed in the TextBox attached to this data control. A *recordset* is a custom list of data extracted from a database. For example, if you ask, "Let me see a list of all authors who live in Alaska," the result you get back is called a *recordset.* It's often a subset of all the data, though you can also request a recordset that includes *all* the data (every record) in a table. (See Chapter 2 for examples.)

15. **Click the TextBox to select it.**

Figure 1-4:
Visual Basic
knows
about, and
shows you,
all the
tables in a
database;
all you do is
click one.

16. Keep double-clicking the TextBox's DataField property in the Properties window until *Author* appears.

You have now specified that the Author field (of the three available fields in the Authors table) will be the one displayed in the TextBox.

17. Press F5.

Your application runs, and you see the first record in the BIBLIO.MDB database, as shown in Figure 1-5.

Figure 1-5:
You did it!
Your
application
displays the
first record
from the
selected
database.

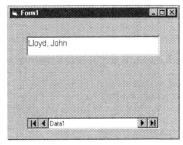

Chapter 2

Databases 101: How Databases Work

. . . .

In This Chapter

▸ Using tables, fields, and records

▸ Understanding the value of indexes

▸ Using the VisData utility to create a new database

▸ Adding data to a database

▸ Defining new tables

▸ Why not just make a list?

▸ Retrieving the data people actually want: recordsets

. . . .

A database is a collection of information that's organized in some fashion and stored in a computer. If you have an address book at home, it's *almost* a database. All it needs to get formal recognition as a proper database is for you to copy its information into a computer and save it — in some orderly way — in a file.

But consider what actually happens when you take the names, addresses, and phone numbers of all your friends and relatives and copy that data into the computer. Just randomly typing data isn't going to result in an organized store of information. You must first define a database structure. It can be similar to the structure in your address book.

This chapter takes you through the components of a database. You see what the various database terms mean — *record, index, field, view, query*, and a few others. As you'll see, the vocabulary of database terms is small.

Understanding Tables, Fields, Records, and All the Rest

Various database designs exist, but this book concentrates on what is by far the most popular type of database — the *relational* database. A relational database has three primary qualities:

- ✔ Data is stored in tables (which are subdivided into fields).
- ✔ You can attach (*join,* in a relationship) tables so that you can later extract data from more than one table at a time.
- ✔ You can query (request data from) tables, getting back *recordsets* (subsets of a table or tables).

Read on.

Records are filled with information

Say that your address book holds information about one person per page. Each page, after it's filled in with the information, would then be the equivalent, in database terms, of a *record.*

As shown in Figure 2-1, the top line on each page of your address book is labeled *Name*, the next several lines are labeled *Address,* and the last line is labeled *Phone.* In database terms, these labels are called *fields.*

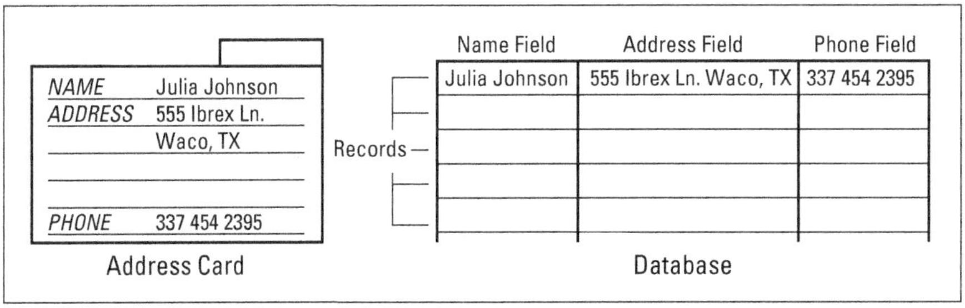

Figure 2-1:
A single page in an address book is equivalent to a single record in this database.

	Name Field	Address Field	Phone Field
	Julia Johnson	555 Ibrex Ln. Waco, TX	337 454 2395

NAME   Julia Johnson
ADDRESS   555 Ibrex Ln.
Waco, TX

PHONE   337 454 2395

Records —

Address Card   Database

Fields are labels

You can think of a field as a *type* of information; each field has its own name — a label like *TotalSales*. But a record has no name. It contains the actual data — like *156* — the specific information that fills the fields ($156 total sales, for instance).

Each record usually has several fields. In my address book example, each record has three fields: Name, Address, and Phone. Here's an example of a *record* in this database:

```
Julia Johnson    555 Ibrex Ln., Waco, TX    337 454-2395
```

 In database terminology, a record is sometimes referred to as a *row*, and a field is sometimes called a *column*. One way to think of the relationship between records and fields is to think of a baseball scoreboard. Across the top are two labels: Home and Visitor. Those are the fields, and they describe the columns of data beneath them. The row contains the data: a 2 under the Home label, and 4 under Visitor, for example, as you can see in Figure 2-2.

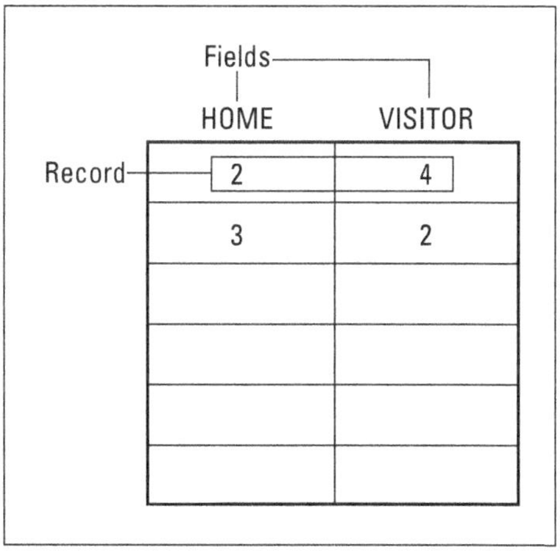

Fields——

	HOME	VISITOR
Record—	2	4
	3	2

Figure 2-2:
A baseball scoreboard is a kind of table, with fields and records.

 Depending on what kind of programming you're doing, if a field's name is two words, like *Personality Drawbacks*, you may need to enclose it in brackets or, sometimes, single quotes. So, if you're having trouble with a two-word field name when programming, try enclosing it in brackets or single quotes: [Personality Drawbacks] or 'Personality Drawbacks'. (The Access-style databases you work with in this book do permit spaces. Note, however, that most relational databases do not permit spaces, so with them you have to resort to underscore characters to separate words: Personality_Drawbacks.)

Tables are made up of fields

Back to the address-book-as-database illustration. The whole thing — an entire address book — is equivalent to a *table* in a computer database. Tables are relatively large-scale collections of data, such as your entire address book, but a database can contain several tables. (You define the contents of a database when you're creating it, so you determine how many tables it has and what fields each table contains.)

Maybe you've marked the birthdays of all your friends and relatives on your calendar. You could put this data into a second table in your database named, perhaps, *Gifts*. Maybe you would define five fields for this table: Name, Birthday, [Favorite Color], [Shoe Size], and Comments.

Notice that both your Addresses table and your Gifts table have a Name field in common. This characteristic will come in handy later. It enables you to *join* the tables, as it's called. You can, in this way, ask to get information (query) from both these tables at once. You can use a query such as: What is Marie's address and birthday? Both tables contain Marie in the name field, so they can provide their respective additional information about Marie: her address from the Addresses table and her birthday from the Gifts table. The result of this query (the information you get back) is made available in what's called a *recordset*. (I explore recordsets at length in the section "Using Recordsets to Work with Data," later in this chapter.)

Why use multiple tables?

Why have two tables — Addresses and Gifts? Why not just put all the data into one big table? Bulging, single-table databases are less flexible and less efficient than multiple, smaller tables — both when in use and from a programmer's point of view. You separate data into tables for the same reason that most people have a divided silverware drawer: It's easier to store, retrieve, and, in general, manage the contents of that drawer than an undivided jumble of tableware.

Of course, if the database is small, its organization doesn't much matter. You don't have to worry about dividing up your little address book database into several tables because it doesn't have that many entries. You're not *that* popular, are you? But if you're designing a multi-user database with 250,000 records, every little efficiency matters. By creating several tables, you can improve the organization of the database, write programming for it more easily, and generally make retrieving records faster. Why? Primarily because putting everything into one big database can result in dreadful redundancies.

To understand how and why to use several tables rather than one big one, consider the sample BIBLIO.MDB database that comes with Visual Basic. It's divided into four tables: Authors, Publishers, Title Author, and Titles. If all this information were stored in a single table, serious redundancy would result. Why? The database contains data about approximately 100 publishers and perhaps 8,000 books. Do you want to repeat the publisher's name, address, and phone number for each record for each of the 8,000 books? Or would you rather just have a separate table for Publishers, listing each publisher's name, address, and phone number only once? And a single PublishersName field in the Titles table? That makes much more sense.

When you look up a title in the Titles table, the publisher's name is part of each title's record (so you do have to provide the publisher's name 8,000 times). But if you want the publisher's address, phone number, and other details, no problem — the Publisher's table and the Titles table both contain a PublishersName field. That way, you can get the other details about a publisher by matching the name fields in the two tables. You store each publisher's address and phone number only once because you have separate tables.

Tangled relationships: Using unique data to tie tables together

When you specify a relationship between tables while designing a database, you're saying: I might need additional information about this fellow, and if I do, it can be found in this *other* table using a field — the primary index — that is identical in both tables.

So, assume that in one table John Jones has an ID number of 242522 (two tables in this database each have this same ID field). To find out more about Mr. Jones, I look up that same ID number in the second table, and I can find additional information on him that's stored in this second table. (I explain the reasons for storing information about the same guy in separate tables in the previous section, titled "Why use multiple tables?" And you can find a discussion of using keys with multiple tables in Chapter 18.)

Let the database do it for you: AutoNumber fields

Often, you let the database automatically generate a unique ID number for each record. These serial numbers start with 1 when you add the first record, and they go up by one for each new record entered into the database. (Some database programmers insist that *every table* should have a field with a unique serial number so that beyond any doubt every record will be unique. All the other fields in a record might be duplicated, but the serial number won't be.)

Such database-generated serial numbers are put into what's called an *AutoNumber field.* This auto-incrementing serial number (such as Pub_ID or Au_ID in the BIBLIO.MDB database) is an *index* (it's maintained in a sorted list), but its main function is to permit tables to be linked together. The primary index makes it possible to identify related records in various tables. This feature works because you specify during database design that these unique *keys* (they are special fields) should be included in two tables as a way of joining the tables.

An AutoNumber field isn't just any ordinary old index, though. (I describe ordinary indexes in the next section.) Unique keys like this are called *primary* index keys. They differ from other indexed fields (which may contain repeating data). An ordinary index might have ten records with the LastName field containing Jones. That LastName field cannot, therefore, be made a primary index and used to create relationships between tables.

Often, a naturally occurring unique value exists that you can use as a way to build relationships between tables without having to generate an ID-style key. Examples include ISBN numbers, Social Security numbers, and other nonrepeating data. The database may contain information about two people named Joe Jones, but they'll both have unique Social Security numbers, so you could use the Social Security number field as the primary index.

Indexes — A Key to Success

Information in a relational database is not automatically stored alphabetically (or by numeric order, if the field is numeric). In a Name field, *Anderware* can follow *Zimbare.* Or maybe not. It doesn't matter.

The point is, you can't expect the records to be in any particular order. When someone adds a new record to a database, it's just put at the end of a table. No attempt is made to place it in some particular position. When a record is deleted, who cares? A relational database has a real la-ti-dah attitude about all this activity. When designing a database, however, you can specify that some of its fields are to be *indexes.*

An index is somewhat like those cut-out, thumb-sized indentations in the side of a dictionary: Each cutout is stamped with a different letter of the alphabet. You can get right to Q real fast by sticking your finger directly into the indentation labeled *Q.*

Imagine non-alphabetic yellow pages

If the user wants to search for a particular record in a field that's not indexed, the database software must search every record until it finds the right one.

How would you like it if the yellow pages in the phone book were *not* alphabetized? You'd be turning pages all night, hoping to stumble on the right page.

An *index* in a relational database is the one exception to the blithe, uncaring order I've just described. An indexed field solves the problem of finding a particular record in the jumble of data. The database software can quickly locate a specific record if a field is *indexed*. So, when you're designing a database, you need to decide which fields should be indexed. (Unindexed data can be searched; it just takes longer.)

Here's the general rule: You should index any fields that are likely to be searched. In the example address book database earlier in this chapter, you are far more likely to search some fields than others:

Fields likely to be searched	Fields not likely to be searched
Name	Favorite Color
Birthday	Shoe Size
	Comments

So, for this database, you might specify that the Name and Birthday fields should be indexed. You leave the others alone, unindexed; they're unlikely to be searched. But what happens if you later buy some size 8 blue shoes on sale and you want to search the database to see if any of your friends or relatives wears that size (you hope) and likes blue? No problemo: The database can still conduct searches on unindexed fields; the database software just takes longer to find the information you need. That's all.

The database software will automatically create and maintain the indexes you specify — you need do nothing more than say which fields should be indexed and after that you're home free.

Hey, let's index every field

Some of you, dear readers, are thinking, "Why not index *all the fields*? That would be super efficient." Wrong. When publishers create an index for a book, they don't index all the words in the book, do they? They include the words likely to be searched for, not words such as *the* or *twelve*. An index of all the words would suffer from several drawbacks. In particular, it would be bigger than the book, and most of the index would be of little use to anyone. A quick scan of the book itself would be faster than slogging through a massively bloated index.

You don't index every field in a table for a similar reason: Too much of a good thing is a bad thing. Efficiencies start to degrade, storage space gets tight, multi-user traffic jams can occur, and other bugaboos arise. Each index always slows down updates to a database, at least a little.

Just remember, index only those fields that make sense. Pop Quiz: Would you index the Male/Female field in a database? Answer: No. Who would ever search on that field? And imagine the work you're asking the database to do to maintain that field in "order" where the only order is either/or. You're saying, "Sort this data (imagine the database has 100,000 records) into *two piles*." And nobody is ever going to actually *use* this indexing anyway. What came over you, asking that a binary (two-state) field be indexed?

Building a Database

But enough theory. Time to get your hands out of your pockets and build this address book. That way, you discover exactly what these terms mean: field, record, table, database, relationship, query, and recordset. After you know what these terms mean, you understand the major concepts underlying databases.

VB includes a handy utility named the Visual Data Manager (VisData, for short). With it, you can create a new database or examine and adjust the structure of an existing database.

You want to create a database with two tables:

- ✔ tblAddresses contains three fields: Name, Address, and Phone.
- ✔ tblGifts contains five fields: Name, Birthday, [Favorite Color], Shoe Size, and Comments.

This database is small, and its fields don't really lend themselves to being divided into two tables anyway. But to illustrate the mechanics of establishing relationships between tables, you create two tables in the following examples.

By convention, table names are signified by using the prefix *tbl*.

To create a database with two tables that contain information about your friends and relatives, follow these steps:

1. **With VB running, choose File⇨New Project.**

   The New Project dialog box opens.

2. **Double-click the Standard EXE icon in the New Project dialog box.**

   The dialog box closes.

3. **Choose Add-Ins⇨Visual Data Manager.**

   The Visual Data Manager (VisData) appears.

4. **In VisData, choose File⇨New⇨Microsoft Access⇨Version 7.0 MDB.**

   The Select Microsoft Access Database to Create dialog box appears.

5. **In the File Name text box, type** Friends.

   FRIENDS.MDB will be the name of your new database.

6. **In the dialog box, move to a folder where you want to store your new database.**

7. **Click Save.**

   The dialog box closes, and you see two child windows in VisData: Database Window and SQL Statement, as shown in Figure 2-3.

8. **From the group of three buttons on the left end of the VisData toolbar, click the button for the type of recordset that you want to use in your application.**

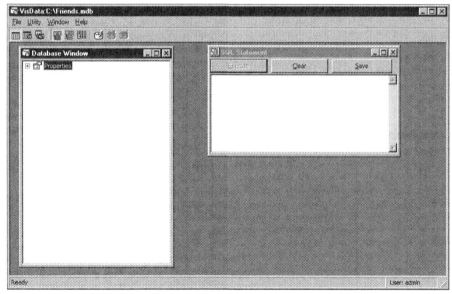

Figure 2-3:
To create your new database, you use the Database Window on the left.

9. **Right-click the word *Properties* in the Database Window.**

   A context menu pops out.

10. **Click New Table in the context menu.**

    The context menu closes, and you see the Table Structure dialog box shown in Figure 2-4.

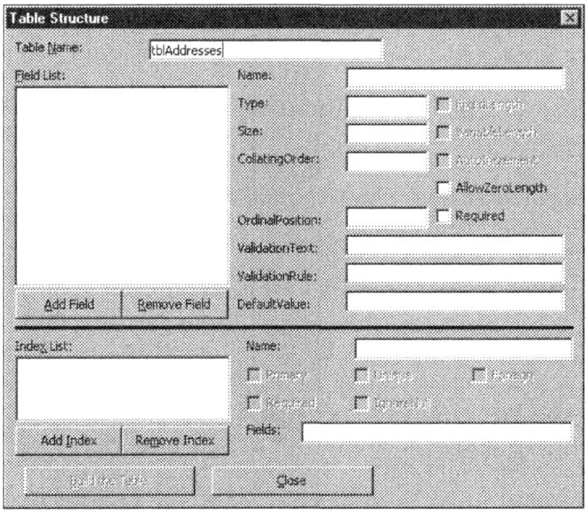

Figure 2-4:
Build a
new table
using this
dialog box.

11. **Type** tblAddresses **as the Table Name in the dialog box, as shown in Figure 2-4.**

12. **Click Add Field.**

    You see the Add Field dialog box.

13. **As shown in Figure 2-5, type** Name **as the name of your first field, change the Size property to** 100, **deselect the AllowZeroLength check box, and select the Required check box.**

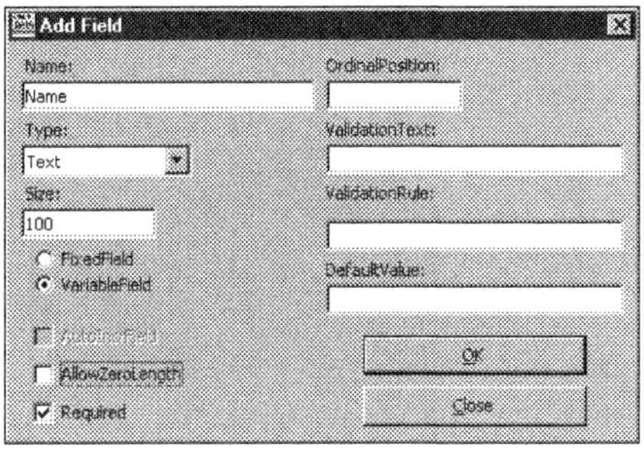

Figure 2-5:
Use this
dialog box
to add fields
to a table
and to
describe the
properties
of each
field.

You want to force people adding records to this database to include a Name in both this table and another table (named tblGifts) you'll later create. They can leave out the phone number, the shoe size, and all the other info, but the Name must be there, repeated in both tables. The Name field is used as a primary index (as I describe earlier in this chapter).

These Name fields in both tables can be used to *join* these tables (create a relationship). So, whatever else they do, users *must* fill in at least the Name field for each new record. That's why you select the Required option in Step 12.

14. Click OK.

The new field is added to the table, and the Add Field dialog box is reset to its default conditions, ready for you to enter another field.

15. Type Address **as the name of your next field, set its length to 200, and then click OK to add this field to the table.**

16. Type Phone **as the name of a new field and then click OK to add this field.**

17. Click Close.

The Add Field dialog box closes.

18. In the Table Structure dialog box, click the Build the Table button.

After a brief pause, your new database table is created.

19. Click Close.

The Table Structure dialog box closes.

20. Click the small + icon next to tblAddresses and the small + icon next to Fields.

You see the structure of your table, as shown in Figure 2-6.

Figure 2-6:
These are the tables and their fields in your database.

Entering Some Data Into Your Database

You can use the Visual Data Manager that you use in the previous example to enter actual records (data) into your new database. To add some data, follow these steps:

1. **Follow all the steps in the previous example.**

   You have created a new database named Friends.

2. **Double-click tblAddresses in the Database Window of the VisData utility.**

   The Table data entry dialog box appears.

3. **Type in a name and, optionally, the address and phone number, as shown in Figure 2-7.**

Figure 2-7:
You can
type in
records
using this
dialog box.

4. **Click the Update button on the dialog box.**

   A message box appears, asking if you want to add this new record.

5. **Click Yes.**

   The message box goes away, and your new record is added. The label 1 Rows appears in the scrollbar at the bottom of the Table data entry dialog box.

6. **Click the Add button.**

   The three field text boxes go blank, ready for you to type in another record.

7. **Type in a second record and click the Update button, adding the new record.**

8. **Click the Close button in the Table data entry dialog box.**

   The data is saved to the database file (FRIENDS.MDB), and the Table data entry dialog box closes.

Adding a New Table

Nothing could be easier than adding a second table to your new database. Follow these steps:

1. **Complete the steps in the section "Building a Database," earlier in this chapter.**

You have a database with a single table in it.

2. **Right-click Properties in the Database Window.**

A context menu pops out.

3. **Choose New Table from the context menu.**

The context menu closes, and you see the Table Structure dialog box shown in Figure 2-4.

4. **Repeat Steps 10 through 19 in the section "Building a Database," earlier in this chapter, only this time, name your database tblGifts and add a different set of fields (except that you do want to repeat the Name field so that both tables include it).**

Why Not Just Make a List?

Why go to all the trouble to define these various tables and then divide those tables into fields? Why all this subdividing a database into neat little boxes? Why not just jot down the information sort of randomly, the way you would in a loose-leaf notebook or on a paper napkin?

Organizing data makes manipulating it far easier, particularly if you have large amounts of data. If your company has 12,000 customers and one of them questions the last bill, you don't want to have to search through a loose-leaf notebook, page by page, to find this customer's records. You want to see an organized, alphabetical list of customer names in a listbox. You can then quickly locate and double-click the name to bring up the records. Alternatively, you could type the name into a textbox and let programming locate the customer. Either interface is far more useful than a drawer full of scribbled napkins.

Using Recordsets to Work with Data

A user does not work *directly* with the data in a database. Instead, when users want to see, or edit, data, they are given a *recordset.* This set of records can be everything in a table (or several tables) or a subset of the data in a table (or tables). But in any case, letting a user simply add records, change data, or delete records from the database itself would be dangerous. And, more importantly, you often want to see only part of the data in a table, not the entire table.

A database *engine* stands between you and the raw data in a database. This engine acts like an interpreter: For example, you give it a query ("Show me a list of movies starring Jude Law"), and it gives you back the result. You don't work with the data directly because the engine takes care of organizing it for you. You talk to the engine, and the engine works with the data.

The benefits of recordsets

Recordsets provide several important benefits:

- A recordset floats free, for a time, from the database from which it originated. Recordsets are used to manipulate, search, navigate, view, and update data. Then, if the recordset has been edited (it was not merely viewed), and if the editing is acceptable to you, the programmer, the revisions can be stored back into the database.

- You, the programmer, can validate data. You can have your program examine what a user enters when the user clicks a button you labeled *Update* or *Enter This Data* in your database application. Before committing the new data to the actual database on the hard drive, your programming can see if the user has made an error. If the user tries to enter a zip code into a phone number field, your programming can detect this error and require that the user fix it before the data is saved into the actual database. Recordsets also permit more than one user to access data from the same database at the same time without causing traffic problems.

- A recordset need not include an entire table of data. A recordset can provide only the data the user needs, not *everything* in a table. If a lawyer needs information about divorces between 1989 and 1991, your application can build a recordset containing only that data:

```
SELECT 'Name'
FROM Divorces
WHERE ('Year' BETWEEN 1989 AND 1991)
```

The recordset produced by this query does not include data from this table on marriages, civil suits, murder trials, and all the other legal activity that might be in the table. The recordset also excludes any divorce data before 1989 or after 1991.

Databases based on the Jet engine (the databases most often used with VB and Access) can provide three kinds of recordsets: Table, Dynaset, and Snapshot. You can choose between them by adjusting a Data Control's RecordsetType property (or by programming), but the default style is the Dynaset. It's the most commonly used style, as well. (See Chapter 14 for more examples of these types of recordsets.)

Each style of recordset specializes in a different kind of data manipulation. A Table-type recordset can read or write to a particular, single table within a database. A Dynaset-type recordset is more flexible. It can read or write to all (or just parts) of various tables, even from various databases; a dynaset is sometimes the product of a query across several tables, providing, for example, all records prior to October 1993 from two different companies. A Snapshot-type recordset is like a Dynaset-type, but is read-only; no data can be edited, added, or deleted in the actual database(s) of which the snapshot was taken. The Dynaset is the most common type, and it's also the default when you're using data components (like the Data Control) or database-related wizards.

Using prewritten queries

Stored queries, views, QueryDefs: All these names refer to the same thing — a prewritten query that sits inside the database itself rather than being sent to the database by an outside database application. You can imagine which typical recordsets might be requested of your database and then put those right there in the database for future use. Recordsets can be predefined in that way. A typical stored query might be *Summary of 1999 Sales* or *Products by Category*. So, instead of having to write the SQL programming that asks for a query, someone using your database just requests the stored query and a recordset comes back to them with the data. In many situations, stored queries can be highly useful. To see the reasons why stored queries are valuable and to see an example showing how to create them and save them into a database, see Chapter 18.

Part II
Making a Connection

The 5th Wave — By Rich Tennant

"NAAAH - HE'S NOT THAT SMART. HE WON'T BACK UP HIS HARD DISK, FORGETS TO CONSISTENTLY NAME HIS FILES, AND DROOLS ALL OVER THE KEYBOARD."

In this part . . .

*I*n Visual Basic 6, Microsoft has assembled tools that offer you many, many shortcuts, including prebuilt components, templates, designers, and wizards. Using these tools, you can often get a jumpstart on a job — for example, load a template that does something like what you want to do, and then just *customize* that template rather than beginning the project from ground zero.

Part II demonstrates all the useful tools and techniques you need for establishing a connection between a database and components, Web pages, or traditional Windows applications. You see how to use the VB Data Controls, and you find out how to work with the powerful Data Environment Designer.

Chapter 3

Getting Connected with Data Controls and the Data Form Wizard

In This Chapter
- Inserting a data control
- Connecting the data control to a database
- Binding other controls to the data control
- Testing your data interface
- Using the Data Form Wizard

onnecting an application to a database may seem formidable, but if you use the tools available in Visual Basic, it's a snap. More precisely, it's a drag and drop.

After you drop a data control into a form, you just answer a few questions: the name of the database, the table of data that you want to use, and the names of the fields in that table. What could be easier?

For many applications, prebuilt components like the data control work just fine. Often, they're all you need for quickly getting a database application up and running. If you need more power than a simple data control, however, you can easily beef up the data control by using the Data Form Wizard. In this chapter, I show you how to work with data controls and the Data Form Wizard.

 Need an industrial-strength database connection? As is so often the case in life — with shoes, furniture, hamburgers, and many other items — making something by hand can sometimes get you the best results. If you're constructing a specialized or heavy-duty database application, you may need to hand-tailor the project. In those situations, there's no substitute for line-by-line programming. Part VI of this book covers this approach in depth. So, if the techniques I describe in this chapter aren't robust enough to handle a job you're working on, take a look at Part VI.

What a Drag (And Drop)!

The quickest way to display information from a database is to drop a data control into a form. The data control does two things:

- ✔ It provides a connection to a database.
- ✔ It gives the user a way of moving around in the database and seeing the records it contains.

This section deals with the DAO Data Control, but if you want to move into the future of database programming, you'll also want to know about ADO. For more information on ADO, see "Using the New ADO Data Control," later in this chapter. Also, be sure to check out Chapters 15 and 16, which examine ADO in more detail.

To connect a database to a Visual Basic project using VB's traditional DAO Data Control, follow these steps:

1. **Start Visual Basic by clicking its icon on your desktop.**

   Depending on how you've specified the Visual Basic startup options, you may or may not see the New Project dialog box. If you don't see this dialog box, choose File⇨New Project.

2. **Double-click the Standard EXE icon in the New Project dialog box.**

   A typical Visual Basic project template appears, with a blank Form1 for you to work with.

3. **Double-click the Data Control icon in the Toolbox.**

   A DAO Data Control appears on Form1, as shown in Figure 3-1.

Figure 3-1:
At runtime, a user can click a data control to move to the next, previous, first, or last record in a recordset.

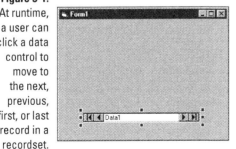

TIP

If the Toolbox isn't visible, choose View➪Toolbox.

4. **Double-click the DatabaseName property in the Properties window.**

The DatabaseName dialog box appears, showing the VB98 folder, as you can see in Figure 3-2. By default, the dialog box lists Microsoft Access-style databases (files with an .MDB extension).

Figure 3-2:
Use this dialog box to locate a database.

TIP

If the Properties window isn't visible, press F4. You should see two sample databases in your VB98 folder (BIBLIO.MDB and NWIND.MDB). If you don't see these names, you may have the data control's Connect property set to some other database type. The solution is to close the dialog box, select Access for the Connect property in the Properties window, and then repeat Step 4.

If you want to use one of the sample databases that comes with VB, but you still don't see BIBLIO.MDB in the dialog box, locate it by clicking the Windows Start button and then choosing Find➪Files or Folders. If you *still* can't find it, rerun Visual Basic's setup program and agree to install all templates and samples.

5. **In the DatabaseName dialog box, double-click the name of the database to which you are connecting the data control.**

If you want to follow along with the examples I present throughout this chapter (and why not follow the examples?), double-click BIBLIO.MDB. The dialog box closes, and the DatabaseName property is set to point to the database that you selected.

REMEMBER

Here's the general rule for deciding whether to use the DAO Data Control or the newer ADO Data Control: Use the DAO version to maintain existing programming, but use the new ADO version if you're creating a new application. In this chapter, I show you how to work with both the DAO version and the new ADO Data Control. For an in-depth discussion of both DAO and ADO, see Chapter 15.

In a Bind: Adding Data-Bound Controls

Connecting to a database is fine, as I explain in the previous section, but you must also find a way to show the data to the user. In some cases, you only want to permit the user to read the information, but not change it — for example, when displaying a product catalog. In other cases, you let the user edit the database.

You can use many of Visual Basic's controls to display data (technically, such controls are called *data-aware* or *data-bound*). You could use a Label or a PictureBox for read-only data, and a TextBox for data the user can edit.

To bind a TextBox to a data control, thereby enabling the user to see and edit the data in the database that's connected to the data control, follow these steps:

1. **Connect a data control to a database, using the steps I describe in the previous section, "What a Drag (And Drop)."**

   If you want to continue the example that I introduce in the previous section, connect the data control to the BIBLIO.MDB database.

2. **Resize the data control and reposition it on the form, as necessary.**

   For my example application, I stretched the data control so it's about two inches wide and positioned it at the bottom of the form, as shown in Figure 3-1.

3. **Add a TextBox to the form by double-clicking the TextBox control on the Toolbox (the icon near the top with ab| in it).**

4. **Reposition and resize the TextBox, as necessary.**

   To follow along with my example, drag and stretch the TextBox so that it looks like the box in Figure 3-3.

   The form is now organized to display data. The TextBox at the top of the form displays data, and the data control at the bottom of the form enables a user to move through the records in the database.

Figure 3-3:
The form
with a
TextBox and
a data
control.

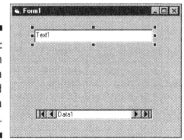

5. **Click the TextBox on the form.**

   The TextBox is selected, as indicated by the stretch tabs (tiny blue boxes) that appear around it. The Properties window displays the TextBox properties. If the Properties window isn't visible, press F4.

6. **Attach the TextBox to the data control by double-clicking the TextBox's Datasource property in the Properties window.**

   The Datasource property changes to Data1, the name of the data control.

   You can put more than one data control on a form, but I advise against it. Data controls eat up lots of system resources. Also, each data control opens up a new connection to the database, so using more than one data control on a form violates the standard that each user session should open only one database connection.

7. **Click the data control.**

   The data control's properties appear in the Properties window. Now you must select the table you want to use.

8. **Click the RecordSource property in the Properties window.**

9. **Click the drop-down arrow icon next to the RecordSource property.**

   A drop-down list appears, displaying all the tables available in the database that you've attached to the data control.

10. **Click the table that you want to select.**

    For example, you may select the Authors table in the BIBLIO.MDB database. The recordset you select becomes the set of records that are displayed in the TextBox attached to this data control.

    You have the freedom to define how your database's data appears to the user. It's all up to you: what you show, how much, from where, and precisely what data. For example, you can put as many different data controls as you want on a Visual Basic form. That way, you can access various tables or even various databases, all on the same form. Similarly, you can attach as many controls, such as TextBoxes, as you want to any particular data control. However, I do recommend that you avoid using multiple data controls.

11. **Click the TextBox to select it.**

12. **Keep double-clicking the TextBox's DataField property in the Properties window until you see the name of the field that you want to display in the TextBox.**

    For example, you may specify that you want to display the Author field (one of the three available fields in the Authors table) in the TextBox.

Trying It Out

As always in Visual Basic, nothing is easier than running an application. Just press F5 and off you go. If you try the example that I present in the previous sections of this chapter, you get the results displayed in Figure 3-4.

Try clicking the right-arrow on the data control to move through the records. Notice that they are not alphabetized. If you change the TextBox's DataField property to Au_ID, the records are displayed in numeric order. Au_ID is the index for this table.

If you want to display the records organized in a different order, you can define a recordset's contents as described in Chapters 14 and 16.

Using the New ADO Data Control

You should use the ADO Data Control for any new projects you start. It replaces both the older DAO Data Control that appears, by default, on the Toolbox (see the previous sections of this chapter) and the remote data control, for RDO. (RDO was used for client/server data. The Internet and intranets divide data from the database application — and cause other divisions. A primary trend today is to work with applications and data that are spread across two or more machines, but that must work harmoniously.)

Data controls offer a quick way to get connected to a database, but sometimes what's quick is also *dirty*. In many cases, you may have good reasons to avoid using data controls entirely and, instead, connect to databases by writing your own programming — see Chapters 14 and 16.

The new ADO control is more flexible than the older DAO control. The ADO control works with both the traditional ODBC and the new OLE DB programming styles. See Chapter 15 for more information about ODBC and OLE DB.

To connect to a database using the ADO Data Control, follow these steps:

1. **Start Visual Basic by clicking its icon on your desktop.**

   Depending on how you've specified the Visual Basic startup options, you may or may not see the New Project dialog box. If you don't see this dialog box, choose File⇨New Project.

2. **Double-click Standard EXE in the New Project dialog box.**

   A typical Visual Basic project template appears, with a blank Form1 for you to work with. You must first add the ADO Data Control to your Toolbox (it's not on the default set of controls).

3. **Press Ctrl+T.**

   A dialog box opens, displaying a list of available components.

4. **Locate Microsoft ADO Data Control 6.0 (OLE DB) in the list, and click to put a check mark in the box next to this component.**

   If you can't find the ADO Data Control in the list, click the Browse button and look for MSADODC.OCX in your SYSTEM32 folder. If you *still* can't find it, rerun VB setup and install all optional database-related components.

5. **Click OK to close the dialog box.**

   The ADO Data Control's icon appears in the Toolbox.

6. **Double-click the ADO Data Control in the Toolbox.**

   VB adds the data control to your form.

7. **Right-click the ADO Data Control on the form and choose ADODC Properties from the context menu.**

   You see three ways to connect (Sources of Connection). For a detailed discussion of these options, see Chapter 5.

8. **Click Use Connection String, as shown in Figure 3-5.**

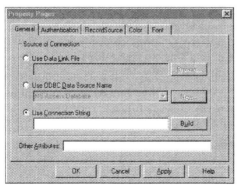

Figure 3-5:
Use this dialog box to describe how you want to connect to a database.

9. **Click the B<u>u</u>ild button to define a connection to a database.**

   You see the Data Link Properties dialog box, as shown in Figure 3-6.

10. **Click Microsoft Jet 4.0 OLE DB Provider, as shown in Figure 3-6.**

    If you don't see Jet 4.0, use Jet 3.51 or whatever version you have.

11. **Click <u>N</u>ext.**

    You see the Connection tab in the Data Link Properties dialog box.

12. **Click the button with three dots (...) in Step 1 on the Connection tab.**

    You see a file browser with the Access-style database file extension (.MDB) as the default.

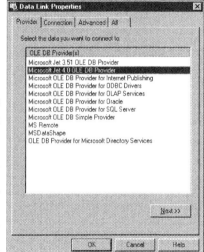

Figure 3-6:
Specify the database provider, and the particular database itself, in this dialog box.

13. **Use the file browser to locate the database that you want to connect to the ADO Data Control.**

    To follow the ADO examples that I describe in this chapter, use VB's sample BIBLIO.MDB database. On most computers, you find the sample BIBLIO.MDB database in C:\Program Files\VB98.

    If you want to use the sample database but you can't find BIBLIO.MDB, locate it by clicking the Windows Start button and then choosing Find➪Files or Folders. If you *still* can't find it, rerun Visual Basic's setup program and agree to install all templates and samples.

14. **Double-click the database that you want to connect to your data control.**

    The file browser closes, and the path to the selected database appears in the Data Link Properties dialog box.

15. **Click OK.**

    The Data Link Properties dialog box closes.

16. **Click the RecordSource tab in the Property Pages dialog box.**

    You see the dialog box shown in Figure 3-7.

17. **Choose adCmdTable as the Command Type and select the table that you want to display, as shown in Figure 3-7.**

    In this way, you specify that you want to use a table, instead of another kind of record source, such as a stored procedure.

    If you want to follow along with my ADO example, select the Authors table.

18. **Click OK.**

    The Property Pages dialog box closes, and you've made your connection to the BIBLIO database and the Authors table within it.

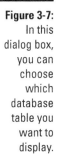

Figure 3-7:
In this dialog box, you can choose which database table you want to display.

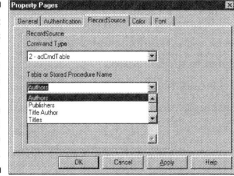

Look but Don't Touch: Binding Labels to a Data Control

To enable a user to view, but not change, the data in a database, you can bind one or more label controls to an ADO Data Control. You use the same process as I describe earlier in this chapter for binding a TextBox to a DAO Data Control. However, in this section, I show you how to bind more than one label so that the user can view several fields at the same time.

To bind several labels to a data control, thereby enabling the user to see (but not edit) data in a database, follow these steps:

1. **Place an ADO Data Control on your form and then connect the data control to a database, using the steps I describe in the section "Using the New ADO Data Control," earlier in this chapter.**

   For example, you may connect the ADO Data Control to the BIBLIO.MDB database.

2. **Resize and reposition the data control, as necessary.**

3. **Double-click the label control on the Toolbox (the icon near the top with an A displayed on it).**

   VB adds a label to the form.

4. **Drag and stretch the label so it's about the same width as the data control.**

5. **Position the label near the top of the form.**

6. **In the Properties window, double-click the label's DataSource property so it reads Adodc1 (the name of the ADO Data Control).**

   The label is now bound to the data control. (If the Properties window isn't visible, press F4, then click the label to select it and cause its properties to be displayed in the Properties window.)

7. **Click the label control to select it and then press Ctrl+C.**

   The label control is copied to the clipboard.

8. **Click the form to select it and then press Ctrl+V.**

   A dialog box appears, asking if you want to create a control array.

9. **Click No.**

   The dialog box closes, and a copy of your label control appears on the form. You now have two labels, and both of them have the same DataSource.

10. **Continue pasting labels on the form until you have one label for each field that you want to display.**

11. **Drag the labels so each is visible.**

12. **Specify which field each label should display.**

    To complete this step, select a label, and in the Properties window, change its DataField property to specify which field the selected label should display. Be sure to set the DataField property for each label on your form.

    If you're following along with my example, click the top label, and in the Properties window, change its DataField property to Au_ID. Then, click the second label, and in the Properties window change its DataField property to Author.

13. **Press F5 to run this project.**

As you click the buttons in the data control, the application displays two fields for each record that you access, as shown in Figure 3-8.

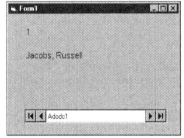

Figure 3-8:
The user can now see two fields, one in each label.

Off to See the Wizard

As I explain in previous sections of this chapter, the data control works for some read-only projects in which the user merely views the information in a database. But what if you want to let users of your application add, delete, update, and refresh database records? That kind of application requires that you add some programming.

You can do the programming the old-fashioned way, by hand, but you might be entirely satisfied with the programming written for you by the Data Form Wizard. It uses the ADO Data Control, but it goes beyond that control's built-in capabilities. The Wizard writes some programming that adds additional features to your project.

You can also tell the Wizard not to use the ADO Data Control if you prefer — it then connects to your database by writing programming code instead. (See Step 7 in the following procedure.)

When the Wizard is finished, you have a form in your project that includes bound controls, CommandButtons, and programming that makes everything work. Based on how you answer the Wizard's questions, you can work with a single table (or query), or a more sophisticated one-to-many relationship (each record in a table can have many records in a different, related table, which is called a *join* or *relationship*). You can also tell the Wizard to display the data in a grid or datasheet, thereby displaying more than one record at a time.

To use the Data Form Wizard, follow these steps:

1. **Choose Project⇨Add Form.**

   The Add Form dialog box appears.

2. **Double-click the VB Data Form Wizard icon.**

   The Data Form Wizard Introduction dialog box appears.

3. **Click Next.**

   (You won't be using a saved profile. A profile enables you to quickly reproduce the same data form in the future, without having to answer all the questions the Wizard asks.)

   The Data Form Wizard – Database Type dialog box appears, as shown in Figure 3-9.

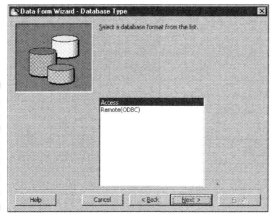

Figure 3-9:
Choose the type of database to which you're connecting.

4. **Leave the default type (Access) selected and click Next.**

   The Data Form Wizard – Database dialog box appears.

5. **Click Browse.**

   As shown in Figure 3-10, the Access Database dialog box opens, enabling you to locate the database you want to use on your hard drive.

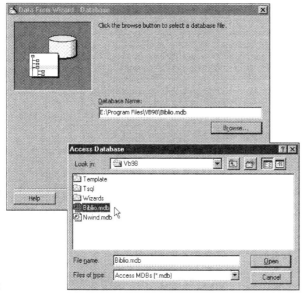

Figure 3-10:
Locate a
database
with this
dialog box.

If you want to use the sample database but you don't see BIBLIO.MDB in
the default directory after clicking Browse, locate it by clicking the
Windows Start button and then choosing Find➪Files or Folders. If you
still can't find it, rerun Visual Basic's setup program and agree to install
all templates and samples.

6. Double-click the database that you want to use.

The Access Database dialog box closes, and the path to the selected
database appears in the TextBox.

7. Click Next.

The Data Form Wizard – Form dialog box appears, as shown in
Figure 3-11.

Notice in Figure 3-11 that you can select three Binding Types. I describe
the ADO Data Control connection earlier in this chapter, in the section
"Using the New ADO Data Control." The second option, ADO Code,
avoids the control and simply writes the programming necessary for
connecting to a database in VB's traditional code. And, instead of using
the data control to permit the user to move through the records, four
CommandButtons and a label replicate the look of the data control. With
the third option, Class, the Wizard writes the programming necessary
for building a data-aware class.

How do you want the user to view the records in the database? You have
several choices: a single record at a time, two kinds of grids, a chart, and
a Master/Detail format. In the example that I describe in this section,
you use the default Single Record format. See Chapter 7 for examples of
the other formats.

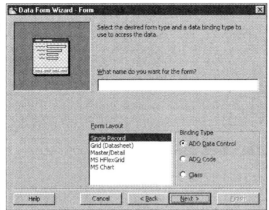

Figure 3-11:
Decide
which kind
of display
the user will
see, as well
as what kind
of connec-
tion to make
to the
database.

8. **Leave the defaults (Single Record and ADO Data Control) selected and click Next.**

   For the example, you can also leave the TextBox blank, and VB names the form frmAuthors because in the next step you select the Authors table as your record source.

   The Data Form Wizard – Record Source dialog box appears, as shown in Figure 3-12.

9. **Choose the table that you want to use as the record source.**

   For the example that I present in this section, use Authors as the record source (it's a table in the BIBLIO database).

   The Available Fields list displays the fields in the selected table.

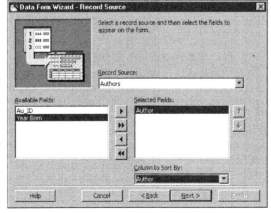

Figure 3-12:
The Data
Form
Wizard's
Record
Source
dialog box.

10. **In the Available Fields list, double-click the name of the field that you want to display.**

    A field that you select moves from the Available Fields list to the Selected Fields list.

11. **In the Column to Sort By drop-down list, select the field that you want to use as the index for sorting records.**

    For example, select Author. The alphabetized Author field serves as the index for the single records (by default, the Au_ID field is the index).

12. **Click Next.**

    The Data Form Wizard – Control Selection dialog box appears, as shown in Figure 3-13. You can remove any of these options by clicking the check box next to it to deselect it.

13. **Click Next, leaving all five buttons selected.**

    The Data Form Wizard — Finished! dialog box appears.

14. **Click Finish.**

    A dialog box appears, telling you that the form has been created.

15. **Click OK.**

    The dialog box closes and the Wizard closes.

If you've followed along with the example I describe in this section, you can test your new data form: Double-click Form1 to get to the code window and then type this code into Form1's Load Event:

```
Private Sub Form_Load()
    Hide
    frmAuthors.Show
End Sub
```

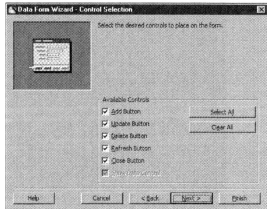

Figure 3-13: The Data Form Wizard's Control Selection dialog box.

This code hides the main form (Form1) and shows the form that contains the data. In a real-world application, you would probably change the startup form to frmAuthors by choosing Project⇨Project1 Properties and then changing the Startup Object.

Now press F5 to run your application. You see the results shown in Figure 3-14.

Figure 3-14:
This form
gives the
user access
to the
database.

Chapter 4

Using the Data Environment Designer

*I*n Visual Basic, you have lots of ways to connect to a database. You can do it with programming that you write by hand (see Chapters 14 through 16) or you can drop a data control on your form (see Chapter 3). You can also connect to a database by using the new VB 6 Data Environment Designer, which I describe in this chapter.

The Data Environment Designer has several strengths compared to alternative ways of connecting an application to a database. In fact, this Designer should usually be your first choice of connection. For example, it enables you to reduce the amount of code necessary to manipulate a database, but (unlike the Data Control) the Designer offers you greater freedom to define how the connection, and your application, manage the data. Not convinced yet? Keep reading to discover more benefits that this Designer brings you.

Previous versions of Visual Basic offered a similar tool, the UserConnection Designer, which performed some of the same tasks as the new Data Environment Designer. However, the Data Environment Designer offers everything the UserConnection did, as well as such new features as drag and drop. Among other things, you can simply drag a table from the Data Environment Designer and drop it onto a VB form. If you do that, data-bound controls (such as paired Labels and TextBoxes for each field) automatically appear on the form, and Visual Basic automatically binds those controls to your DataEnvironment.

Other improvements offered by the Data Environment Designer include multiple data connections, new OLE DB data sources (along with the older ODBC sources), the capability to bind a DataEnvironment connection directly to controls, and features for contacting and managing the DataEnvironment with programming. The Designer also enables you to connect to multiple tables or queries through only a single connection to your database. Therefore, you can write programming using the standard client/server conventions in which a single user session usually opens only one database connection. Finally, the older UserConnection technology exposed RDO objects; the Data Environment Designer uses ADO objects (see Chapter 15 for details on this distinction).

Adding a Data Environment Designer to a VB Project

You may be a bit mixed up by two terms used in this chapter: *Data Environment Designer* and *DataEnvironment* object. They're really nearly the same thing: Whenever you add the Designer to a VB project, a DataEnvironment object is automatically created and placed into your Project Explorer. Double-click that object, and you see the Designer — a special window in which you can define connections, commands, and other relationships. The Designer and the object are, in a sense, two ways of looking at the same thing in the VB editor — both define the object that, when the application runs, is used to connect the application to a database or databases.

Many of the database-related features in VB 6 rely on the Data Environment Designer (for example, the Query Designer, the Data Form Wizard, the DataReport Designer, and the Data Object Wizard). So, exploring how to use the Data Environment Designer is worth your time.

To add a Data Environment Designer to a new VB project, follow these simple steps:

1. **Choose File⇨New Project.**

   The New Project dialog box appears.

2. **Double-click the Standard EXE icon to start a typical, traditional VB project.**

   The New Project dialog box closes, and you see a blank form.

3. **Choose Project⇨Add Data Environment.**

   Wait a minute — you probably don't see the Add Data Environment option on your Project menu! (VB is full of these little surprises — it's a good way to discourage novices and casual users.) Steps 4–7 show you how to add this option to the Project menu. If you *do* see the Add Data Environment option, go to Step 8.

4. Choose Project⇨Components.

The Components dialog box appears.

5. Click the Designers tab, as shown in Figure 4-1.

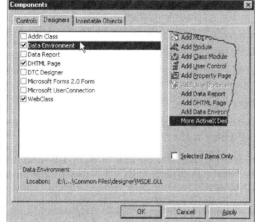

Figure 4-1:
You add
the Data
Environment
Designer to
a project by
selecting
the Data
Environment
in the
Designers
list.

6. Click the check box next to Data Environment, as shown in Figure 4-1.

7. Click OK.

The Components dialog box closes, and the Add Data Environment option is now available on the Project menu.

8. Now you can choose Project⇨Add Data Environment.

A new DataEnvironment is added to your project, and it includes a connection object named *Connection1,* as shown in Figure 4-2.

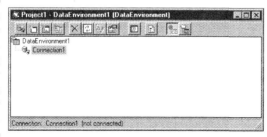

Figure 4-2:
A brand-new
Data
Environment
Designer
now awaits
your
instructions.

Connecting to a Database

After you have a Data Environment Designer up and running in your project (see the previous section in this chapter), you need to connect the DataEnvironment to a database. Technically, you define the properties of a *connection object* and then use that object to access the database. And, you can create more than one connection object.

Follow these steps to create a connection object:

1. **Add a Data Environment Designer to your VB project by following the steps I describe in the previous section of this chapter.**

   You see the Data Environment Designer window, as shown in Figure 4-2, as well as a new category in the Project Explorer named Designers. And in that category, you see DataEnvironment1 (DataEnvironment).

2. **In the Properties window, change the name *Connection1* to a more descriptive name, if you want.**

   For example, if you want to use the connection object with the sample Northwind database that's supplied with VB 6, you might name the connection object **conNWind**.

   The name changes in the Data Environment Designer.

3. **Right-click the connection object in the DataEnvironment window.**

   A context menu pops out, as shown in Figure 4-3.

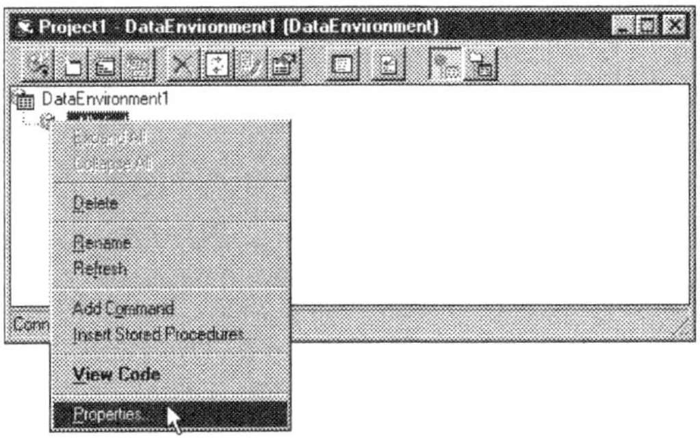

Figure 4-3:
This menu
enables you
to manage
a data
connection.

4. **Click Properties on the context menu.**

   The Data Link Properties dialog box appears.

5. **On the Provider tab in the Data Link Properties dialog box, click Microsoft Jet 4 OLE DB Provider (or use whatever version is available, if Jet 4 isn't in your list).**

The Jet provider option is highlighted. (I use Jet in this book, for all the examples. See Chapter 5 for a discussion of Jet's advantages over alternative engines.)

6. **Click the Connection tab.**

   Figure 4-4 shows the Connection tab in the Data Link Properties dialog box.

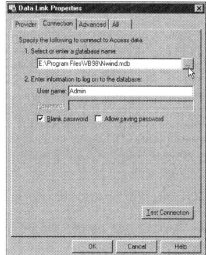

Figure 4-4:
Specify the database's path in this Data Link Properties dialog box.

7. **Click the button with the three dots (...) on the Connection tab.**

   A file selection dialog box appears.

8. **Browse your hard drive until you locate the database that you want to use.**

   (To find the NWIND.MDB sample database, look in the Program Files\Microsoft Visual Studio\VB98 directory.)

9. **Double-click the name of the database you want.**

   The file selection dialog box closes.

   Some databases require *authentication* — that is, entry of a valid name and password — before you're allowed access. As you can see in Figure 4-4, the Data Link Properties dialog box has a provision for supplying log-on information.

10. **Click OK.**

   The Data Link Properties dialog box closes.

You're now connected to a database, but you need to specify the data that you want to see — tables, fields, stored procedures, or whatever. To do that, you add a *command object.*

Adding a Command Object

After you add a Data Environment Designer to a VB project and then attach a database to a connection object in the Designer, you're ready to specify which information you want to access. A command object defines the data that your application exposes to the user. A command object can be a SQL query or a database object (such as a stored procedure or a table).

A command is like a *method* in other objects: You define the input parameters and define what it returns. By adding a command to the DataEnvironment object, you make the method (what the command *does*) available at runtime. In other words, you can write programming that triggers the command, in the same way as you can write Form.Show to trigger the Show method of the Form object in VB.

To create a command object that connects to a particular table in a database:

1. **Add a Data Environment Designer to your project and then specify which database you want to access.**

   For all the details on adding a Data Environment Designer and connecting to a database, see the previous sections in this chapter.

2. **In the Data Environment Designer, right-click the connection object.**

   (If you named your connection *conNWind* in the previous section, for example, right-click that connection object.)

   A context menu pops out.

3. **Choose Add Command.**

   A new command is added, with the default name of Command1. Now you need to specify what this Command1 object does.

4. **Right-click Command1.**

   A context menu pops out.

5. **Choose Properties.**

   The Command1 Properties dialog box appears, as shown in Figure 4-5.

Figure 4-5:
You can
define many
ways to
access
information,
as well as
how that
data should
be organized.

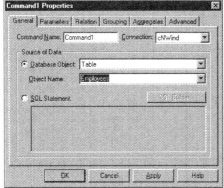

As you can see in Figure 4-5, a command object's Properties dialog box includes several tabs — among them, Relation, Grouping, and Aggregates. These often-useful features enable you to refine recordsets of data, or even, in the case of Aggregates, perform some calculations on data (such as adding up, spreadsheet-style, the total money spent by all current customers). I cover these features in Chapter 19.

6. **Click the down-arrow icon on the ListBox next to Database Object and then select Table from the drop-down list.**

7. **Click the down-arrow icon on the ListBox next to Object Name and then select the table you want from the drop-down list of tables.**

8. **Click OK.**

The Command1 Properties dialog box closes. Notice the small plus sign (+) that now appears next to Command1 in the Data Environment Designer. This symbol tells you that the command object now contains something — something you can see if you click the +.

9. **Click the small +.**

You see a list of all the fields in the table that the command object defines, as shown in Figure 4-6.

10. **Right-click Command1.**

A context menu pops out.

11. **Choose Rename from the context menu.**

The name Command1 is highlighted and surrounded by a box, indicating you can type in that box.

12. **Rename Command1, giving it a more descriptive name.**

For example, you might rename Command1 as tEmployees.

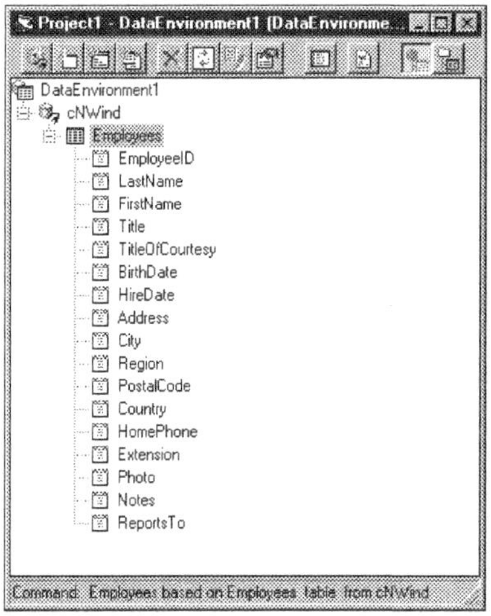

Figure 4-6:
This
command
object
is attached
to the
Employees
table in the
NWind
database.

Adding a Command Object the Easy Way

You can quickly add a command object to a connection if you use the Data
View window. This feature is one of the drag-and-drop shortcuts now available in Visual Basic 6. Here's how you drag a table from the Data View
window and drop it on a command object in the Data Environment Designer:

1. **Add a Data Environment Designer to your project, specify which database you want to access, and create a command object.**

   For all the details on completing this step, see the previous sections in
   this chapter. If you want to try this process with the Northwind sample
   database that comes with VB 6, you can use the Employees table and
   create a command object named tEmployees.

2. **Right-click the command object.**

   A context menu pops out.

3. **Choose Delete from the context menu, to remove this command
   object.**

   (You want to see how to add a new command in this section, so you can
   get rid of this old command.) A dialog box appears, asking if you're sure
   you want to delete this object.

4. **Click Yes.**

   The dialog box closes, and the command object disappears from the
   Data Environment Designer.

5. **Choose View➪Data View Window.**

   The Data View window opens.

6. **Click the + symbol next to Tables in the Data View window.**

   The Data View window lists all the tables in your Data Environment connection, as shown in Figure 4-7.

Figure 4-7:
You can
drag and
drop tables
and stored
procedures
from this
Data View
window into
a Data
Environment
Designer.

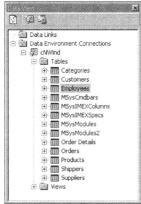

7. **Drag the table you want from the Data View window and drop it on the name of your connection object in the Data Environment Designer.**

   If you're following along with the examples that I present throughout this chapter, drop the Employees table on the conNWind connection object. A new command object appears in the Data Environment Designer. (In my example, the command object is named *Employees.*)

Making Magic Reports

Ready for a little VB magic? In the previous section, I show you how to create a command object by dragging a table from the Data View window and dropping it into the Data Environment Designer. In this section, you drag a command object from the Data Environment Designer and drop it onto a VB form. What will happen, I wonder? VB automatically creates a set of Labels describing each field in the command object, and also creates a set of TextBoxes to hold the data for each field.

Follow these steps to put VB 6 to work, generating a report display for you:

1. **Add a Data Environment Designer to your project, specify which database you want to access, and create a command object.**

I describe the procedures for completing these tasks in previous sections of this chapter. If you want to follow along by using the Employees table in the sample Northwind database that comes with VB 6, create a command object named Employees.

2. **If the Data View window isn't visible, choose View➪Data View Window.**

   The Data View window appears (see Figure 4-7, earlier in this chapter).

3. **Drag the table you want to use from the Data View window and drop it onto Form1.**

   Pay no attention to the man behind the curtain! Right before your very eyes, Form1 is populated with a Label and a TextBox for every field in the selected table, as shown in Figure 4-8.

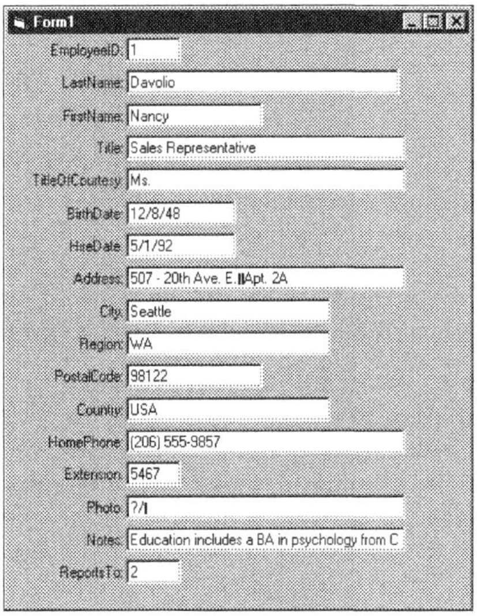

Figure 4-8:
Visual Basic automatically creates this data-entry display, after you drop a table onto the form.

4. **Press F5 to run this application.**

   The TextBoxes fill with the data from the first record in the selected table.

5. **Click the X in the upper right corner of Form1.**

   The application stops running, and you're back in VB design mode.

6. **Click a TextBox to select it.**

   The Properties window displays the TextBox's properties.

7. Look at the DataSource property.

You see that the source of data for the TextBox control is DataEnvironment1.

Also notice that the DataMember property identifies the table you're using, and the DataField property differs for each TextBox.

Displaying Views

A database can contain *stored procedures.* Usually, a stored procedure is a SQL statement that provides a specialized, organized subset of the data in a database. In plain English, a stored procedure may show you, for example, all the hotels with rooms available in New York City next Wednesday.

One kind of stored procedure is a *view.* A view is stored on the database server. It's essentially like a table and is updated each time you request the view. However, unlike a true table, a view's data isn't stored together in the database — instead, it's extracted from other tables as required when the view is requested. A view is sometimes called a *query result set.*

A view is not read-only — data changed to a view can be stored to update the tables from which the view was extracted. Most ODBC-compliant databases can offer views.

As I explain in Chapter 17, you can use SQL to specify particular types and ranges of data that you want to extract from a database. The difference between a stored procedure and a SQL statement in a typical VB database project is that the stored procedure resides within the database (usually on a server), whereas a SQL statement resides on the client machine. In other words, if you find a stored procedure you can use, you don't have to create a SQL query in your application.

To look at a view, follow these steps:

1. Create a connection object by completing the steps I describe in the section "Connecting to a Database," earlier in this chapter.

If you're following along with the examples that I present throughout this chapter, you're now connected to the NWIND.MDB sample database.

2. Right-click Connection1 in the Data Environment Designer. (If you've renamed it to conNWind or something, right-click whatever name you gave it.)

A context menu pops out.

3. **Choose Add Command.**

   A new command is added, with the default name of Command1. You can now specify what this Command1 object does.

4. **Right-click Command1.**

   A context menu pops out.

5. **Choose Properties in the context menu.**

   The Command1 Properties dialog box opens.

6. **Click the down-arrow icon on the ListBox next to Database Object and then select View from the drop-down list.**

7. **Click the down-arrow icon on the ListBox next to Object Name and then select the view you want from the drop-down list.**

   For example, you may select Customers and Suppliers by City.

8. **Click OK.**

   The Command1 Properties dialog box closes.

9. **Click the small + next to Command1 in the Data Environment Designer.**

   You see a list of all the fields in the view.

10. **Drag Command1 and drop it on Form1.**

    If you're following along with my example, the four fields in the *Customers and Suppliers by City* view are reproduced on the form, with a label and a text box for each field.

11. **Press F5 to run the program.**

    You see the first record in the view, as shown in Figure 4-9.

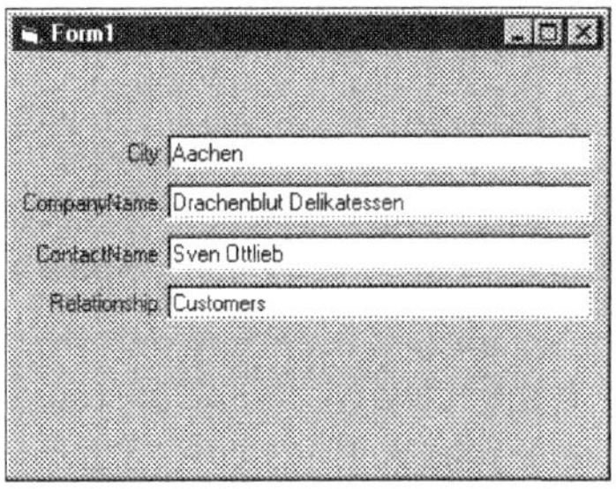

Figure 4-9:
This is a record from a "virtual table," also known as a *view*.

Manipulating a DataEnvironment with Programming

As I explain in previous sections of this chapter, you can put a DataEnvironment into a VB project and use it, along with the Data View window, to easily create connections and commands that tap into a database's innards. But can you manage a DataEnvironment object by writing programming code? Sure.

Chapters 15 and 16 focus on VB's database programming language and the new ADO technology. However, if you want to work with a little programmatic DataEnvironment manipulation, you can try the process I describe in this section.

You can programmatically create Connection, Command, and Recordset objects by using ADO programming (see Chapter 16). Or, as this chapter explains, you can create them by using the Data Environment Designer. The third possibility is to create the objects with the Data Environment Designer and then manipulate the objects with programming. This third approach avoids the need for writing programming that explicitly opens the connection or any commands. (Note that you need not use commands — you can always just use recordsets by themselves. Commands are useful mainly for executing a stored procedure.)

To create an instance (an object) of your DataEnvironment and then display data from a recordset contained within that object, follow these steps:

1. **Choose File⇨New Project.**

   The New Project dialog box opens.

2. **Double-click the Standard EXE icon to start a typical, traditional VB project.**

   The New Project dialog box closes, and you see a blank form.

3. **Choose Project⇨Add Data Environment.**

   If you don't see the Add Data Environment option on the Project menu, complete Steps 4 through 8. If you see the Add Data Environment option on your Project menu, choose it and then proceed to Step 9.

4. **Choose Project⇨Components.**

   The Components dialog box opens.

5. **Click the Designers tab.**

6. **Click the check box next to Data Environment.**

7. **Click OK.**

   The Components dialog box closes, and the Add Data Environment option is now available on the Project menu.

8. **Now choose Project⇨Add Data Environment.**

9. **Right-click Connection1 in the Data Environment window.**

   A context menu pops out.

10. **Choose Properties.**

    The Data Link Properties dialog box opens.

11. **On the Provider tab in the Data Link Properties dialog box, click Microsoft Jet 4 OLE DB Provider (or use whatever version is available, if Jet 4 isn't in your list).**

    The Jet provider option is highlighted.

12. **Click the Connection tab.**

13. **Click the button with the three dots (...) on the Connection tab.**

    A file selection dialog box opens.

14. **Browse your hard drive until you locate the database you want to use.**

    (To find the NWIND.MDB sample database, look in the Program Files\Microsoft Visual Studio\VB98 directory.)

15. **Double-click the name of the database.**

    The file selection dialog box closes.

16. **Choose View⇨Data View Window.**

    The Data View window opens.

17. **Click the + symbol next to Connection1 in the Data View window.**

    The Tables and Views folders appear.

18. **Click the + symbol next to Tables in the Data View window.**

    The Data View window lists all the tables in the Data Environment.

19. **Drag the table you want to use from the Data View window and drop it on the name Connection1 in the Data Environment Designer.**

    A new command object (named *Employees,* if you're using the example I suggested) appears in the Data Environment Designer. The command object has the same name as the table you dropped on Connection1.

20. **Click Form1 to give it the focus and then double-click the ListBox icon in the Toolbox.**

    A listbox appears on Form1.

21. **Drag the corners of the listbox so it nearly fills Form1.**

22. **Double-click Form1.**

    The code window appears, with the Form_Load event displayed.

23. **Type the following programming into the Form_Load event:**

```
Private Sub Form_Load()
Dim DE As New DataEnvironment1
DE.employees
DE.rsEmployees.MoveFirst

Do While DE.rsEmployees.EOF = False
List1.AddItem DE.rsEmployees.Fields(1)
DE.rsEmployees.MoveNext
Loop

End Sub
```

In this source code, replace, if necessary, *Employees* and *rsEmployees* with the name of the recordset you're using.

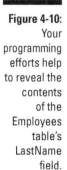

Although the ADO connection has not yet opened, when you execute a command in the DataEnvironment, the recordset object is automatically created for you and the ADO connection is also opened.

24. **Press F5.**

    The program runs and you see the results shown in Figure 4-10.

Figure 4-10:
Your
programming
efforts help
to reveal the
contents
of the
Employees
table's
LastName
field.

You thought that the object model (the syntax required to access a DataEnvironment and its components) would be straightforward and recognizable from previous programming you've done? You thought you could string together `DataEnvironment1.Command1` and create an object that way?

Not in this universe. Alas, many object models have varying syntax. Makes life interesting. Also results in lots of head-banging.

The preceding code has two profoundly weird pieces. Here's one:

```
DE.employees
```

This totally new syntax points the DataEnvironment object to the Employees command object.

For every command that returns recordsets, the DataEnvironment creates an object with that command's name and the prefix rs. That new object points to the recordset returned by the command. This recordset becomes available only after you've executed the command, just as you would any other method in an object.

The Microsoft help engine offers the following explanation for the rs nuisance:

> In the Data Environment, the names of ADO Recordset objects are prefaced with "rs" to distinguish them from their corresponding Command objects. For example, a Command object named Customers creates a Recordset object named rsCustomers. By default, Recordset objects are closed. When the Recordset object's corresponding Command method executes, the Recordset object opens. For example, executing the Customers method opens the Recordset object of "rsCustomers." In addition, you can open a Recordset object directly using the ADO Open method. Using this method, you can manipulate a Recordset object before it is opened.

Now, consider one of the points being made at the very end of this help text. You are told that you can "open" a Recordset and thereby manipulate it "before it is opened." Hmm.

In some respects, I'm glad that this kind of perplexing information appears in documentation. That kind of foggy thinking (along with the many, many disabled — missing — Example hyperlinks in the help engine) make it possible for authors like me to spend two days puzzling out some syntax and offer it to you in a book. I did spend the better part of two days trying to figure out how to programmatically manipulate a DataEnvironment. (I describe another programmatic approach in the following section.)

Recordsets are now independent objects and are not tied exclusively to the hierarchy. You can even build recordsets from scratch. Recordsets are objects, like everything else, and they sport properties and methods, one of them being Open. You can open and manipulate a recordset object independently before you open it against the database that populates it with data.

Manipulating a DataEnvironment with Programming, Revisited

Microsoft usually offers many and various ways to get a job done — many languages, object models, components, add-ins, wizards, and other paths to a goal. For example, here's a different way to write programming that manipulates a DataEnvironment object:

1. **Follow Steps 1 through 22 in the previous section, "Manipulating a DataEnvironment with Programming."**

2. **Move your cursor above the Form_Load event.**

   You're now in the General Declarations section of Form1.

3. **Type this code in the General Declarations section of Form1:**

```
Dim cnn As ADODB.Connection
Dim cmd As ADODB.Command
Dim rs As ADODB.Recordset
```

4. **Type this code in the Form_Load event:**

```
Private Sub Form_Load()

Set cnn = DataEnvironment1.Connection1
Set cmd = New ADODB.Command
cnn.Open
Set cmd.ActiveConnection = cnn

cmd.CommandText = "Employees"
cmd.CommandType = adCmdTable
cmd.CommandTimeout = 15

Set rs = cmd.Execute()

Do While Not rs.EOF
    List1.AddItem rs!LastName
    rs.MoveNext
Loop

rs.Close
cnn.Close

End Sub
```

5. **Press F5, and you see the same result as shown in Figure 4-10.**

In this example, you build three objects: a connection, a command, and a recordset object. The command object, however, isn't something you created using the Data Environment Designer.

Instead, you build the command in the code by defining some of its properties: its CommandText (in this case, the name of a table in the database) and
its CommandType (table) property. Then, you "execute" the command, which
dumps the resulting recordset into a Recordset object named rs.

A Form is never itself bound to a DataEnvironment. You open an ADO connection (cnn.Open in the preceding example). When you add a data-bound control
(the TextBox in the example) to a form, because the control is linked to an ADO
command in the DataEnvironment, that command is executed when the form is
loaded. When commands are executed in the DataEnvironment object, the
ADO connection is automatically opened for you.

You must open the connection in your code (cnn.Open) before setting the
ActiveConnection property or else an error occurs. This is a great feature
because (unlike the Data Control) it enables you to decide where and when
your connection is to be opened. And because opening database connections
takes a long time — in computer terms — and gobbles up resources, this feature enables you to code intelligently and remain in control of what goes on,
and where and when things happen in your applications.

When you run a VB project that contains a DataEnvironment, each command
you've specified in the Data Environment Designer generates a command
object, just as each connection generates a connection object. By default,
command objects are "Recordset Returning" so a recordset object is also
generated for each command object at runtime. (You can deselect the
Recordset Returning option on the Advanced tab of a command's Properties
dialog box.)

If you are interested in binding data-aware controls (such as a TextBox) to a
DataEnvironment, note that at this time, some VB controls recognize the
DataEnvironment as a proper conduit to a database, and some controls don't.
You can tell by attempting to assign your DataEnvironment to the DataSource
Property of the control you're interested in.

In some cases, you want to refresh a recordset so you can see exactly how
the data currently exists in the database. You use the Requery method, as in
this example:

```
DataEnvironment1.rsCustomers.Requery
```

A Requery is the equivalent of closing and then reopening the recordset.
However, following a Requery, you *must* rebind any data-bound controls.
Here's an example:

```
With Text1
    Set .DataSource = DataEnvironment1
    .DataMember = "Customers"
    .DataField = "ContactName"
End With
```

Chapter 5

A Collection of Connections

*W*hen you think about working with databases, a primary question is: Which kind of database engine should I use? Jet? Oracle? Access? SQL Server? This chapter describes the uses of the Jet engine and then goes into *data sources* in depth.

A *database engine* is the software that actually manages the database — only the engine has direct access to the data in a database. By itself, a database file is merely an orderly collection of information. It's not usually an executable program that can, by itself, *do* anything. So, you need an engine that can look at your request — such as "get me a list of all employees' last names" — and then go to the database and extract that information for you. You can think of a database as the books and the engine as a smart research librarian.

True enough, some databases contain stored procedures (and some databases don't reside in simple, passive data files). But stored procedures — and their cousins, views — are not actually programming that executes. Instead, they are merely built-in queries. With a stored procedure, instead of handing the database engine a SQL statement, you hand the database engine the name of the stored SQL statement. In either case, it's the engine that runs, not the database.

The current versions of Jet and the DAO programming technology (see Chapter 15) are doomed to be the last versions. At least, that's the plan. (Sometimes, Microsoft doesn't follow the plan, so you'll have to wait and see.) Microsoft does not plan to revise or expand them, though it will support them indefinitely. Why? Because Access and, to a lesser extent, Visual Basic use them, and vast numbers of users, developers, and programmers depend on them.

The Little Engine That Could

The Jet engine (get it?) acts essentially like a high-level language (such as Basic itself). You provide Jet with a command, such as MoveNext, and it takes care of the low-level details necessary for performing the command — for example, moving to the next record in the database.

For your purposes (finding out how to work with databases), Jet is the engine of choice for several reasons:

✔ It's a solid, established technology.

✔ It's the world's most popular database engine.

✔ It works with Visual Basic and Access.

✔ It's the right scale: Jet is specially designed to be highly efficient with desktop and smaller intranet database applications.

Actually, and ironically, Excel is the most popular database around, even though it's not a "real" database. It is nonetheless often used as one. Access is number two.

For large-scale database applications, consider SQL Server or Oracle. Jet works great unless you go beyond, say, 600 records in a given table or recordset, or you go beyond approximately four or five users. Past that point, you are likely to run into some performance degradation and user-traffic problems. If you need a powerhouse, you go on to what's called a *client/server* solution, such as SQL Server (which does come with the Enterprise edition of Visual Basic 6). Some databases with 100,000 plus records actually *are* reported to run smoothly under Jet, but don't push it by allowing more than a few users simultaneously. Multi-user traffic is not Jet's strong point.

Jet does support multiple users, but each request is handled by the client computer that's making the request. Nothing on the server executes requests or returns the data those requests want. With a client/server database engine, you have something called a *back end*. (No rude comments, please.) A back end simply means that programming resides on the server to provide security features, manage multiple users, and retrieve and temporarily store data.

To understand a bit more about what the Jet connection means to a VB data-base programmer, consider Jet in relation to Access. Access is a Microsoft application — part of the Microsoft Office suite of applications. Access is a standalone database manager that works with relational databases. Access uses both the Jet engine and, among others, the Data Access Objects (DAO) technology (see Chapter 15).

Technically, DAO is a library of objects that stands between Access, or some other database manager application, and the Jet engine, providing relatively high-level communication between the application and the down-and-dirty, low-level behaviors of the Jet engine itself.

If your application uses a Jet database, you don't need to have Access installed on the user's computer. When you use the Visual Basic setup utility to create an installer program, setup includes the Jet libraries within your Visual Basic application, so people who use your database program have everything they need.

All About Data Sources

In Visual Basic 5 and earlier versions, you had to put a data control on a form and then connect the data control to a database. Then, you would bind other controls — such as a text box — to the data control.

Visual Basic 6 offers you more flexibility. You can create a *data source* and bind (connect) any data-aware control directly to the data source, bypassing a data control entirely, if you want. You can even create a set of data sources, which can be in special data link files on the hard drive, or they can reside in the Registry. A data source is not a control; instead, it is a description of a connection to a database.

The three main connections

Visual Basic gives you three fundamental ways to connect a control to a database:

- ✔ Creating a new connection string
- ✔ Referencing a data link file
- ✔ Using an existing data connection

Each approach has its uses. In this chapter, I show you examples of each kind of connection. (Chapter 4 describes the Data Environment Designer, which offers a somewhat different approach to creating a data source.)

In the following sections, I show you how to create data sources and then connect them to the new ADO Data Control. But remember that you can directly connect *any* control to a data source in Visual Basic, as long as that control has a DataSource property.

Creating a new connection string

A *connection string* is a path to a database, and the string can also include information about security and other features of the database. Think of a connection string as similar to the programming you would write to attach a database to a VB application.

To create a new connection string to attach an ADO Data Control to a database, follow these steps:

1. **Choose File⇨New Project**

   You see the VB New Project dialog box.

2. **Double-click the Standard EXE icon.**

   A standard VB project is started.

3. **Right-click the VB Toolbox and choose Components.**

   The Components dialog box opens.

4. **In the Controls listbox, find the Microsoft ADO Data Control 6.0 (OLE DB) and click the box to the left of this control's name.**

   A check appears in the box, indicating that the ADO Data Control will be loaded onto the Toolbox.

5. **Click OK.**

   The dialog box closes.

6. **Put an ADO Data Control on Form1.**

7. **Double-click the ConnectionString Property in the Properties window.**

   The Property Pages dialog box for the data control appears, as shown in Figure 5-1.

8. **Click the option button next to Use Connection String to select it, as shown in Figure 5-1.**

   If you know what you want, you can type a connection string into the Use Connection String TextBox. However, the Build wizard is usually a real help.

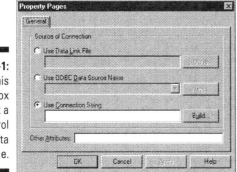

Figure 5-1:
Use this
dialog box
to connect a
data control
to a data
source.

9. **Click Build.**

   The Data Link Properties dialog box opens, as shown in Figure 5-2.

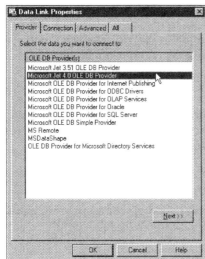

Figure 5-2:
Use the
Data Link
Properties
dialog box
to specify
which data-
base engine
you want to
use, and to
specify a
particular
database.

10. **Select Microsoft Jet 4.0 OLE DB Provider (or use whatever version you have if 4.0 is not listed).**

11. **Click Next.**

    The Connection tab is displayed, as shown in Figure 5-3.

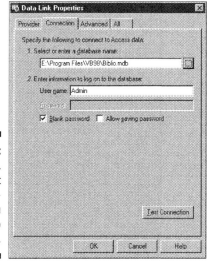

Figure 5-3:
On this tab, you select the database you want to connect to.

12. **Click the button with the three dots (...) to the right of the Select Or Enter A Database Name TextBox on the Connection tab.**

    A Select Access Database dialog box appears, enabling you to locate an .MDB file.

13. **Locate and then double-click the name of the database that you want to use.**

    (The sample BIBLIO.MDB file is usually in your VB98 directory.)

    The dialog box closes, and the path to the selected database appears in the Select Or Enter A Database Name TextBox.

14. **If your database requires that you log on and provide a password, you can fill in those fields on the Connection tab as well.**

15. **Click OK.**

    The Data Link Properties dialog box closes.

Take a look at the connection string that you built in the Property Pages dialog box. It should look something like this example:

```
Provider=Microsoft.Jet.OLEDB.4.0;Data Source=C:\Program
        Files\VB98\Biblio.mdb;Persist Security Info=False
```

Advanced connection options

When you use the Data Link Properties dialog box, as demonstrated in the previous section, the properties shown on the various tabs depend on the database engine to which you're connecting.

Visual Basic endeavors to simplify the creation of a connection string. For example, if you click the Advanced tab in the Data Link Properties dialog box following the previous example, you see the tab shown in Figure 5-4.

Figure 5-4:
Some options on this tab are disabled (gray) because they don't apply to this connection string.

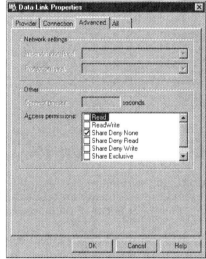

Notice in Figure 5-4 that you can define the level of access. Can users of your database application only read data, or are they also allowed to write (change) that data? You can also specify various levels of permission for other users who can access the data (share).

All connection options

Try clicking the All tab on the Data Link Properties dialog box. You see the dialog box displayed in Figure 5-5.

In some cases, a database provider might require a bit of tweaking to the connection. If the provider's documentation tells you to do so, you might need to adjust some of the settings on the All tab. Simply double-click the setting that you want to edit. An Edit Property Value dialog box opens, and you can click a Property Value drop-down list to see and select from among the available settings.

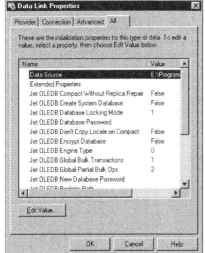

Figure 5-5:
On this tab,
you can edit
any element
of the entire
connection.

Creating an ODBC file data source

The data link you define in the preceding section uses ADO. In this section, you look at a different approach. All these acronyms can get confusing. If you're anxious to understand the differences between them, see Chapter 15.

A second major way to connect a data control to a data source is by creating an ODBC data source, which you can then use as your connection. After you create a data source, it remains available for other connections in the same or future VB projects. In effect, it becomes permanently available — reusable.

To create a data source and then use it to connect a data control to the database described by the data source, follow these steps:

1. **Complete Steps 1 through 7 in the previous section, "Creating a new connection string."**

   You see the Property Pages dialog box shown in Figure 5-1.

2. **Click the Use ODBC Data Source Name option button.**

3. **Click the down-arrow button next to the Use ODBC Data Source Name TextBox.**

   A drop-down list appears, listing the existing data sources currently available on your system, as shown in Figure 5-6. In this section, you create a new data source, but you don't add it to this list. (In the warning at the end of this section, I explain why you're not adding this data source to the list.) I show you how to create one to add to this list in the section "Creating a user data source," later in this chapter.

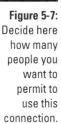

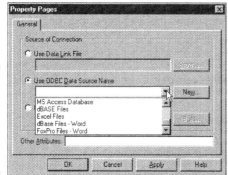

Figure 5-6:
You can
choose a
data source
from this
list.

4. **Click New.**

The Create New Data Source wizard appears, as shown in Figure 5-7.

Figure 5-7:
Decide here
how many
people you
want to
permit to
use this
connection.

5. **Leave the default option button selected.**

You are creating a file-based data source that can be used by others, on other machines.

6. **Click Next.**

The wizard displays a page for selecting the driver (essentially the same idea as an *engine,* which I discuss earlier in this chapter).

7. **Leave the default Microsoft Access Driver (.mdb) option selected. Click Next.**

You see the page on which you can specify where you want to save the file data source. By default, it is saved in \Program Files\Common Files\ODBC\Data Sources. Save it there.

8. **Type in a name for this connection.**

For the examples that I show in the next few figures, I used the name *conBib*. The prefix *con* identifies it as a connection, and the name *Bib* stands for Biblio.

9. **Click Next.**

You see details describing your new connection, as shown in Figure 5-8.

Figure 5-8:
You're almost done. This page displays the details you've specified about the connection you're building.

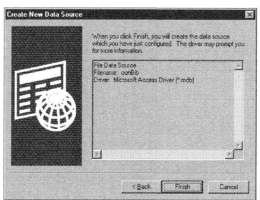

10. **Click Finish.**

The ODBC Microsoft Data Access Setup dialog box appears. This dialog box differs for each ODBC connection type. Based on your selections in the previous steps, you see the one devoted to Access-style databases.

11. **Click Select.**

The Select Database file-browsing dialog box appears.

12. **Locate and then double-click the database you want to use.**

The dialog box closes, and the path to the selected database appears in the ODBC Microsoft Data Access Setup dialog box.

13. **Click OK.**

The ODBC Microsoft Data Access Setup dialog box closes, and you're back in the Property Pages dialog box shown in Figure 5-1.

14. **Click OK.**

The Property Pages dialog box closes.

At last, your new connection is available. In the next section, I show you how to link it to a data control.

The connection you just created is *not* listed in the Use ODBC Data Source Name drop-down list. That's because in Step 5 you chose to make the connection a *File Data Source*. As a result, the connection must be made using the Use Data Link File option, as I describe in the next section.

Referencing a data link file

In the preceding section, I show you how to create a .DSN (Data Source Name) file (also called a *data link file*). This file is a machine-independent data link that can be used by people even on other machines. In Step 5 in the previous section, you choose to create a File Data Source rather than one of the machine-specific sources (a User Data Source or a System Data Source).

A .DSN file describes how your application can be connected to a specific ODBC database. The file contains the necessary connection information to permit the ODBC Driver Manager to make the connection when required. A quite similar file, ending with .UDL (a User Data Link Name file), can be built for the same purposes as a .DSN file. To see one way that you can create a .UDL file, see the section "A Wacky Trick," later in this chapter.

To connect an ADO Data Control to a .DSN File Data Source, follow these steps:

1. **Complete the steps I list in the previous section to create a file data source.**

   If you want to follow along with my example, name the data source conBib.

2. **Follow the steps I describe in the section "Creating a new connection string," earlier in this chapter, to place an ADO Data Control onto Form1.**

3. **Double-click the ConnectionString Property of the ADO Data Control in the Properties window.**

   The Property Pages dialog box for the data control opens (refer to Figure 5-1).

4. **Click the Use Data Link File option.**

5. **Click the Browse button to locate your .DSN file.**

   You see the Select Data Link File dialog box, as shown in Figure 5-9.

6. **Change the Files of Type listbox to ODBC DSNs (*.dsn), as shown in Figure 5-9.**

   You're likely to find your .DSN file in this path:

   ```
   C:\Program Files\Common Files\ODBC\Data Sources\
   ```

7. **Double-click the name of your .DSN file when you locate it.**

   The Select Data Link File dialog box closes, and the path to your .DSN file appears in the Use Data Link File TextBox.

8. **Click OK.**

   The Property Pages dialog box closes, and your ConnectionString Property is set to the correct link.

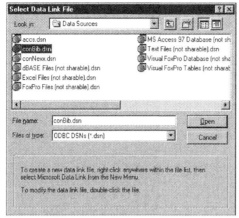

Figure 5-9:
This file-
locating
dialog box
can help
you locate
all data link
files you've
created.

Using an existing data connection

In previous sections of this chapter, I show you how to create a data link file and a connection string — two means for linking to a database. The user data source (or its close cousin, the system data source) is the third kind of connection that can link to databases.

A user data source works only on your machine and only for you. A system data source is similar — working only on your machine — but can be used by others who log onto your computer. After you create a user data source, a new connection appears in the ODBC Data Source list when you double-click a data control's ConnectionString property.

To create a user data source, follow these steps:

1. **Complete Steps 1–4 in the section "Creating an ODBC file data source," earlier in this chapter.**

   You see the Create New Data Source wizard (see Figure 5-7).

2. **Click the User Data Source (Applies to this machine only) option.**

3. **Click Next.**

   You see the Create New Data Source dialog box, as shown in Figure 5-10.

4. **Leave the default Access Driver (Jet engine) selected.**

   You might see a different version of the Jet engine listed. Go ahead and use whatever version you have.

5. **Click Next and then click Finish.**

   You see the ODBC Microsoft Access Setup dialog box.

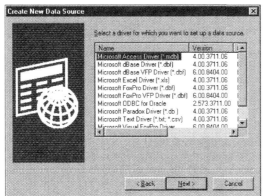

Figure 5-10:
Specify
which
database
engine you
want to use.

6. **Click Select.**

   The Select Database file-browsing dialog box appears.

7. **Locate and then double-click the name of the database you want to use.**

   The dialog box closes, and the path to the selected database appears in the ODBC Microsoft Data Access Setup dialog box.

8. **In the Data Source Name TextBox at the top of the ODBC Microsoft Access Setup dialog box, type the name of your new data source.**

   In the examples for this chapter, I use conBibx as the name of the new data source.

9. **Click OK.**

   The ODBC Microsoft Data Access Setup dialog box closes, and you're back in the Property Pages dialog box, shown in Figure 5-1. Now your new connection is available.

10. **Click the drop-down list titled Use ODBC Data Source Name.**

    You see your new data link in the list, as shown in Figure 5-11.

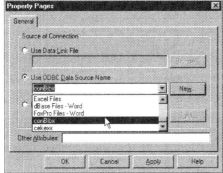

Figure 5-11:
There's
conBibx, the
database
connection I
defined in
my example.

A Wacky Trick

This chapter focuses on ways to create the various kinds of data links. Yet another way exists, and it's a bit odd. It works from Windows Explorer! I guess the idea is that you may be browsing your hard drive one day and say to yourself, "Hey! I think I'll create a new data link."

If you expect that feeling to come over you someday, review the steps I describe in this section to see how it works. You can create a new data link by right-clicking the right pane in Windows Explorer. It doesn't matter what directory you're in. Just click, and off you go! Here's how to do it:

1. **Open Windows Explorer.**

2. **Right-click the right pane.**

   A context menu pops out.

3. **Choose New⇨Microsoft Data Link, as shown in Figure 5-12.**

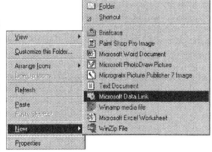

Figure 5-12:
This create-a-datalink option is available in Windows Explorer.

The context menus disappear, and a new .UDL file appears in Explorer. It's selected, indicating to you that you may want to rename it.

4. **Type in a name for your new Data Link file — for example,** MyNewLink.UDL.

5. **Click anywhere in Explorer *other* than on the new file.**

   The file is deselected.

6. **Double-click the filename of your new .UDL data link file.**

   A Data Link Properties dialog box appears, very similar to, but not identical to, the one shown in Figure 5-3.

7. **If you're interested in continuing to define this new data link file, follow the previous sections in this chapter that explain how to create a data link using a connection string or a data source name.**

Creating Data Connections in Control Panel

If you've been reading along from the beginning of this chapter, you're probably thinking that I've covered all possible ways to create a database connection, aren't you? Well, you have one more way: You can create data connections (and manage existing ones) from Control Panel!

In Windows 95/98, the icon is named ODBC(32bit), and in NT 4, the icon is named ODBC Data Sources — other machines call it 32bit ODBC. Whatever it's called, it's an organizer for data connections. To use it, follow these steps:

1. **Click Start➪Settings➪Control Panel.**

   Control Panel opens.

2. **Double-click the ODBC(32bit) icon (or if you use NT, the ODBC Data Sources icon).**

   The ODBC Data Source Administrator appears, as shown in Figure 5-13.

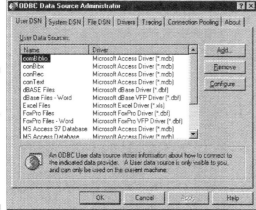

Figure 5-13: This Administrator helps you manage your ODBC data connections.

3. **Click the first three tabs in turn — User DSN, System DSN, and File DSN (Data Source Name).**

   You see each kind of data connection listed in separate pages in the Administrator.

Each of the first three tabs includes Add, Remove, and Configure buttons. The Add and Configure buttons bring up wizards and Property Pages that you'll recognize right away if you've experimented with the various examples in this chapter. The Remove button speaks for itself.

The Drivers tab lists all the database engines registered on your computer. The Tracing tab features tools to assist you in debugging. You can create a log file of calls to ODBC functions and then look at that file to see how one of your database connections is working with those functions. The Connection Pooling tab enables you to specify that a particular database engine can use existing handles, to save time. You can also request Performance Monitoring on this tab. Finally, the About tab lists the primary ODBC dynamic link libraries.

Part III
Contacting
the User

The 5th Wave   By Rich Tennant

Re·al Pro·gram·mers

Real Progammers don't use micros. If it weren't for mainframe delays, there wouldn't be time to go to the bathroom or talk to all the other Real Programmers.

In this part . . .

*1*f you need to make databases work for other people (and that always seems to be part of any programming job), you want to know how to design effective, friendly user-interfaces. Your database needs to be filled with data, so you have to provide bullet-proof ways for users to enter data. And after it's filled with data, you often have to generate reports, displaying subsets of the data in an organized, easily understood manner.

The chapters in this part show you how to get good data into your databases, and how to get good data out of them. Always remember the old programmer's axiom: What goes in must come out.

Chapter 6

Reports — Plain and Fancy

A report is, in its simplest form, just a printout of information from a database. Your application can display the report on-screen, but more often, you send the report to the printer. Of course, like most anything, reports can range from simple to complex.

This chapter demonstrates how to use Visual Basic's new DataReport Designer to make constructing reports a snap. I explain how you can easily display and group data into logical lists called *groups* (such as displaying customers grouped by the state where they live). You also find out how to create groups within groups to make the report even easier to understand. And by simply clicking the Export button on the DataReport Designer, you can translate a report into HTML so you can add it to a Web page. The DataReport Designer writes all the HTML code for you — and there's tons of code when HTML displays tables of data. "Your hands never get the least bit soiled," as the ads used to say.

What Is a Report?

Usually, you need to create a report because the boss says something like this: Let me have a list showing the sales figures for each customer. List them alphabetically but give me a separate list for each country.

Your job, should you feel like doing it (ha!), is to mentally translate the word *list* into *report* and then extract the requested information from a database.

Most reports involve three elements:

- ✔ **The basic query.** The preceding example involves this basic query: Get each customer's name field and sales figure field.
- ✔ **The sort order.** In this example, it's alphabetic.
- ✔ **Grouping.** The example has a group (of customers) for each country.

How can you create the report you need? The quickest and easiest way to get a report flowing out of the printer is to use Visual Basic's new DataReport Designer.

Adding a DataReport Designer to Your Project

New to Visual Basic 6 is the DataReport Designer, a surprisingly easy-to-use tool that generates reports of sufficient complexity for many tasks. What's more, you can even send the resulting reports to HTML files (.HTM) for displaying in Web pages. The DataReport Designer fits in very well with the Visual Basic IDE, and it works with a data source (I cover data sources in depth in Chapters 4 and 5).

To add a DataReport Designer to a VB project and then attach the Designer to a data source, follow these steps:

1. **Create a data source that connects to the database that you want to use.**

   For all the details on creating a data source and connecting it to a database, see the following sections in Chapter 4: "Adding a Data Environment Designer to a VB Project" and "Connecting to a Database."

   You now have a data source — or a *connection,* as it's called in the Data Environment Designer.

   Although the two terms are sometimes used interchangeably, technically, a *data source* is the actual file(s) that contains data, and a *connection* is the link between the client application and the data source. The relationship between the two terms is similar to the relationship between *water* and *pipe:* You don't say "turn on the pipe," though that would be more technically correct.

2. **In the Properties window, change the name Connection1 (or whatever it's called) to a more descriptive name.**

   For example, if you're creating a report that uses the sample Northwind database, you might name your connection object *conNWind.* When you change the name in the Properties window, it also changes in the Data Environment Designer.

3. **Right-click Command1 in the Data Environment Designer.**

   A context menu pops out.

   If you don't see Command1 under the connection object, right-click the connection object and then choose Add Command from the context menu. Name the command object **Command1**.

4. **Choose Properties on the context menu.**

   The Command1 Properties dialog box opens.

5. **Click the Database Object option button.**

6. **Select Table from the Database Object drop-down list.**

7. **Select the table you want to use from the Object Name drop-down list.**

   For example, with the Northwind sample database, you may decide to create a report by using information from the Employees table.

8. **Click OK.**

   The Command1 Properties dialog box closes.

9. **Choose Project⇨Add Data Report.**

   A new DataReport Designer appears, as shown in Figure 6-1.

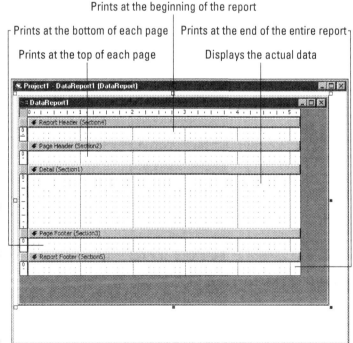

Prints at the beginning of the report

Prints at the bottom of each page | Prints at the end of the entire report

Prints at the top of each page | Displays the actual data

Figure 6-1:
An empty
DataReport
Designer,
ready to be
connected
to a data
source.

If you don't see Add Data Report on the Project menu, choose Project⇨Components. A Components dialog box appears. Click the Designers tab. Click the box to the left of Data Report so a check appears in the box, as shown in Figure 6-2. Click OK to close the Components dialog box. Now, complete Step 9 to add a DataReport Designer to your project (it's available on the Project menu now).

Figure 6-2:
Use this
Components
dialog box
to add the
DataReport
Designer
to your
Projects
menu if the
Designer
isn't already
available
there.

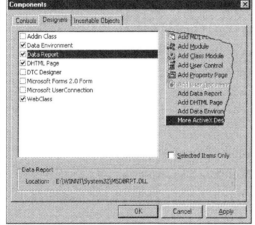

10. **In the Properties window, click the DataReport Designer's DataSource property and set it to point to DataEnvironment1, your Data Environment.**

    The Data Environment Designer must be open, or you can't set the DataSource property to point to the DataEnvironment.

11. **In the Properties window, click the DataReport Designer's DataMember property and set it to point to Command1, a command in your DataEnvironment.**

    You've now successfully added a DataReport Designer to your project and attached it to a data source.

Crafting a Report with the DataReport Designer

Here's how you construct a report with the DataReport Designer:

1. **Add a DataReport Designer to your project and then attach it to a data source, as I describe in the preceding section.**

In the example that I mention in the preceding section, a DataEnvironment Designer's connection named conNWind contains the data source.

2. **Right-click the DataReport Designer.**

   A context menu pops out, as shown in Figure 6-3.

Figure 6-3:
From this context menu, you can manage the options and features of the DataReport Designer.

3. **Choose Retrieve Structure from the context menu.**

   A dialog box appears with the mysterious threat that the "existing report layout" is about to be replaced. Because you have no layout yet, just laugh sullenly and then click Yes. The dialog box closes.

When you *Retrieve Structure* in the DataReport Designer, you're synchronizing the report with the current contents of the DataEnvironment's commands. Any controls you've placed on the report are removed. (Pressing Ctrl+Z restores them, though, if you didn't mean to synchronize.)

Notice that when a DataReport has the focus, the Toolbox contains six specialized report controls: rptLabel, rptTextBox, rptImage, rptLine, rptShape, and rptFunction. Each of these controls behaves as its ordinary (non-rpt) version, with the exception of the rptFunction, which I describe in the section "Using Aggregates, Functions, and Other On-the-Fly Calculations," later in this chapter.

4. **Put a rptLabel in the Report Header section of the DataReport.**

5. **In the Properties window, change the rptLabel's Caption property.**

   For a report using information from the Employees table in the Northwind database, you might set the Caption property to EMPLOYEES REPORT.

   This label in the ReportHeader will be printed only at the start of the report.

   Now the fun part: creating the page headers and the data.

6. **Click DataEnvironment1.**

   DataEnvironment1 is selected.

7. **Click the + next to Command1 in the DataEnvironment.**

   VB displays the fields in the Employees table (or whatever table you're using).

8. **Drag the first field for your report from the DataEnvironment and drop it into the Detail section of the DataReport.**

   For example, drag the FirstName field from the Employees table over to the Detail section. You see a label named (by default) Label2 and a rptTextBox named txtFirstName.

9. **Drag Label2 and drop it into the Page Header zone in the DataReport.**

   In the example that I'm describing in this section, this label will act as a title for the FirstName column of the entire page (instead of repeating each time within each record).

10. **Move the rptTextBox over so it's still in the Detail zone, but is underneath the Label2.**

11. **Repeat Steps 8 through 10 to add the other fields to your report.**

    If you want to follow along with the example, add LastName, Title, and HomePhone Labels and rptTextBoxes, as shown in Figure 6-4.

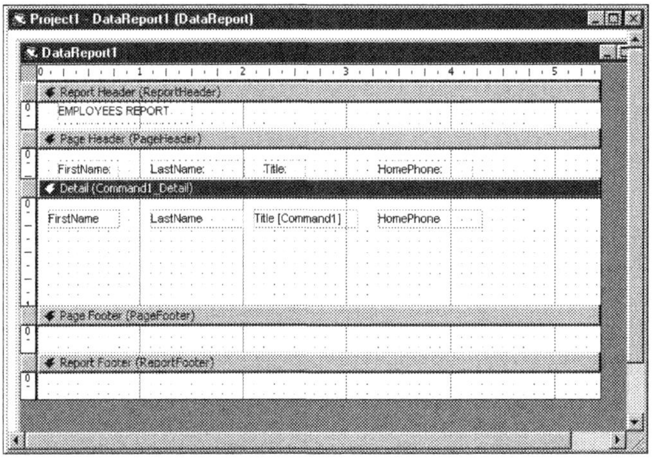

Figure 6-4:
Your report is taking shape. You have the header, and four rptTextBoxes to display the data.

12. **Double-click Form1 to get to its code window and then type the following code into the Form1_Load event:**

```
Private Sub Form_Load()
DataReport1.Show
End Sub
```

You need this code because the DataReport Form doesn't automatically display itself when you run this program.

13. **Press F5 to see how your report will appear on-screen, as shown in Figure 6-5.**

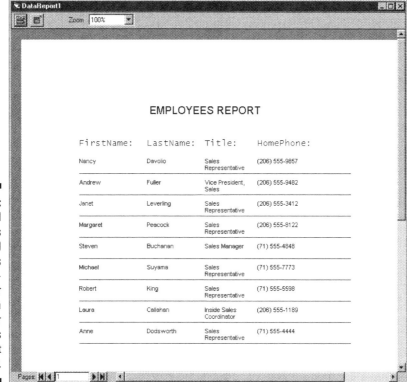

EMPLOYEES REPORT

FirstName:	LastName:	Title:	HomePhone:
Nancy	Davolio	Sales Representative	(206) 555-9857
Andrew	Fuller	Vice President, Sales	(206) 555-9482
Janet	Leverling	Sales Representative	(206) 555-3412
Margaret	Peacock	Sales Representative	(206) 555-8122
Steven	Buchanan	Sales Manager	(71) 555-4848
Michael	Suyama	Sales Representative	(71) 555-7773
Robert	King	Sales Representative	(71) 555-5598
Laura	Callahan	Inside Sales Coordinator	(206) 555-1189
Anne	Dodsworth	Sales Representative	(71) 555-4444

Figure 6-5: The final result: Users can scroll through this report on-screen, or view it in a browser such as Internet Explorer.

Notice that the report displays the Detail section repeatedly, showing as many records as will fit on each page. You might want to fiddle with the Font Properties of the Report Header, Page Header, and Detail TextBoxes to distinguish between the titles and the data. To create the lines between records, put a rptLine control in the Detail zone of the DataReport Designer.

The DataReport is an object and you can query it with programming. The Print, Export, and Zoom features are already programmed for you. However, if you want, you can access a DataReport in other ways via programming. For example, here's how you can find the names of the sections and controls on a DataReport:

```
Private Sub Form_Load()
DataReport1.Show
MsgBox DataReport1.Sections(2).Name
MsgBox DataReport1.Sections(2).Controls(2).Name
End Sub
```

Note that the Sections and Controls collections of a DataReport start with an index of 1, not 0.

Exporting a Data Report

Nothing could be easier than displaying a report in an intranet or Internet Web site. Follow the steps in the preceding section and then press F5 to run the report. Click the Export button and save the file to your hard drive as RP.HTM or whatever name you want to give it. Then, in Explorer, double-click the filename RP.HTM, and it will load into your browser, ready to be viewed by all and sundry, as shown in Figure 6-6.

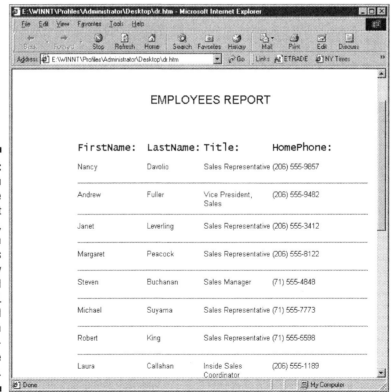

Figure 6-6:
When you click the Export button, a data report is automatically converted into HTML and saved as a browser-viewable .HTM file.

Getting Fancy with DataReport Controls

You might have wondered if you can cause the DataReport Designer to print page numbers on each page of the report. Yes, as shown in Figure 6-7, the Designer comes with a set of specialized controls you can employ by right-clicking to see the context menu and then choosing Insert Control.

Figure 6-7:
Use this context menu to add page numbering, date or time stamping, the sum of pages in the report, or a title for the report.

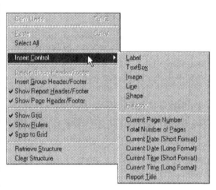

Note that the Title control is programmable. After you place a Title control into the Report Header section of the DataReport, for example, you can either change the Title property *of the DataReport* (not the Title control) by using the Properties window, or you can program a change to the title, as in this example:

```
Private Sub Form_Load()
DataReport1.Show
DataReport1.Title = "MARA LAGOON PROPERTIES"
End Sub
```

You can force page breaks in any of the zones in a DataReport. For example, if you want to print the Report Header on a separate page, just click the Report Header section in the DataReport Designer. Then, in the Properties window, change the ForcePageBreak property to rptPageBreakAfter.

Working with Advanced DataReport Features

You can use the DataReport Designer to display more complex relationships and groups of data than those mentioned in the examples throughout previous sections in this chapter.

Organizing data into groups

Assume that you want to create a report that shows each company name and, in a list under each name, the date of each order from that company. To create this kind of complex report, follow these steps:

1. **Create a DataEnvironment with a connection to your database and then add a DataReport with its DataSource property pointing to the DataEnvironment.**

   For all the details on completing these tasks, see Steps 1 through 3 in the section "Crafting a Report with the DataReport Designer," earlier in this chapter.

2. **In DataEnvironment1, right-click the connection to your database.**

   (In my example application, conNWind is the connection to the NWind database.)

   A context menu pops out.

3. **Choose Add Command.**

   The context menu disappears, and a new command, named Command2, appears in the DataEnvironment.

4. **Right-click Command2.**

   Its context menu pops out.

5. **Choose Properties.**

   The context menu closes, and the Command2 Properties dialog box appears.

6. **Change the Database Object to Table.**

7. **In the Object Name drop-down list, select the table that you want to use.**

   For the example application, change the Object Name to Customers.

8. **Click OK.**

   The dialog box closes.

9. **Right-click Command2 and then choose Add Child Command from the context menu.**

   You see that a new command, named Command3, has been added, but it's listed under Command2 rather than under the connection. (In my example, conNWind is the connection.)

   Being able to add child commands under other commands is an important feature of ADO 2.0 and the Data Environment Designer. It enables you to easily create relationships between separate tables, without having to write any programming.

   When you add a child command, you're creating a relationship between the child and parent commands (sometimes called *data shaping* or *hierarchical commands*). It's similar to joining two tables (see Chapter 19), but hierarchical commands produce hierarchical recordsets instead of a flat table. The child command (or commands — there can be more than one) becomes a field in the parent command. The example I'm constructing in this section displays each company name (the parent command), but then expands a list under each company name to show the date of each order from that company (the child command).

10. **Right-click Command3.**

    Its context menu pops out.

11. **Choose Properties.**

    The context menu closes, and the Command3 Properties dialog box opens.

12. **Change the Database Object to Table.**

13. **In the Object Name drop-down list, select the name of the table that you want to use for the child command in this hierarchical relation you are building.**

    (In my example, the hierarchy is a list of companies, with each one having its own sublist of order dates.)

    The example application uses the Orders table.

14. **Change the Command Name to a more descriptive name.**

    For the example, type the name **cmdOrders**.

15. **Click the Relation tab and ensure that the Relate to a Parent Command Object option is checked.**

16. **Click Add.**

    You have established the relationship between Command2 and the child command (cmdOrders, in the example).

17. **Click OK.**

    The Command3 Properties dialog box closes.

18. **Right-click in the space between the Page Header and the Detail bars in the DataReport.**

    A context menu pops out.

19. **Choose Insert Group Header/Footer.**

    A Group Header and a Group Footer appear on the DataReport.

    These specialized "Group" headers act like frames around other, inner sets of data. The innermost repeating data is in the Detail section of the report, but you can subdivide the report into one or more nested groups, as this example illustrates.

    What you're doing here is similar to the GROUP BY section of a SQL query, which is used to group queries by categories based on the foreign keys of a parent table. For details on SQL GROUP BY, see Chapter 19.

20. **Drag the field that you want to use for organizing the grouped data from Command2 and drop it into the space below the Group Header.**

    For the example application, drag CompanyName from Command2 and drop it into the space below the Group Header. A Label and a TextBox appear.

    If this technique doesn't work (if you can't drag and drop the field you want), use the Properties window to change the DataReport's DataSource property to DataEnvironment1 and its DataMember property to Command2. If that fails to solve the problem, use the Project Explorer to delete the DataReport, create a new one in the Project menu, and then set its DataSource and DataMember properties as described in this tip.

21. **Separate the Label and TextBox so they don't overlap.**

22. **Drag the field you want to use from the child command in the DataEnvironment and drop it into the Detail section.**

    In the example, you drag the OrderDate field from the cmdOrders command and drop it into the Detail section.

23. **Separate that field's Label from the associated TextBox so the whole job looks like Figure 6-8.**

24. **Press F5.**

    You see each parent (the CompanyName) followed by the date of every order the company has submitted.

The relationship in this example is the equivalent of a query that makes this request: Display each order date for each CompanyName.

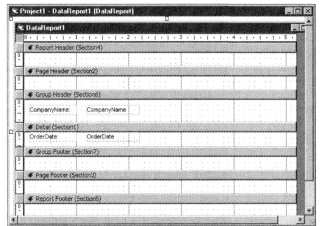

When you press F5, if you only see Form1, make sure that you've got this
code in Form1's Load Event:

```
Private Sub Form_Load()
DataReport1.Show
End Sub
```

Grouping groups: Taking it up a level

There's yet another way to group data using the DataEnvironment, beyond
the one illustrated in the preceding section. Microsoft uses the term *group* in
several ways in its applications and operating systems. Even when used with
a DataReport, the word *group* has two meanings:

   ✔ Group Headers (and Footers) added in the DataReport Designer, in addi-
     tion to relationships. This approach groups data based on a table in a
     database. (The example in the preceding section of this chapter illus-
     trates this kind of grouping.) To accomplish this kind of grouping, you
     must first create a new command in the DataEnvironment (I called it
     cmdOrders in the preceding example). Then, you make a relationship
     between the parent and child commands. Finally, you drag and drop
     fields from the parent and child commands into the DataReport.

     For details on using hierarchical commands, see Step 9 in the preceding
     section.

   ✔ The second approach to grouping is to use the Grouping feature of the
     Data Environment Designer. This feature enables you to group data
     based on a field in a table. No new command is added to the
     DataEnvironment. (I illustrate this kind of grouping in the following
     example.)

In this example, the goal is to take the data displayed in the previous example and an additional grouping, further organizing how the data is displayed. In the previous example, order dates are grouped by company name. Now, you take those groupings and add a new Group Header/Footer that further segregates the data into sets grouped by Country. In other words, the company names will, themselves, be grouped.

To achieve this additional level of grouping, complete the following steps:

1. **Complete all the steps in the previous section, "Organizing data into groups."**

   You have a DataEnvironment with a connection to a database (I use the NWind sample database for my example) and a DataReport with its DataSource property pointing to the DataEnvironment. In the example application, you also have a command named Command2 that represents the Customers table in the NWind database, and a child command named cmdOrders.

2. **Double-click DataEnvironment1 in the Project Explorer.**

   The DataEnvironment comes to the top and gets the focus.

3. **Right-click Command2 in the DataEnvironment.**

   A context menu pops out.

4. **Choose Properties.**

   The context menu closes, and you see the Command2 Properties dialog box.

5. **Click the Grouping tab.**

6. **Click Group Command Object.**

   Visual Basic assigns a Grouping Command Name, Command2_Grouping, to your new group.

7. **In the Fields In Command box, double-click the name of the field that you want to use for grouping the data.**

   For the example application, double-click Country. The Country field moves into the Fields Used for Grouping listbox.

8. **Click OK.**

   The Command2 Properties dialog box closes.

9. **Look at the Data Environment Designer.**

   You see that Command2 is now renamed to Command2 Grouped Using Command2_Grouping. You also see two folders: Summary Fields in Command2_Grouping and Detail Fields in Command2, as shown in Figure 6-9.

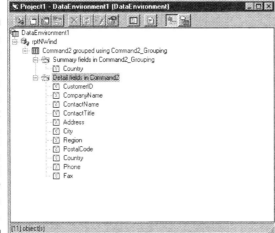

Figure 6-9:
When you
create a
group in
the Data
Environment
Designer,
your original
command is
renamed
and new
folders are
added.

10. **Double-click DataReport1 in the Project Explorer.**

    The DataReport Designer comes to the top and gets the focus. Delete
    any Group Headers and Footers, and any controls such as Labels and
    TextBoxes that might be on the DataReport from previous examples.

11. **Right-click the DataReport Designer in the Page Header section.**

    A context menu pops out.

12. **Choose Insert Group Header/Footer.**

    An Insert New Group Header/Footer dialog box appears, as shown in
    Figure 6-10.

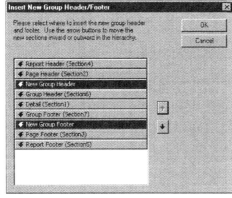

Figure 6-10:
Use this
dialog box to
position a
new Group
Header/
Footer pair
within the
existing
report
structure.

13. **Click the up-arrow in the Insert New Group Header/Footer dialog box
    until the New Group Header moves to the outermost position in the
    Group Header hierarchy, as shown in Figure 6-10.**

14. Click OK.

The dialog box closes, and Visual Basic inserts a new Group Header and Footer into the report.

15. Click DataReport1 in the drop-down list in the Properties window.

The DataReport (as a whole, not one of its sections) is selected, and its properties are listed in the Properties window.

16. In the Properties window, change the DataReport's DataMember property from Command2 to Command2_Grouping.

Now, your DataReport structure reflects the grouping by Country that you've defined in the DataEnvironment.

17. Double-click DataEnvironment1 in the Project Explorer.

The DataEnvironment comes to the top and gets the focus.

18. Click the + symbol next to the Summary Fields in Command2_Grouping folder in the Data Environment Designer.

The Country field in this folder is displayed.

19. Drag your field from the Command2_Grouping folder (not the field in the Detail fields folder) from the DataEnvironment and drop it into the new, outermost Group Header section.

In my example, you would drag the Country field. A Label and a TextBox appear in the new Group Header section, as shown in Figure 6-11.

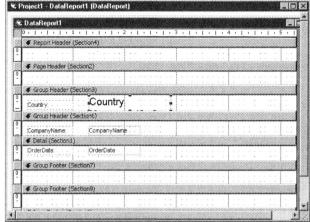

Figure 6-11:
The completed report design, including two pairs of Groups.

20. Click the TextBox.

The Properties window displays the properties for the TextBox. In my example, it's the txtCountry TextBox.

21. **Double-click the Font property in the Properties window.**

    The Font Properties dialog box appears.

22. **Make the font larger, perhaps 16 points.**

23. **Click OK.**

    The Font Properties dialog box closes, and the TextBox's font size is larger. Your DataReport should now look like Figure 6-11.

24. **Press F5.**

    The data report is displayed, as shown in Figure 6-12.

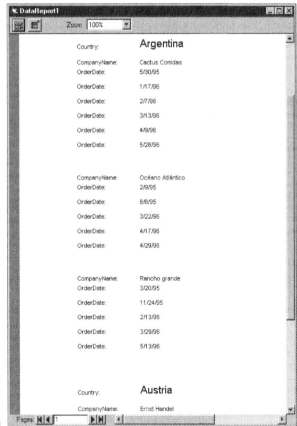

Figure 6-12:
This report features a hierarchy that is subdivided into two levels of grouping: by Country and then, within countries, by Company Name.

You can use the techniques illustrated in the two previous examples to subdivide the data in your report as many times as you want. Grouping is an easy and effective way to organize data in a report, making the report easier to read and understand.

Using Aggregates, Functions, and Other On-the-Fly Calculations

Displaying calculated data in a report is often useful. For example, your bank statement is a report, and it contains calculated data, such as Previous Balance, Current Balance, and Total Number of Checks. In the examples earlier in this chapter using the NWind database, it would probably be helpful to display the total number of orders from each company, the total money spent by each company, and the grand total of money paid by all companies.

You can calculate in several ways: aggregates, the Function control in the DataReport Designer, and, above all, SQL itself. However, these various kinds of calculations are more easily understood in the context of an in-depth exploration of SQL. So, if you want to include calculated values in a report, look at the examples in Chapter 19.

VB includes a specialized report-generating application named Crystal Reports. This application includes both a report designer and a special ActiveX Control that displays the report in your VB application when the application runs. Some VB programmers prefer to use Crystal Reports rather than the DataReport Designer that I examine in this chapter. If you want to try it out (it's relatively easy to learn and to use), locate its setup program, CRYSTL32.EXE, on your Visual Basic CD. It's located in this path on the CD: \COMMON\TOOLS\VB\CRYSREPT.

Crystal Reports also features a free report designer that fits inside a Visual Basic project, much like the report designer I describe in this chapter. It must be downloaded from the Seagate Software Web site (www.seagate.com) and installed separately, but it provides great reporting features similar to those I show in this chapter, but using the Crystal Report Engine.

Crystal Reports in VB6 is the same version as in VB5. Microsoft has not licensed an upgrade from Seagate Software. If you frequently need to produce complex reports, you may want to consider upgrading to the Pro version of Crystal Reports (Version 7). Also take a look at ActiveReports, from DataDynamics (www.datadynamics.com). It is a more recent product, but it has matured quickly.

Visit these company's Web sites and give their products a test run. You'll find that most third-party developers now offer free, downloadable evaluation versions of their products, so you can try before you buy.

Chapter 7

Designing a User Interface

* *

In This Chapter

▶ Using the classic components

▶ Moving through records

▶ Preventing overshooting of recordset boundaries

▶ Working with specialized, data-aware controls

▶ Controlling user input with the Masked Edit control

* *

*C*reating the user interface ranks as one of the more important jobs that any computer programmer or developer undertakes. The interface should make it easy for a user to view and, sometimes, change information. The key word is *intuitive* — the tools the user sees on-screen should be, as much as possible, self-explanatory and easily employed. To that end, Microsoft has created dozens of user-interface tools called *controls* or *components.* Microsoft's user-interface experts have carefully thought out these predesigned objects, such as the TextBox and the DataRepeater, constructing them with familiar tools like scrollbars so the user can easily see how they work and what they do.

This chapter focuses on the components most useful for database work. Some of these components that you can drop into your Visual Basic projects have been around for years; others are brand-new in VB 6.

Don't neglect the important job of designing the user interface. Having those controls sitting there on the VB Toolbox, right next to that naked, vulnerable form is just too tempting for many programmers. So, instead of thinking through the user interface and making practical decisions, some programmers just start populating the form with whatever components they think they need, and position those controls where they look good. True design is a science and an art that is all-too-often ignored. You can get considerable assistance with the design job by looking at Microsoft's *Windows 95 User Interface Design Guide.* It's available from MSDN Online for free on the Internet.

Using the Classic Components

Visual Basic's classic components are those controls that appear on the Toolbox automatically (you don't have to press Ctrl+T, bringing up the Components dialog box so you can add additional controls). These controls are sometimes called *intrinsic* controls. Whatever. Most of them have been there on the Toolbox since day one, and they do most of the work. But, as you'll see, you can add some great new components to the Toolbox, too, for specialized database user interfaces.

Of the 20 classic components, seven are *data-aware* — capable of being linked to a Data Control or a DataEnvironment. The data-aware classic controls are

- ✔ TextBox
- ✔ Label
- ✔ CheckBox
- ✔ PictureBox
- ✔ Image
- ✔ ComboBox
- ✔ ListBox

Attaching a data-aware control

The TextBox is one of the VB workhorses. It's a mini–word processor, enabling users to view or edit text. In this section, I show you how to attach a TextBox to a database by setting the TextBox's DataSource property to point to a DataEnvironment. Then, you point to a field in that database with the TextBox's DataField property.

To attach a control to a data source, follow these steps:

1. **Choose File⇨New Project.**

   The New Project dialog box appears.

2. **Double-click the Standard EXE icon in the dialog box.**

   The dialog box closes, and the basic VB project type is available.

3. **Add a Data Environment Designer to your project, and attach it to the database that you want to use.**

   I describe the steps for completing these tasks in Chapter 4, in the sections "Adding a Data Environment Designer to a VB Project" and "Connecting to a Database." In that chapter, and here, my examples use the NWind sample database.

4. **Add a command object to your project, pointing to the table that contains the data you want to display.**

   For all the details on completing this step, see the section "Adding a Command Object," in Chapter 4. If you want to follow along with the examples that I describe in this chapter, set the command object to point to the Employees table within the NWind database.

5. **Put a TextBox on Form1.**

6. **Double-click the TextBox's DataSource property in the Properties window.**

   The DataSource property changes from blank to DataEnvironment1 (or whatever name you may have given the DataEnvironment). It's the only data source in this project at this time, so when you double-click the property, it is automatically selected as the data source.

7. **Double-click the TextBox's DataMember property in the Properties window.**

   Command1 (or whatever name you entered for this command) appears as the DataMember property. Notice that a DataEnvironment can have multiple commands, so you need to set the DataMember property. It tells VB which command, of potentially several, should be used as the source of data.

8. **Complete the connection between the database and the TextBox by clicking the TextBox's DataField property in the Properties window. Then click the down-arrow icon in the property box.**

   You see a list of all the fields in the table you're using. (Employees is the table used in my example.)

9. **In the Properties window, click the name of the field that you want to display in the TextBox.**

   For the example, specify that you want the TextBox to display the contents of the LastName field.

10. **Press F5.**

    VB runs the project, and the TextBox displays the data — in the example, `Davolio`.

Moving through records

You sometimes want to permit the user to move to the next, or previous, records in a database. In this section, you find out how to use the MoveNext and MovePrevious commands, how to attach a TextBox to a Data Control, and how to prevent the user from falling off the end of the earth.

It is usually preferable to avoid using the VB Data Control, and instead use the Data Environment Designer and supplement it by writing your own programming. However, for one-user desktop database management, or otherwise simple applications, the Data Control works fine. For more on hand-programming, see Chapter 14.

To permit the user to navigate forward or back through a set of records, follow these steps:

1. **Add a TextBox to Form1 in a new VB project.**

2. **Add a Data Control and two CommandButtons to Form1.**

   Just use the Classic Data Control that's always on the Toolbox when you run VB.

3. **Click the Data Control.**

   The Data Control is selected, and the Properties window lists its properties.

4. **Click the button with the three dots (...) next to the DatabaseName property in the Properties window.**

   A file-browser dialog box appears.

5. **Locate the database you want to use and double-click it.**

   For the example application, use the NWIND.MDB database. The dialog box closes, and Visual Basic attaches the selected database to your data control.

6. **Click the RecordSource property in the Properties window and click the down-arrow icon next to that property.**

   You see a list of all the tables in the selected database.

7. **Click the name of the table that contains the data you want to display.**

   Click the Employees table to follow my example. The list closes, and your selection becomes the table for this data source.

8. **Click the TextBox to select it, and change its DataSource property in the Properties window to Data1, the Data Control.**

9. **Also in the Properties window, change the TextBox's DataField property to the name of the field that you want to display.**

   For my example application, change the DataField property to LastName.

10. **Put two CommandButtons on the Form, with Command1 on the left and Command2 on the right, using the layout shown in Figure 7-1.**

11. **Change the CommandButtons' Caption properties to PREVIOUS and NEXT, as shown in Figure 7-1.**

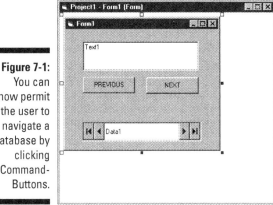

12. **Double-click the CommandButton captioned** NEXT.

    You see the Click event for this CommandButton in the code window.

13. **Type this programming into the code window:**

```
Private Sub Command2_Click()
Data1.Recordset.MoveNext
End Sub
```

    This programming causes the TextBox to display the LastName field of
    the next record in the Employees table.

14. **Press F5 to run this program and click the NEXT button about 10 times.**

    Whoops! You went off the end of the earth. Your programming makes no
    provision for the user clicking beyond the number of available records.
    This omission will crash your application and seriously puzzle most
    users. You see the error message box shown in Figure 7-2.

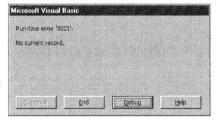

This problem has two solutions:

✔ **You can use the Data Control instead of CommandButtons to permit the user to navigate your database.** The Data Control has an EOFAction property that, by default, is set to `MoveLast`. In other words, if the EOF (end of file) is reached, simply move to the last record. The BOFAction property handles the parallel problem — going off the beginning of the recordset. (BOF, as you probably guessed, stands for beginning of file.)

✔ **You can write a little programming to detect the BOF or EOF conditions and react appropriately, as I explain in the next section.**

Avoiding overshooting of recordset boundaries

As the previous example illustrates, users may attempt to navigate beyond the available records. They might try to go *previous* to the first record or past the last record. You can prevent this error by checking the BOF or EOF properties of a recordset.

The solution is to insert some programming like this, to check for a problem *before* you use the MoveNext or MovePrevious commands:

```
Private Sub Command2_Click()
If Data1.Recordset.EOF = True Then Exit Sub
Data1.Recordset.MoveNext
End Sub
```

Or, to prevent falling off the beginning of a recordset:

```
Private Sub Command1_Click()
If Data1.Recordset.BOF = True Then Exit Sub
Data1.Recordset.MovePrevious
End Sub
```

For more information on this frequent error, see Chapter 17.

Working with other classic controls

Clearly, making a Line, Frame, or Shape control data-aware would be pointless. But what about the other controls?

How about CheckBoxes?

You're probably suspicious about the utility of the CheckBox as a data display device. However, a CheckBox actually has some uses. It has only two states: on and off, checked or unchecked. However, you can use it to let the user define certain kinds of data. For example, if someone is filling out a reservation form for a hotel, you might set a CheckBox's caption to `Non-smoking`. By clicking that box, the user demands a room so wholesome, so uncontaminated, that no one has *ever* lit tobacco anywhere near it. The way people jump to sue these days, a wise hotelier would likely also include several additional CheckBoxes, including exclusions for peanuts and fish.

Using Labels for read-only displays

You may also wonder about the utility of the Label control. However, if you want to display data that the user cannot change, the Label is one way to do it. A Label also uses up fewer resources than a TextBox and has some special properties you might want, such as AutoSize, which adjusts the container to fit the contained data, and BackStyle, which can permit the underlying form, including any graphics, to show through underneath the text.

Understanding ListBox limitations

Applications usually display a ListBox as a kind of menu, from which the user selects an item by clicking it. After that, your application can expand the selection. This feature can be useful in database work because you could, for example, show a list of product names. When the user clicks a particular product, the application can display details about its price, availability, weight, color, and so on. You can also use a ListBox to provide options when someone is filling out a form. For example, you could provide a list of four shipping options, with their different costs, from which the user can click to select.

However, ListBoxes (and their cousins, ComboBoxes) have several limitations when used with databases:

- ✔ They don't hold unlimited amounts of data.

- ✔ They *will* attempt to draw in thousands of records, if that's what's asked of them — until they shut down the application (at the very least).

- ✔ They don't automatically display data when attached to a data source (as does, for example, a TextBox). Instead, you must write programming to populate a ListBox.

Visual Basic does include a database-specialized DBListBox control — which does automatically display a field from the first record — and this control can handle huge lists. However, if you use the DBListBox, you must then supply it when you distribute your project; it's not an intrinsic component of VB.

To populate a standard (intrinsic) ListBox by using the AddItem command, follow these steps:

1. **Add a ListBox to Form1 in a new VB project.**

2. **Add a Data Control to Form1.**

   Just use the classic Data Control that's always on the Toolbox when you run VB.

3. **Click the Data Control.**

   The Data Control is selected, and the Properties window lists its properties.

4. **Click the button with the three dots (...) next to the DatabaseName property in the Properties window.**

   A file-browser dialog box appears.

5. **Locate the database you want to use for this project and double-click it.**

   The dialog box closes, and Visual Basic attaches the selected database to your data control. I use the NWIND.MDB sample database (you find it in your VB98 directory) for testing.

6. **Click the RecordSource property in the Properties window and then click the down-arrow icon next to that property.**

   A list of all the tables in the selected database appears.

7. **Click the name of the table that you want to use.**

   As in previous examples, you can use the Employees table in the NWIND.MDB database. The list closes, and Employees becomes the table for this data source.

8. **Click the ListBox to select it and then change its DataSource property in the Properties window to Data1, the Data Control.**

9. **Also in the Properties window, select the field you want to use for the ListBox's DataField property.**

   For the example, change the ListBox's DataField property to LastName.

   If you press F5 at this point, the ListBox remains empty. You must write some programming.

10. **Double-click Form1.**

    The code window is displayed.

11. **In the Form's Activate event, type this code:**

    ```
    Private Sub Form_Activate()
    Do While Data1.Recordset.EOF = False
        List1.AddItem Data1.Recordset.Fields(1)
        Data1.Recordset.MoveNext
    Loop
    End Sub
    ```

This code loops through the records in the data source (the recordset) until EOF (end of file) is reached. Each time through the loop, the LastName data is added to the ListBox.

12. **Press F5 to run the project.**

    You see the ListBox filled with the LastName field for each record in the Employees table in the NWind database.

Exploring the Specialized, Data-Aware Controls

In the past couple of versions, VB has added various database-related components. These components generally endeavor to display records in a more flexible or elaborate fashion than as single-record TextBox clusters or single-field ListBox lists. In this section, you try several data-aware components that are new to Visual Basic 6. (These components are not available in the Learning version of Visual Basic — only in the Professional and Enterprise versions.)

Unlike the classic (intrinsic) VB components, the specialized, data-aware components must be distributed along with your VB project when you give it to others for their use. However, the VB Package and Deployment wizard usually makes this process relatively painless. This wizard detects the use of any nonstandard components and ensures they are included in the setup package. The only problems I've run into with add-on, specialized components is that they are sometimes replaced with newer (and incompatible) versions, which can present problems. It's sometimes safer to stick with the intrinsic components, despite their limitations.

Using the DataRepeater — a mega-ListBox

Of the new data-aware components in Visual Basic 6, the DataRepeater is one of the more intriguing. It's kind of a mega-ListBox, displaying a scrollable list of entire controls rather than single lines of text. However, demonstrating this component requires that you build a custom component (one of your creation!) and then use that component on the Repeater container. Therefore, I leave the DataRepeater to Chapter 10, which tells you all about creating custom data-bound ActiveX UserControls.

The DataGrid, a faux spreadsheet, shows mega-data

If you want to cram lots of information onto the screen, try the new DataGrid, which replaces the older DBGrid control. You have to use the new ADO Data Control with the DataGrid (instead of the intrinsic Data Control you use in the previous examples in this chapter). You can also use other ADO-based data sources, such as a DataEnvironment.

When you give users a DataGrid, they not only see a spreadsheet-like mass of data, but also have the ability to resize the columns to suit their needs. Also, the DataGrid is highly customizable by you, the programmer. It resembles Access's datasheet view.

Any programming you wrote for the VB 5 DBGrid control will work fine with the new VB 6 DataGrid, except for the unbound mode feature. The DBGrid is based on Apex's True DBGrid, and that product has evolved greatly between VB5 and VB6. It now supports multiple unbound modes, one of them being a copycat of a VB3 implementation that Apex brought back to life. Essentially, the latest version supports multiple unbound modes, whereas the old VB5 version had only one or two.

To use the DataGrid component, follow these steps:

1. **In a new VB Standard EXE project, press Ctrl+T.**

   You see the Components dialog box.

2. **Click the check box next to Microsoft ADO Data Control 6.0 (OLEDB) and the check box next to Microsoft DataGrid Control 6.0 (OLE DB) in the Components dialog box.**

   Don't confuse the DataGrid control in the Components dialog box with the Microsoft Data Bound Grid Control 5.0 (SP3).

3. **Click OK.**

   The Components dialog box closes, and Visual Basic adds the ADO Data Control and DataGrid Control icons to your Toolbox.

4. **Double-click the ADO Data Control's icon on the Toolbox.**

   It's added to your Form1.

5. **Right-click the ADO Data Control on Form1.**

   A context menu pops out.

6. **Choose ADODC Properties from the context menu.**

The Property Pages for the ADO Data Control appear, as shown in
Figure 7-3.

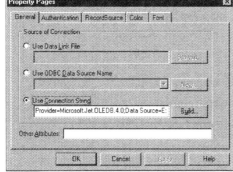

Figure 7-3:
You can
make a
database
connection
in this set of
Property
Pages.

7. **Click the Build button next to the Use Connection String option in the
   Property Pages.**

   You see the Data Link Properties dialog box.

8. **Click the Provider tab and select Microsoft Jet 4.0 OLE DB Provider
   (or select whatever version number of Jet you have available on your
   machine).**

9. **Click the Connection tab and then click the button with the three dots
   (...) next to the Select or Enter a Database Name text box.**

   A Select Access Database dialog box appears.

10. **Locate the database you want to use on your hard drive and double-
    click it.**

    The Select Access Database dialog box closes, and the Connection tab
    lists the path to the selected database.

    If you want to follow along with my example, but you can't find
    NWIND.MDB, locate it on your VB6 CD and copy it to your hard drive.
    Then redo Step 10.

11. **Click OK.**

    The Property Pages reappear with your newly defined Connection
    String, which should look something like this example:

    ```
    Provider=Microsoft.Jet.OLEDB.4.0;Data Source=C:\Program
                Files\VB98\Nwind.mdb;Persist Security Info=False.
    ```

12. **Click the RecordSource tab in the Property Pages.**

13. **Choose 2 – adCmdTable as the Command Type.**

14. **Click the Table or Stored Procedure Name down-arrow icon.**

    A list drops down, displaying all the tables in the database you're using.

15. **Select the table that you want to attach.**

    For the example, select the Customers table.

16. **Click OK.**

    The Property Pages dialog box closes.

17. **Double-click the DataGrid icon on the Toolbox.**

    A DataGrid appears on Form1.

    You *hope* a DataGrid appears on Form1! Even though I used it a few weeks ago in another project, when I tested it for this example by double-clicking the DataGrid, it failed to appear. Instead, for reasons of its own, it decided to display the error message shown in Figure 7-4.

Figure 7-4:
This dreaded message tells you, in a polite way, that you're trying to use an *illegally obtained* control.

If this happens to you — and there's no telling when it might — your best bet (if, indeed, you *do* have a legal copy of VB 6) is to simply rerun the VB 6 Setup program and choose the Reinstall option. This approach should clear up the problem, reregistering the component. If that fails, try uninstalling and then completely reinstalling VB 6. That procedure almost certainly will resolve the difficulty.

18. **In the Properties window, change the DataGrid's DataSource property to the name of the ADO Data Control (by default, its name is Adodc1).**

19. **Press F5 to run the project.**

    Whoa! This isn't your father's TextBox data display. A DataGrid is among the most data-intensive user interfaces available, as you can see in Figure 7-5.

    Try dragging the columns by adjusting the title bars to make them wider or narrower.

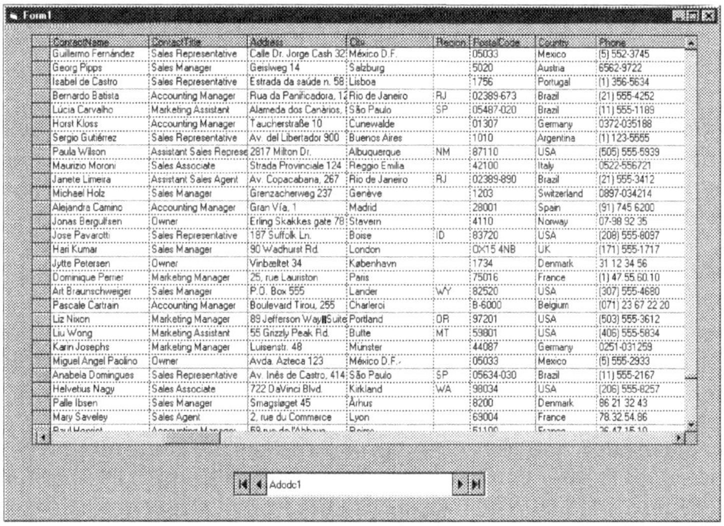

Figure 7-5:
Users get an
eyeful of
data when
you let them
use the
DataGrid.

After you stop the application, and you're in design mode, right-click the DataGrid and choose Retrieve Fields in the context menu. You can now see the titles of all columns, as they will appear when the application runs. You can also right-click the DataGrid again and choose Edit from the context menu. When you're in this mode, you can resize the column widths yourself. Also, try right-clicking and then managing which fields are displayed by using the Insert, Delete, Cut, Copy, Paste, and Append features. Right-click one last time and choose Properties. Now you can see the Property Pages dialog box, where you can adjust many qualities of the DataGrid, including fonts, text wrapping, colors, time and date formatting, and various other customizations.

Managing user input with the Masked Edit control

Often, you want to limit how users enter data, or provide them with visual cues. Databases can be fairly picky about how an application punctuates such information as dates and phone numbers.

The Masked Edit control can assist you in ensuring that users enter data correctly. The control has two properties that contribute to good data:

- The Format property can modify the user's input after the fact, adding, for example, commas to separate thousands. If the user enters 12456, the Format property can change it to 12,456.

- The Mask property can coerce user input while the user is typing. If you use the mask ##### (useful for zip codes), the user can only enter digits.

Nothing happens if the user types a letter of the alphabet — only numbers are accepted. What's more, nothing happens if the user types more than five digits.

To see how the Format and Mask properties work together, assume that you want phone numbers formatted using parentheses around the area code and a hyphen within the local number. To enforce this formatting, you can change the Mask Edit control's Format property to this setting:

```
(###) ###-####
```

The # symbol means *digit* and the other symbols (the parentheses and the dash) are considered *literals*, meaning they will be added to the digits (in the proper positions) the user enters if the user forgets them.

The Mask Edit control's Format property uses the same modifiers as the traditional VB Format command, such as ##,##0.00, which changes an input of 2429.1 into 2,429.10. The 0 symbol in the format string has this meaning: Even if no number is entered, at least display a 0 in this location in the string. The # symbol means any digit, but if nothing is entered in this location in the string, nothing will be displayed.

To see how to use the Masked Edit control, follow these steps:

1. **In a new VB Standard EXE project, press Ctrl+T.**

   You see the Components dialog box.

2. **Click the check box next to Microsoft Masked Edit Control 6.0 in the Components dialog box.**

3. **Click OK.**

   The Components dialog box closes, and VB adds the Masked Edit control icon (##|) to your Toolbox.

4. **Double-click the Masked Edit control's icon on the Toolbox.**

   A Masked Edit box is added to your Form1.

5. **Double-click the CommandButton's icon on the Toolbox.**

   A CommandButton is added to your Form1.

6. **Right-click the Masked Edit control on Form1.**

   A context menu pops out.

7. **Choose Properties.**

   VB displays the Property Pages for the Masked Edit control.

8. **Type (###) ###–#### into the Format text box in the Property Pages.**

9. **Click OK.**

The Property Pages close.

10. **Double-click the CommandButton.**

The code window opens.

11. **Type this code into the CommandButton's Click event:**

```
Private Sub Command1_Click()
MsgBox MaskEdBox1.Text
MsgBox MaskEdBox1.FormattedText
End Sub
```

12. **Press F5 to run this project.**

13. **Type** 1234567890 **into the Masked Edit control.**

14. **Click the CommandButton.**

A message box appears, displaying 1234567890, and a second message box appears, displaying (123) 456-7890.

Notice that if you want to store the formatted version of the data in your database, you use the FormattedText property of the Masked Edit control. That property contains the result *after* the Format property does its job.

15. **Erase 1234567890 from the Masked Edit control.**

16. **Type** abcdefghijklm **into the Masked Edit control and then click the CommandButton.**

You see two message boxes, both displaying abcdefghijklm. This example demonstrates that users can enter characters or anything else, and nothing prevents them from entering improper data. The Format property merely adds punctuation or formatting, if it can, to the user's input. The Format property does not in any way restrict the user's input. That's the job of the Mask property.

17. **Click Properties in the context menu.**

VB displays the Property Pages for the Masked Edit control.

18. **Type ########## into the Mask text box in the Property Pages.**

19. **Click OK.**

The Property Pages close.

You've now told the Masked Edit control that users can only enter digits, and can only enter nine of them.

20. **Press F5 to run the project and try to type in** abcd.

Nothing happens; the Masked Edit control refuses to accept anything other than numbers. However, each time an incorrect character is typed (a character not permitted by the Mask property), the Masked Edit control's ValidationError event is triggered. You can write programming in this event to display a message box with an error message explaining the problem to the user.

The Masked Edit control can be data-bound, so you can use it to display fields from a database or enable the user to edit those fields to change the data in the database. Think of the Masked Edit control as a specialized TextBox.

Do be careful to avoid punctuation chauvinism. When using masks for dates, time formats, and currency formats, some programmers have a tendency to assume the whole world uses the US formats. It's a big, big world, and people in different parts of the world do things differently. For instance, US dates are expressed month/day/year, but other countries use a day/month/year format. In Control Panel (click the Regional Options icon), and also during Windows setup, you can choose the format you prefer for date, time, currency, numbers, and other such issues. This information is held in the Windows Registry and when you're programming in VB, you can employ a set of functions to figure out how users have set these Regional Options. Use the FormatCurrency, FormatDateTime, and FormatNumber functions. Just look them up in Help to see how they work.

Part IV
Building a New Database

"YOU'VE PLUGGED YOUR MOUSE INTO THE
ELECTRIC SHAVER OUTLET AGAIN."

In this part . . .

Sure, there are lots of databases sitting around, and you often just generate reports out of those existing databases, or otherwise manage existing data. But there comes a time in every database programmer's life when he or she is called upon to climb the stairs to the next level. When that happens to you, you'll be ready if you use the information in this part of the book. The chapters in this part show you how to design and build a database from scratch.

You get to know VB's excellent Visual Data Manager, experimenting with building new databases, and seeing how easy it is to modify the structure of existing ones. You also discover how to use indexes to speed up searches for data, and how to check data entry to make sure that users don't enter a license number when they're supposed to enter their phone number (you'd be surprised how many people get area code confused with zip code — because both words end in *code,* I guess). Anyway, this part also illustrates how you can build your own custom data-bound ActiveX UserControls.

Chapter 8

Creating and Manipulating a New Database

. . . .

In This Chapter

▶ Designing a new database

▶ Creating a new database

▶ Creating a user interface

▶ Understanding the limitations of the Visual Data Manager

. . . .

*C*reating a new database can be quite easy in Visual Basic. You simply choose <u>A</u>dd-Ins⇨<u>V</u>isual Data Manager, and you're only a few steps away from completing a new table. When you finish that table and its fields, do another table if you want. You can't define relationships in the Visual Data Manager or add other complexities, but you can get a good start and then, if you decide to, add programming code or use Access to make subsequent adjustments.

Of course, a tool like the Visual Data Manager is only as good as the brain on the other side of the keyboard. Building a database involves numerous important considerations, including the user interface, which fields should be available, and the properties of each field (how many characters? what kind of data will it hold?). I cover those topics in this chapter, as you discover how to create a database from scratch by using Visual Basic.

And after you build a database, you can edit it, using the Visual Data Manager to make some adjustments. Chapter 9 shows you how to validate data and how to define indexes.

Designing a New Database

Before you fire up VB's excellent database tool, the Visual Data Manager, to create a new database, you want to spend at least five minutes thinking about the design of that database — or maybe more than five minutes.

You get to decide how you approach the job of creating a structure for a new database. Some people like to write down each table, field, and field type (currency, date, text, and so on). They define all that information, as well as indexes and any relationships between tables, on paper before they ever turn on their computers. Other developers prefer to sketch the structure while actually building it, using Access, VB's Visual Data Manager, or a specialized program like Visio.

Two useful products that can assist you in designing and building complex database systems are Powersoft's PowerDesigner DataArchitect (www.powersoft.com) and Platinum's Erwin (www.platinum.com/products/products.htm).

Of course, entire books are devoted to the topic of database design. The topic goes far, far beyond the scope of this book. So, this chapter assumes that you can design one or will learn the techniques elsewhere. In this chapter, you see how to construct a relatively simple database structure with VB's Visual Data Manager.

Creating a New Database

To explore the process of creating a new database in Visual Basic, assume that you have a CD collection and you want a database that catalogs your collection. You make a list of the smallest units of information that your database will contain: title, artist, and quality, with quality being a judgment ranging from 0 to 10. This example seems to require only one table that contains three fields.

To create a new database, follow these steps:

1. **Choose File⇨New Project.**

   The New Project dialog box appears.

2. **Double-click the Standard EXE icon in the New Project dialog box.**

   The dialog box closes.

3. **Choose Add-Ins⇨Visual Data Manager.**

   The Visual Data Manager appears, as shown in Figure 8-1.

4. **In the Visual Data Manager (you see VisData in its title bar), choose File⇨New⇨Microsoft Access⇨Version 7.0 MDB.**

   The Visual Data Manager displays the Select Microsoft Access Database to Create dialog box.

5. **Type a filename for your new database in the File Name text box.**

   For the CD catalog example, name the database **CD**.

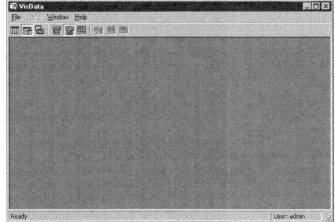

Figure 8-1:
The Visual
Data
Manager,
ready for
you to
design your
masterpiece
database.

6. **In the dialog box, move to the folder where you want to store your new database.**

7. **Click Save.**

The dialog box closes, and you see two child windows in VisData: Database Window and SQL Statement, as shown in Figure 8-2.

8. **From the group of three buttons on the left end of the VisData toolbar, click the button for the type of recordset that you want to use in your application.**

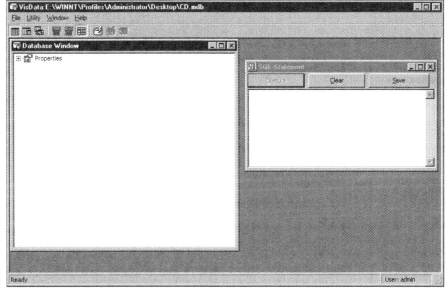

Figure 8-2:
Build the
design of
your data-
base in the
Database
Window
and define
queries in
the SQL
Statement
Window.

For the CD example, click the button on the far left in the VisData tool-bar. This button selects a Table-type recordset.

The Table-type recordset connects you to a single table. The next button over on the VisData toolbar represents the Dynaset-type recordset, which can connect to more than one table at a time. The Snapshot-type recordset (the third button) is read-only. It's useful for reports, but no data can be updated in the underlying database. For more details on these three recordset styles, see the section "Editing Records" in Chapter 14.

9. **Right-click Properties in the Database Window.**

   A context menu pops out.

10. **Choose New Table from the context menu.**

    The context menu closes, and you see the Table Structure dialog box, shown in Figure 8-3.

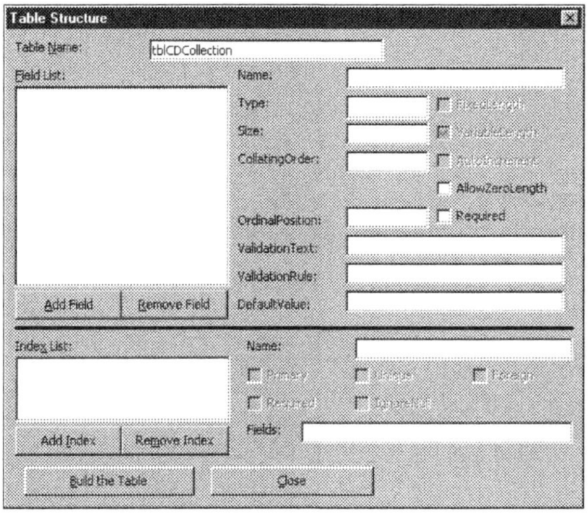

Figure 8-3:
Build a
new table by
using this
dialog box.

11. **Enter a name for the new table.**

    For the example application, type **tblCDCollection** as the Table Name in the Table Structure dialog box, as shown in Figure 8-3.

12. **Click Add Field.**

    You see the Add Field dialog box, shown in Figure 8-4.

13. **Type in the name of the first field in your table.**

    For the CD example, the first field is Title.

14. **Change the data type, size, or any other property of this field, as appropriate to your needs.**

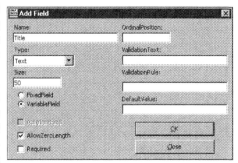

Figure 8-4:
Here's
where you
can add a
field to a
table and
describe its
various
properties.

You determine these field properties when designing your database. I describe the various properties you can define for a field in the sidebar "Setting field properties," later in this chapter. For more information about the ValidationText and ValidationRule properties, see Chapter 9.

For the example application, leave the data type and the other properties set to their defaults (text, 50 length, and so on).

15. Click OK.

VisData adds the new field to the table and then resets the Add Field dialog box to its default conditions, ready for you to enter another field.

16. Type in the name of your next field, specify its type, length, and other details, as necessary, and then click OK to add this field to the table.

The next field in the example is Artist.

17. Continue adding new fields, as detailed in the preceding steps, until you have completely defined your table.

For the CD example, you need to define only one more field: Quality. In the Add Field dialog box, change the Type for the Quality field to Integer.

This field now holds only numbers between –32,767 and +32,768 as its data.

18. Click Close.

The Add Field dialog box closes.

19. In the Table Structure dialog box, click the Build the Table button.

After a brief flurry of activity behind the scenes, your new database table is created.

20. Click Close.

The Table Structure dialog box closes.

21. In the Database Window, click the small + icon next to your table (tblCDCollection in the example) and then click the small + icon next to Fields.

You see the structure of your table, as shown in Figure 8-5.

Figure 8-5:
Tables and
their
fields are
displayed in
this tree
structure.

Setting field properties

When you add a field to a database, you can specify various properties of that field:

✔ **Type:** Specifying a data type enables the database to store and manage its data more efficiently. You can specify the following data types for a field in a VB database application: Binary, Boolean, Byte, Currency, Date/Time, Double, GUID, Integer, Long, Long Binary, OLE Object, Memo Single, Text, and VarBinary. This list is similar, but not identical, to the data types in VB itself for non-database programming. Choose the data type based on the kind of data that you plan to store in that field.

Clearly, if a field can contain only the digits 0–10, there's little point in wasting space by choosing a 50-byte storage space (the default size for the text data type) when you can store this field's data as an integer type, which takes up only two bytes.

✔ **Size:** For some data types, you can specify a particular size. For example, the Text data type can be a *fixed-length* type, meaning it isn't dynamically sized; you specify its length (it can range from 1 to 255 characters). Again, there is no point in specifying 50 characters for a zip code field.

✔ **FixedField or VariableField:** With some fields, you can choose *whether* you want to

specify their length or let them resize dynamically to fit the data assigned to the field. Choose FixedField or VariableField to determine this behavior.

✔ **AutoIncremental:** If you make a field AutoIncremental (it must also be a Long data type), the first record in the database (with this field as part of the record) automatically gets a value of 1 in this field, the second record added to the database gets a 2 in this field, and so on, up beyond 2 billion. (Some programmers believe that every table should include such a field.) The result is that each record is guaranteed to be unique because at least *this* field will hold a unique value. Fields like this are sometimes called AutoNumber fields, and they can be used to create *joins* — relationships between tables.

✔ **ZeroLength:** This option specifies whether a zero-length string is permitted ("" is the VB symbol for empty string). In other words, can this field be empty of text? A zero-length string is not the same thing as a NULL value.

✔ **Required:** This option specifies whether a NULL value is permitted in this field.

Creating a User Interface

You'll be startled by how easily you can get a user interface out of the Visual Data Manager. However, when using the Visual Data Manager's Data Form Designer, you're limited to building a form that uses a Data Control.

The Visual Data Manager's toolbar has three buttons: Data Control, Don't Use Data Control on New Form, and DataGrid. However, these options refer to the kind of user interface you work with when typing data into the database from within the Visual Data Manager. These three buttons have nothing to do with building a form for use in a VB project. You can build only one style of user interface for a VB project, and it's based on the Data Control.

To create a form that uses a Data Control as its primary user-navigation tool, follow these steps:

1. **Open the Visual Data Manager and create a database.**

   I cover all the details for completing this step in the preceding section of this chapter.

2. **With the Visual Data Manager running and your database loaded into it (you can use the example CD.MDB database that I show you how to create in the previous section), click the fourth button from the left on VisData's toolbar.**

   This button has an icon that is identical to the Data Control in the VB Toolbox.

   You have now instructed VisData that you want to build your user interface around the Data Control.

3. **Choose <u>U</u>tility⇨Data <u>F</u>orm Designer.**

   VisData displays the Data Form Designer, shown in Figure 8-6.

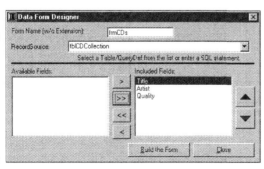

Figure 8-6:
You can
define
a user
interface by
using this
dialog box.

4. **In the Form Name text box, type a name for your user-interface form.**

   For the CD example, name the form **frmCDs**.

5. **Click the down-arrow icon next to the RecordSource text box.**

   A list of tables drops down (you have only one table in your example database).

6. **Click the name of the table you want to use.**

7. **Specify which fields you want to include in your user interface by moving selected fields from the Available Fields list to the Included Fields list.**

   To move all fields from the Available Fields list to the Included Fields list, click the second button down with the >> icon on it.

   For the example, move all three fields from the Available Fields list over to the Included Fields list.

   If you don't see the three fields in the Available Fields list, you must shut down the Visual Data Manager and rerun it. You can then choose its File⇨Open Database⇨Microsoft Access option to reload CD.MDB from your hard drive.

8. **Click Build the Form.**

   There's a brief outbreak of activity as VisData constructs your new form. You might see your VB Properties window flutter. Remain calm.

9. **Return to VB.**

   You see the new frmCDs now available in your project, as shown in Figure 8-7.

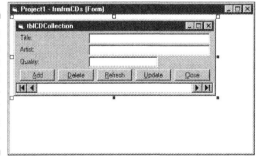

Figure 8-7:
VisData
created this
Data
Control–
based user
interface
for you.

10. **Double-click Form1.**

   You see Form1's Load Event in the code window.

11. **Type this code into Form1's Load Event:**

```
Private Sub Form_Load()
frmfrmCDs.Show
End Sub
```

This programming causes Form1 to display your new database user interface when this project is run. Form1 is the startup object by default. (If you want your database interface form to be the startup object — and thereby not have to use this frmfrmCDs.Show code — you can change the startup object by choosing Project⇨Project1 Properties.)

What's this frmfrm? In the VisData Data Form Designer, you were told to leave off the filename extension .FRM when you typed in the name. You did that, but VisData automatically adds the frm prefix without telling you — hence, frmfrm. If this convention bothers you, change the name of frmfrmCDs in the Properties window.

12. **Press F5.**

The project runs, and you see the data form ready to display existing data or accept new data input.

13. **Type in the data for a record in your database, as shown in Figure 8-8.**

Figure 8-8:
The user can now add new records to your database.

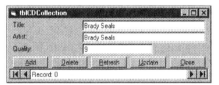

14. **Click the Add button on your data form.**

Whoops. You see the error message shown in Figure 8-9.

Figure 8-9:
As time goes on, error messages are likely to become more specific.

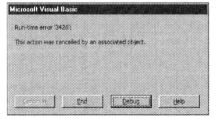

The culprit is the Data Control, which tends to choke when all records are removed from a table or when the user moves below or above a recordset. You're now in the dreaded *boundary error condition,* which is that spooky place that slices between two realities.

The problem: You have absolutely no data at all in the table. The quick (but very, very dirty) cure: Add a record so you have at least one in the database. A much better solution: If a table has no records, your application should simply *display no data.* That lets the user see the situation vividly. And, you should also disable (set their Enabled properties to False) all controls on your form that move through the table, or update or delete records. This way, the user cannot attempt to navigate the (non-existent) records.

The only control that you should leave enabled (not gray and unresponsive) on your form is the button or other control that's labeled Insert (or Add, or whatever you label it) — the button that's used to add a new record. (You want to let users do that, if they want.) For a complete code example demonstrating how to avoid this problem, see the section "Avoiding overshooting of recordset boundaries," in Chapter 7. Or, for a cunning alternative way around this problem, see the section "No current record" in Chapter 17.

Understanding the Visual Data Manager's Limitations

The Visual Data Manager isn't very helpful if you want to change many properties of the fields in a table. If you select the Design option in the Visual Data Manager, you see the Table Structure dialog box. It enables you to change the name of a field, for example, but prevents you from adjusting its Type or Size property. The solution is to delete the field and then add a new field to replace it, featuring the properties you want. (I cover this topic in Chapter 9.)

Another limitation of the Visual Data Manager is that you cannot define relationships in it. Instead, you could write programming to create a relationship in VB, or switch to Access to specify relationships.

The third major drawback is that the user-input form created for a VB project when you use the Visual Data Manager's Data Form Designer (described earlier in this chapter) is fairly simple and limited. For alternatives to this user-input form, see Chapter 7.

Chapter 9

Validating and Indexing Your Data

In This Chapter

▶ Validating user input at the source

▶ Using the ValidationRule property

▶ Indexing your data

*D*ata validation attempts to ensure that a database contains useful, accurate data. Of course, the old saying "garbage in, garbage out" is the truth. Most so-called "computer errors" are either programming or data entry errors. And I use the phrase *attempts to ensure* because no amount of data validation can prevent someone from entering 1 as his or her age.

Indexing is important to database design, too. It speeds things up, as you'll see, in much the same way that an index in a book speeds up finding specific information. When you specify that a field should be indexed, you're requesting that the data in that field be maintained in an organized, easily searched list.

In this chapter, you see how to validate within data-input forms, as well as how to validate by using a feature of the Jet database engine called the ValidationRule property. You also find out why and how to index *some* fields in a table. You may be tempted, but you don't want to index *all* the fields. Too much of a good thing, as they say.

Validating User Input at the Source

Usually, you need to check data before it gets stored in a database. If someone types in a three-digit zip code or forgets to enter a credit card number, money can be lost. Some database applications don't accept certain kinds of bad data.

When you're designing a database, you can sometimes employ features of the database engine, such as the Jet engine's ValidationRule property, to accept or reject data. I describe this technique in the section, "Using the

ValidationRule Property," later in this chapter. An alternative is to check the data at the point of entry — that is, the user-input form or the other component used to permit the user to type in data. I describe techniques for catching errors at the point of entry in this section.

The most common way to see whether a user has typed in appropriate data (a zip code, for example, instead of an area code) is by simply checking the data when the user indicates that he or she is finished entering it. For example, you can write programming to test the length of a zip code, like this code:

```
Private Sub Text1_LostFocus()
L = Len(Text1)
If L < 5 Then
    MsgBox "A zip code must be at least 5 characters long.
        But you! You entered only " & L & " characters. Do
        try again."
End If
End Sub
```

You can use the LostFocus event (of the control where the data is entered) to write the programming to validate data entry. If you do detect bad data, display a clear error message to the user and also use the SetFocus command to restore the focus to the same data entry control where the error occurred. This is only courteous, and speeds things up. (The control with the focus is the one that is ready to accept typing from the keyboard.)

You could put your validation programming into whatever button on your data-entry form the user clicks to move to the next record. The button might be captioned SUBMIT, SAVE, ADD, NEXT, or some such way for the user to say, "I'm done entering this record, so save it into the database." This approach works, but you can use some better methods for handling data validation. For one thing, this approach only checks the record after all the fields have been filled in and the user is ready to move to the next record.

Instead, you should validate each field as soon as the user moves to the next field. This approach enables you to leave the insertion cursor still blinking in the problem field, so users don't have to move their hands from the keyboard to the mouse in order to click the invalid field and thus put the cursor back into that TextBox. To validate in this way, use the LostFocus event and the SetFocus command, as I explain earlier in this section.

Validating a zip code

How does your application know that the user has typed in a zip code and then pressed the Tab key to move to the next TextBox, which means that your application should now validate the zip code? In the past, some programmers used the GotFocus event of the next TextBox. The flaw in this approach is that users don't always proceed from TextBox to TextBox in a data-entry form, entering data in each field in order: Name, Address, City, State, Zip, and so on.

As I explain in the preceding section, a better approach puts validation code in the LostFocus event of the ZipCode TextBox. With this approach, your application checks each field's entry when that field *loses the focus* (is no longer the container where characters will be displayed when the user types). A field loses the focus when the user presses the Tab key, moving to the next input component based on the TabIndex property, or when the user clicks any component capable of input, with the mouse. For another effective validation technique, see the following section.

Using the Validate event

The primary problem with the technique I describe in the preceding section is that by the time you get around to checking the data for validity, the focus has already moved to a new TextBox or other control. You *could* set up a virtual array to keep track of TabIndexes, or otherwise programmatically return the focus to the bad input until the user gets it right, but you don't have to use such complicated techniques. Visual Basic 6 has a pair of complementary members that make validation easy.

The Validate event is triggered when the user tries to shift the focus to another control (by clicking or pressing Tab), but before that focus actually shifts. So, if a user enters 244 in the ZipCode TextBox and then presses Tab, trying to get to the Country TextBox, the Validate event is triggered, but the LostFocus event doesn't yet occur. And, the LostFocus event doesn't occur (because the focus remains on the ZipCode TextBox) if your application finds a problem with the data and therefore sets the Cancel parameter to True.

To test for a valid zip code by using the Validate event, follow these steps:

1. **Start a new Standard EXE program in Visual Basic by choosing File⇨New.**

2. **Put two TextBoxes on the form, named by default Text1 and Text2.**

3. **Double-click Text1.**

   The code window opens.

4. **In the right drop-down list in the code window, choose Validate.**

   You see the Validate event Sub in the code window.

5. **Type this code into Text1's Validate event:**

```
Private Sub Text1_Validate(Cancel As Boolean)
If Len(Text1) < 5 And Text1 <> "" Then
    MsgBox "Zip codes are 5 digits long. Try again
        please."
    Cancel = True
End If
End Sub
```

You test to see if Text1 is blank (<> " ") because you do want to permit a user to tab past a data entry field. Sometimes, users want to enter data in an order other than the one you assume; they may want to come back later and fill in the zip code, for instance. You should therefore permit data fields to remain blank during the data entry process.

6. **Press F5 to run this program.**

7. **Try typing** 1234 **into Text1. Then press Tab (or click Text2), attempting to move the focus to Text2.**

An error message is displayed, and the focus remains in Text1.

By setting the Cancel argument to True, you prevent Text1 from losing focus.

If you want to explore a more heavy-duty validation system, take a look at the section "Managing user input with the Masked Edit control," in Chapter 7.

Using the CausesValidation property

In the previous section, setting Cancel to True in Step 5 prevents the user from shifting the focus to *any* input component, including CommandButtons. If your form has a button labeled Help, the user should be able to click that button no matter what a TextBox's Validation event thinks of the bad data in that TextBox. To avoid putting the user into the unhappy position of not being able to click a Help button, you can set that CommandButton's CausesValidation property to False. That way, clicking the CommandButton does not trigger the TextBox's Validation event (or any other Validation event). Instead, the user gets help.

Using the ValidationRule Property

When using the Visual Data Manager to create a new database (see Chapter 8), you can specify several properties for each field of data. These properties include

⊭ Allow Zero Length

⊭ ValidationRule

⊭ Default Value

In this section, I show you how to use the ValidationRule and ValidationText properties to prevent the user from typing in the wrong kind of data for a particular field. (These properties work only with Microsoft Jet-based databases, such as those created by Access and Visual Basic, with the .MDB extension.)

Of course, you can write code to analyze a user's input, and then reject bad input and display a message alerting the user about how to correct the problem (see the previous sections in this chapter). However, the two Validation properties that I describe in this section are simple to use. To ensure that users enter only what you want them to, follow these steps:

1. **Open your database with the Visual Data Manager, as I describe in Chapter 8.**

   If you're following along with the examples I present in Chapter 8 and in this section, you have a database (CD.MDB) and a table defined, you have three records in that table, and you're running the Visual Data Manager.

2. **In the Visual Data Manager's Database Window, right-click the table you're interested in validating.**

   A context menu pops out. If you completed the CD example in Chapter 8, you can use the tblCDCollection table.

3. **Choose Design.**

   You see the Table Structure dialog box, as shown in Figure 9-1.

   It's possible that you don't see the Table Structure dialog box after you choose Design from the context menu. A bug in the VisData program sometimes causes this problem. If you see the error message shown in Figure 9-2, simply click No and then choose File⇨Close to shut down the Visual Data Manager. In Visual Basic, choose Add-Ins⇨Visual Data Manager to rerun the Visual Data Manager. Now you can repeat Steps 1 through 3 in this example, and everything will work fine. No harm done.

4. **Click the field you want to validate (for example, Quality) in the Field List in the Table Structure dialog box.**

5. **Type a description of the validation rule into the ValidationText TextBox.**

   If you're following my example, type **Number must be between 1 and 10.** You want a user to type in only numbers within this range.

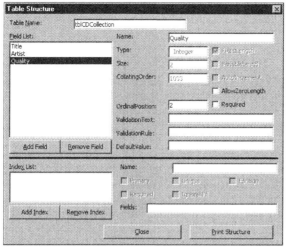

Figure 9-1:
You can
modify a
table and
its fields
and their
properties
in this
dialog box.

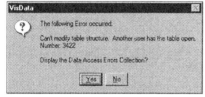

Figure 9-2:
If you
see this
message,
restart the
Visual Data
Manager.

6. **In the ValidationRule TextBox, type the actual rule you want used to test the user's input.**

   To follow my example, type **BETWEEN 1 AND 10**.

   Your application uses the words you enter to test whether the user types in acceptable data. The words are a SQL WHERE clause, but you leave out the word *WHERE* (and you don't use quotation marks). For an in-depth discussion of SQL, see Chapters 18 and 19.

7. **Click Close.**

   The Table Structure dialog box closes.

8. **In the Database Window of the Visual Data Manager, double-click the name of your table.**

   To follow my example, double-click tblCDCollection. A user interface data-entry form appears, as shown in Figure 9-3.

Figure 9-3:
You can test
your valida-
tion scheme
by entering
a new
record in
this form.

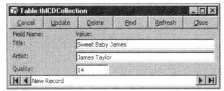

If you don't see the same user interface shown in Figure 9-3, click Close
to close the user interface and then click the fourth button from the left
on the Visual Data Manager's toolbar. This button selects the Data
Control-style user-input form. Now repeat Step 8 to bring up the form
shown in Figure 9-3.

9. **Click the Add button on the data-entry form.**

   The fields' text boxes go blank, and the phrase New Record appears in
   the Data Control.

10. **Type in data to fill all the fields, entering invalid data for the field
    you're testing.**

    To follow my example, type in a Title, an Artist, and the number **14** as
    the Quality. Because 14 isn't a valid entry for Quality, the database
    should respond to this error.

11. **Click Update.**

    A message box appears, asking if you want to save the new record.

12. **Click Yes.**

    The message box disappears, but a new message box appears, displaying
    the ValidationText you typed in Step 5, as shown in Figure 9-4.

Figure 9-4:
The Quality
field only
accepts
numbers
from 1 to 10.

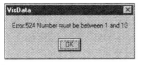

13. **Click OK.**

    The error message disappears.

14. **Enter valid data in the field where you're testing validation.**

    Enter **10** in the Quality field, if you're following my example.

15. **Click Update.**

    A message box appears, asking if you want to save the new record.

16. **Click Yes.**

    This time, the database agreeably absorbs your data, or in the case of my example CD database, it accepts your assessment that this CD is worth a 10 in the Quality field.

Indexing Your Data

When you design a database, you can designate some of its fields as indexes. Information in a relational database is not automatically stored alphabetically (or by numeric order, if the field is numeric). When someone adds a new record to a database, it's just put at the end of a table. No attempt is made to place it in some particular position.

However, if you do specify that a particular field, or fields, are to be indexed, they will be kept in an ordered list. This makes searching them far faster (for the same reason that you can find a particular topic faster in a book that has an index). For an in-depth discussion of indexes, see Chapter 2.

An index speeds up data access for the field that you index, so you usually design a database with at least one index. For example, if you usually display the names in your address book database sorted by the LastName field, you would want to index the LastName field. By doing so, you speed up the process of displaying this alphabetized list. Or, if you expect to frequently request specific records based on birthdays, you'd probably want to index the BirthDate field.

Why not index every field?

So, if you think data will be accessed primarily from *several* fields in a table, you can index each of these fields. "A-ha!" you say. "Why not index *every* field? Then, no matter what, the display of data must be ultimately swift." Nope, sorry. The use of indexes involves a tradeoff: If you index everything, you cancel the indexing efficiencies. So, use indexes only in moderation.

One reason that you don't index every field is that sometimes a quick table scan is faster than analyzing a query, identifying the right index, loading that index, and querying against it. The main reason though is that for every index you have, whenever an update is done to the data, the indexes relative to that data must be updated, too. So, indexes speed up searches but always slow down updates. Indexing a database properly is an art and requires performing a detailed analysis of your users' behaviors to detect what operations are done more often — read or write — and adapting the application and configuring the database to reflect this. Here are some excellent sources you should check out if you want more information on this topic:

- *Microsoft Jet 3.5 Performance Overview and Optimization Techniques* (a White Paper by Kevin Collins, Microsoft Jet Program Management)
- *Microsoft Jet Database Engine Programmer's Guide,* a Microsoft Press book (available free in MSDN Online at Microsoft's Web site)

The special primary index

One special index, called the *primary key,* ensures that the records in the database can be distinguished from each other. In other words, no two records can have identical data in the primary key field.

If you use a LastName field as your primary key, you can't enter two records with the same last name. Of course, that would be impractical. (If you create an index on a field such as LastName or FirstName, don't select the Unique property for either of those kinds of fields, which are likely to have duplicate values.) A more sensible field to use as the primary key would be taxpayer identification number, because, by design, no duplicate numbers exist. Everyone gets a unique taxpayer identification number. For additional details on the primary key, read on or look at the discussion of indexing in Chapter 2.

Not only must each record have a distinct value (distinct content) in its primary key field, but each record must also have *some* content in the primary key field. This field cannot be empty. (Technically, a field with no data is said to contain a *null* value.)

Every table should have a primary key field. Often, the most practical kind of primary key isn't some data about a person or object, but instead is generated at the time a record is added to the database. To obtain this number, each new record is given a number one higher than the previous record. Usually, such a specialized, generated number is called an ID. The database itself can generate these serial ID numbers for each item of data.

To see how, follow these steps:

1. **Open the Visual Data Manager and load the database that you want to index.**

   If you're following along with the examples I present in this book, you can use the CD database that I describe in Chapter 8. Choose File⇨ Open Database⇨Microsoft Access and load in the CD.MDB database.

2. **In the Database Window of the Visual Data Manager, right-click the table that you want to index (tblCDCollection in the CD example).**

   A context menu pops out.

3. **Choose Design.**

   The context menu closes, and the Table Structure dialog box appears.

4. **Click Add Field.**

   The Add Field dialog box appears.

5. **Type in the name you want to use for your primary key field.**

   For example, you can name this field **ID**.

6. **Select Long from the Type listbox (click the down-arrow icon to see the list).**

   The Long data type is required if you're using the AutoIncrementing feature. This data type can count from 1 to more than 2 billion, which is high enough for most purposes.

7. **Click the AutoIncrField check box to check it.**

   This setting tells VB that you want to use the special automatic incrementing (serial-number generating) feature for this field.

8. **Click the Required check box to check it.**

   This field now requires a non-null value. In other words, users can't leave this field empty when entering a new record.

9. **Click OK.**

   The new field is added to your table.

10. **Click Close.**

    The Add Field dialog box closes.

11. **Click Add Index in the Table Structure dialog box.**

    The Add Index dialog box appears, as shown in Figure 9-5.

12. **Type in the name** PrimaryKey.

13. **Click ID in the Available Fields list.**

    ID appears in the Indexed Fields list.

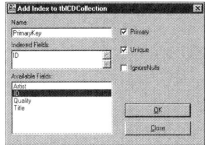

Figure 9-5:
In this dialog box, you define indexes and the primary key.

14. **Ensure that both the Primary and Unique check boxes are checked, as shown in Figure 9-5.**

15. **Click OK and then click Close.**

    The ID field is specified as the primary key in your table, and the Add Index dialog box closes.

16. **Click Close.**

    The Table Structure dialog box closes.

17. **Double-click the table (for example, tblCDCollection) in the Database Window of the Visual Data Manager.**

    The user-input data form appears, as shown in Figure 9-6.

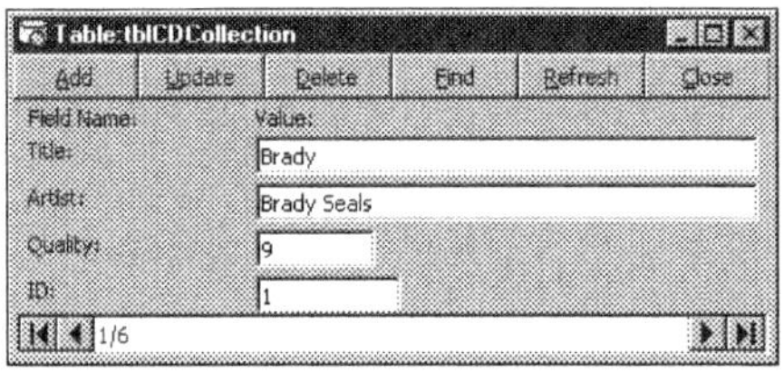

Figure 9-6:
The new ID field in this form automatically assigns a unique number to each record.

18. **Click the arrow buttons on the Data Control to move through the records in this database.**

    As if by magic, each existing record in your table has been given a unique ID number. Now try adding a new record and notice that its ID number is automatically generated, too.

Chapter 10

Creating Custom, Data-Bound
ActiveX UserControls

* *

* *

*S*ometimes, there's no better way to solve a programming problem than building your own controls. You can build them to behave the way you want, instead of having to work within the confines of existing, factory-built controls like the standard CommandButton or TextBox.

Visual Basic has facilities for assisting you in creating various kinds of custom-made controls. You can easily add an ActiveX UserControl to your VB Toolbox and then drag and drop it onto any form in any of your projects. In Visual Basic editions previous to VB 6, you couldn't make UserControls data-aware. Now you can.

In this chapter, you see how to add database connectivity to standard ActiveX UserControls, and how to place data-aware UserControls on the DataRepeater component, a special, new VB 6 component that displays scrollable data by replicating your UserControl. You also find out how to employ one of the cooler new tricks in VB6: dynamic control creation. It's not for the faint of heart, but it can be a powerful tool in the right hands.

VB 6 has an alternative type of user control — the ActiveX *Document* UserControl — that you can easily drop into a Web page, right in there along with the usual HTML code. Because it works compatibly with HTML, a Document-style UserControl enables you to quickly add features that can jazz up your Web pages. Chapter 11 describes the ActiveX Document UserControl.

VB's wizards can create both standard and Document ActiveX Controls. And as you see in this chapter, you can attach both types of controls to a database. But before building a UserControl, you should know that both kinds of ActiveX UserControls come in two flavors: DLL or EXE. You get to choose which flavor you want to employ. This choice involves a tradeoff: DLLs run in-process, but EXEs don't. Unlike an EXE, a DLL doesn't put extra demands on the system by requiring communication across address spaces. And when using DLLs, you can preserve variables' values (maintain state) on a server. On the other hand, DLLs are harder to distribute and require each client container to instantiate a new instance of the DLL.

In-process technically means that calls do not need to be marshaled across process boundaries by the COM library, and therefore calls are faster. The downside is that only one client application can use the same instance of a control from an in-process DLL. DLLs can scale very well if they are thread-safe (as VB makes them) and when they are run in MTS or COM+. Out-of-process EXEs run in a separate process and therefore allow for easier multithreading and process isolation to prevent crashes. The calls to EXEs are a bit slower, because of the necessity to cross process boundaries using a proxy and a stub and sometimes even machine boundaries using DCOM.

UserControls offer the following major benefits:

- You can easily reuse them.
- They encapsulate (hide and insulate from side-effects) your programming.
- You design them, so they offer you the opportunity to provide functionality unavailable elsewhere.
- They can trigger events in the container (form or browser), thereby communicating to their host.
- They are relatively easy to improve later if you decide to modify them.
- The ActiveX Control Interface wizard can be a useful assistant when you're building UserControls.

Creating a Data-Bound UserControl

Before using the new DataRepeater component, you must build a UserControl (which gets repeated when you attach it to the DataRepeater, as you see in the section "Using the DataRepeater," later in this chapter). Creating a data-bound UserControl is a simple matter of building a typical UserControl and then adding some properties that can be made data-aware. In this way, you can bind TextBoxes (or whatever controls you use) to a database via a Data Control on the form or other container that you later use to display your UserControl.

The following steps show you how to create a UserControl you can use to display the fields in a table. (I use an example that displays the products available in the NWind sample database, along with the cost and product ID of each item.) To create a data-bound UserControl that can display this data, follow these steps:

1. **Choose File⇨New Project.**

   The New Project dialog box appears.

2. **Double-click ActiveX Control.**

   The template for an ActiveX Control appears, including a blank UserControl form. In the Toolbox, Visual Basic disables the OLE icon and adds a disabled (for now) UserControl1 icon. This icon represents your UserControl and will shortly become enabled.

3. **Put pairs of Labels and TextBoxes (one pair for each of the fields that you want to display) on the UserControl form by double-clicking their icons on the Toolbox.**

   For my NWind example, I use three Labels and three TextBoxes. Each Label shows the name of the field, and each TextBox shows the actual contents of the field.

   Beware of adding third-party commercial controls to a UserControl. Using third-party controls in this way can cause you problems later if new versions of the third-party control become available, and use of these controls may require licenses on any system to which you distribute your UserControl.

4. **Click each Label in turn on the form to select it and then, in the Properties window, change the Label's Caption property to the names of the fields you want to display.**

   For my example, change the captions to **Product Name**, **Product ID**, and **Unit Cost**. The result should look like Figure 10-1.

Figure 10-1:
Your Labels and TextBoxes now fit into a DataRepeater control.

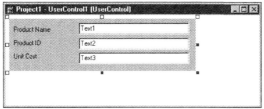

Because you plan to put this UserControl into a DataRepeater, you should resize your custom UserControl to be as compact vertically as possible, as shown in Figure 10-1. A DataRepeater displays each record (one record per UserControl), one after the other, stacked on top of each other. In other words, your program will display a stack of these UserControls, and it's more efficient if they're not too tall.

5. **Change the Name property of each TextBox in the Properties window to some descriptive name relating to the field it displays.**

   For my example, I change the names to txtName, txtID, and txtPrice.

6. **Double-click the UserControl form's background.**

   You see the code window.

7. **Move the cursor to the top of the code window until the ListBoxes at the top of the code window say** (General) (Declarations).

   You can now type in the programming code that adds three properties to your UserControl.

8. **To follow my NWind example, type the following code into the code window:**

```
Public Property Get ProductName() As String
ProductName = txtName.Text
End Property

Public Property Let ProductName(ByVal newProductName As
        String)
txtName.Text = newProductName
End Property

Public Property Get ProductPrice() As String
ProductPrice = txtPrice.Text
End Property

Public Property Let ProductPrice(ByVal newProductPrice As
        String)
txtPrice.Text = newProductPrice
End Property

Public Property Get ProductID() As String
ProductID = txtID.Text
End Property

Public Property Let ProductID (ByVal newProductID As
        String)
txtID.Text = newProductID
End Property

Private Sub txtName_Change()
PropertyChanged "ProductName"
End Sub
```

```
Private Sub txtPrice_Change()
PropertyChanged "ProductPrice"
End Sub

Private Sub txtID_Change()
PropertyChanged "ProductID"
End Sub
```

If you're working with a different set of fields, replace each TextBox name with whatever you named those TextBoxes, and replace each variable I use (ProductName and newProductName, for example) with variable names that describe the fields you're using.

This programming illustrates how you create new properties for a UserControl. The special procedure called `Property Let` permits a programmer who's employing your UserControl to change the property. `Property Get` enables a programmer to see (read) the existing value in the property. The `PropertyChanged` command stores the value of each property when it is changed. For more detail on this topic, see "Adding Properties to Controls" in the VB Help.

9. **Choose Tools⇨Procedure Attributes.**

   You see the Procedure Attributes dialog box.

10. **Click Advanced.**

    Additional options, including data-binding, appear in the dialog box, as shown in Figure 10-2.

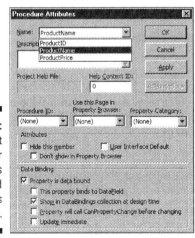

Figure 10-2: Specify that each of your properties is data-bound in this dialog box.

11. **Choose the name of a field in the Name field of the dialog box.**

    In my example, I first choose the ProductID field.

12. **Click both the Property is Data Bound check box and the Show in DataBindings Collection at Design Time check box.**

    Check symbols appear in both check boxes.

    The DataBindings collection option makes it easy for a programmer to assign fields to the TextBoxes in your UserControl, as you see in the section "Using the DataRepeater," later in this chapter.

13. **Repeat Step 12 until you've bound all the fields you want to display.**

14. **Click OK.**

    The Procedure Attributes dialog box closes.

15. **Click the UserControl1 form (not one of the controls on it).**

    UserControl1 appears in the Properties window.

16. **Change the Name property from UserControl1 to a name that's descriptive of the table you're displaying.**

    For my example, I use the name **ctlProducts**.

17. **Right-click Project1 in the Project Explorer.**

    A context menu pops out.

18. **Choose Project1 Properties from the context menu.**

    The Properties dialog box appears.

19. **Change the Name field from Project1 to a name descriptive of the data you're displaying.**

    In my example, I use the name **Products**.

20. **Click OK.**

    The dialog box closes.

21. **Using Windows Explorer, create a new directory to hold your UserControl project and its associated forms, files, and even, as you'll do next, the compiled component (.OCX) itself.**

22. **Choose File➪Save Project.**

    A series of File Save dialog boxes appears. Save all the elements of this project into your new directory. When you're asked to save the .VBP element, change its name to a descriptive name (I used **ctlProducts**) before you save it to the disk.

23. **For my example, choose File➪Make ctlProducts.OCX. (If you aren't following the example, your File menu will display the name of the OCX that you chose in Step 22.)**

The Make Project dialog box appears. At this point, you are actually asking VB to compile and save your UserControl.

24. **Click OK.**

VB saves the compilation (the .OCX file) to your new directory, and as a pleasant by-product of this compilation process, your new UserControl is also registered in the operating system's Registry. That makes it available for use by other projects (such as a project that includes a DataRepeater container component, as you see in the next section).

Congratulations! You now have a reusable component that you can add to the VB Toolbox for use in any future projects.

Using the DataRepeater

One of the more interesting additions to the VB 6 arsenal of tools is the DataRepeater control, which acts like a power-ListBox. Unlike a normal ListBox, it doesn't provide a scrolling list of lines of text. Instead, it displays a scrolling set of UserControls.

You first build a UserControl designed to display a single record, as I describe in the previous section. Then, you place that UserControl on a DataRepeater. When running your program, the user can view multiple records by scrolling the DataRepeater. To see how this control works, follow these steps:

1. **Create and then register a data-bound UserControl named Products.**

   For all the details on completing this step, see the preceding section in this chapter.

2. **Choose File⇨New Project.**

   The New Project dialog box appears.

3. **Double-click the Standard EXE icon in the New Project dialog box.**

   The dialog box closes, and the typical, classic VB project appears.

4. **Right-click the Toolbox.**

   A context menu appears.

5. **Choose Components.**

   The Components dialog box appears, listing operating system components; components added by other languages and applications; VB components; legacy components; and, to your delight, the component which I show you how to build in the previous section in this chapter. (In that section, I named the component Products, but you may have used a different name for your component.)

6. **Scroll the list of components until you see the name of the component you created in the previous section in this chapter.**

7. **Click the check box next to the component's name, as shown in Figure 10-3.**

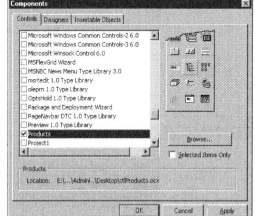

Figure 10-3:
This dialog box lists all the components registered in your computer.

8. **While the Components dialog box is still open, also click the check boxes next to Microsoft DataRepeater Control 6.0 (OLEDB) and Microsoft ADO Data Control 6.0 (OLEDB).**

9. **Click OK.**

The dialog box closes, and VB adds all three requested components to your Toolbox, as shown in Figure 10-4. The DataRepeater icon looks like a honeycomb; the ADO Data Control looks like a scrollbar with a yellow bee attached; your UserControl's icon resembles a pencil touching buttons.

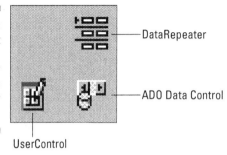

Figure 10-4:
You've just added three new components to your Toolbox.

DataRepeater

ADO Data Control

UserControl

10. **Double-click the DataRepeater icon in the Toolbox.**

A DataRepeater appears on your form.

11. **Stretch the DataRepeater to make it tall enough to display several of your UserControls at a time.**

12. **Click the UserControl icon on the Toolbox and then drag your mouse on the DataRepeater.**

    VB adds your Products UserControl to the DataRepeater, which acts as its container, as shown in Figure 10-5.

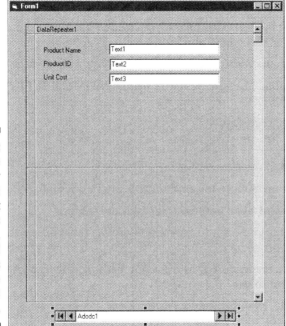

Figure 10-5:
Make the DataRepeater high enough so that when this project runs, several UserControls can be displayed vertically.

13. **Double-click the ADO DataControl icon in the Toolbox.**

    An ADO DataControl appears on your form.

14. **Move the DataControl beneath the DataRepeater, as shown in Figure 10-5.**

15. **Right-click the ADO Data Control.**

    A context menu pops out.

16. **Choose ADODC Properties from the context menu.**

    The Property Pages dialog box appears.

17. **Select Use Connection String.**

    Instead of using an existing data connection, you're going to create a new connection.

18. Click Build.

The Data Link Properties dialog box appears. You see a list of all available database engines.

19. Select Microsoft Jet 4.0 as the OLE DB provider.

If you don't have the Jet 4.0 engine, use whatever version is available. The Connection tab page is displayed. (I use the Jet engine throughout this book.)

20. Click the button with three dots (...).

A file-locating dialog box appears. You need to locate the database you want to use for this connection.

21. Locate and then double-click the database you want to use.

For this example, I use the database named NWIND.MDB. (It's in your VB98 directory.)

The file dialog box closes.

22. Click OK.

The Data Link Properties dialog box closes.

23. Click the RecordSource tab in the Property Pages dialog box.

24. In the Command Type listbox, select adCmdTable.

In this example, you want to get records from a table rather than a text file or stored procedure.

25. In the Table or Stored Procedure Name listbox, select the name of the table you want to use.

In my example, I select Products as the table.

26. Click OK.

The Property Pages dialog box closes.

27. Click the DataRepeater control on the form.

Its properties appear in the Properties window.

28. In the Properties window, select Adodc1 as the DataSource property for the DataRepeater.

29. In the Properties window, click the RepeatedControlName property and then select the name of your UserControl.

In my example, I select Products.CtlProducts from the drop-down list.

The DataRepeater suddenly lives up to its name. It's populated with your UserControl.

30. Right-click the DataRepeater.

A context menu pops out.

31. **Choose Properties.**

    The DataRepeater Property Pages dialog box appears.

32. **Click the RepeaterBindings tab.**

    On this tab, you assign fields to the properties in your UserControl, as shown in Figure 10-6.

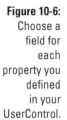

Figure 10-6:
Choose a
field for
each
property you
defined
in your
UserControl.

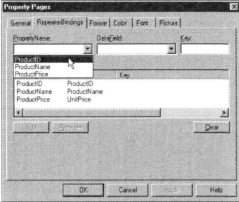

33. **Select the name of a field in the PropertyName drop-down list.**

    In my example, I selected ProductID.

34. **Select the same field in the DataField drop-down list.**

35. **Click Add.**

    The assignment of the field to the property now appears in the RepeaterBindings list.

36. **Repeat Steps 33 through 35 to assign property names to each data field you're displaying.**

    In my example, I assigned ProductName to ProductName and ProductPrice to UnitPrice, as shown in Figure 10-6.

37. **Click OK.**

    The dialog box closes.

38. **Press F5 to run this program.**

    You see the DataRepeater in action, as shown in Figure 10-7.

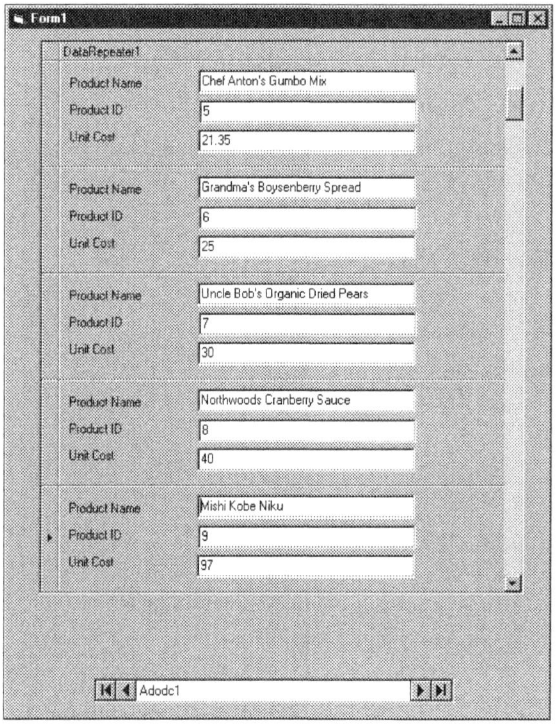

Figure 10-7:
The
DataRepeater
displays
records in
this handy
scrollable
stack.

You might want to set the Visible property of the ADO Data Control to False. You don't have much reason to use it as a navigation tool because the DataRepeater has a scrollbar and it responds to the PgUp, PgDown, Home, and End keys.

If you get into building UserControls, remember that a highly useful wizard with the rather grand name of ActiveX Control Interface wizard can assist you. This wizard can automatically generate most of that nasty `Property Get` and `Property Let` stuff that you would otherwise have to type by hand (see "Creating a Data-Bound UserControl, earlier in this chapter). And it does several other cool things, too.

Exploring this wizard in any detail goes beyond the scope of this book, but you should try it out yourself. When you get to the wizard's Set Mapping page, try selecting Text1 or Command1 from the drop-down list labeled Maps to ... Control. Map some functionality by selecting some of the properties in the Public Name list. Mapping enables you to steal the functionality built into components like TextBoxes and use that functionality in your new UserControl — without having to write code. By the time you've finished, the wizard has generated quite a bit of programming for you.

Creating Controls Dynamically at Runtime

Now for something completely radical. Be warned: If you're given to panic or hysteria, skip this section. What follows is cutting-edge VB programming. In this section, I show you how to fill a VB form with controls while your program is running.

You've probably heard of Control Arrays, a technique that enables you to create *clones* — new TextBoxes born out of an existing TextBox on a form. What I'm describing in this section, though, takes things a step further: It's not necessary to even have a control on a form. You can pop a TextBox into existence while your application is running, even if no other TextBox exists on the form. For example, you can take a look at the set of fields in a table in a database, and then, after you find out which fields you need to display, you can populate the form with the necessary controls and assign properties to those controls as you want.

Think of it this way: Being able to pop objects into existence while a program is running increases the flexibility of your programs. For example, you can let users request to see text in a RichTextBox rather than a TextBox. That way, they can choose to see italics and other formatting possible only in the Rich version of the TextBox. Or, you can populate a form with appropriate components, based on which controls best display the fields in a database or best show the content message sent over the Internet.

But there's more: You can even bring your UserControls into existence — without having them in the VB Toolbox. As long as a component is registered, it's available to be *instantiated,* as it's called, when something seems to appear out of nowhere.

Dynamic control creation, a new VB 6 capability, is still cutting edge, so you won't find lots of support or documentation. You want to explore this technique because it offers exciting possibilities. And you'll remember that it exists if a task in your own work would benefit from this technology.

In addition to the benefits I've already mentioned, consider that you can also use this technique to be selective about which components you include on a form when the form is first loaded — this conserves system resources. And if you have a complicated Property Pages style form, instead of using tabs and switching components' Visible property on and off (also uses up resources), you could merely instantiate and destroy components as necessary. Think of it as components on demand.

To put a couple of TextBoxes on a form during runtime (while an application is running), follow these steps:

1. **Build and then register a UserControl, following the steps I describe in the section "Creating a Data-Bound UserControl," earlier in this chapter.**

   In that section, I show you how to build and register a UserControl named ctlProducts.

2. **Choose File⇨New Project.**

   The New Project dialog box appears.

3. **Double-click the Standard EXE icon in the New Project dialog box.**

   The dialog box closes, and the typical, classic VB project appears.

4. **Double-click Form1.**

   The code window appears with the Form_Load event displayed.

5. **Type this code into the Form_Load event:**

   ```
   Private Sub Form_Load()
       Set ctlExtender =
           Controls.Add("Products.ctlProducts",
           "MyUserControl")
       With ctlExtender
           .Visible = True
           .Top = 1200
           .Left = 900
       End With
   End Sub
   ```

   Here's what you're saying in this code: To the Controls collection in this project (the items on the Toolbox), add this UserControl. In your projects, you should change `Products.ctlProducts` to the name of your own UserControl. The second parameter — `MyUserControl` — can be used in your program to refer to this entity. For instance, you could replace `With ctlExtender` with `With Form1!MyUserControl` or `Form1.Controls("MyUserControl")` in the preceding code.

   You must explicitly set the Visible property to True because dynamically added UserControls are, by default, invisible.

6. **Type this code into the very top of the code window (above Sub Form_Load), in the General Declarations section:**

   ```
   Dim ctlExtender As VBControlExtender
   ```

The ControlExtender is an object that enables you to add a control during runtime even though that control doesn't currently appear in the Toolbox. If you're adding a third-party commercial control, you may need to include licensing information when you instantiate (dynamically create) the control. Use this syntax:

```
Licenses.Add "Products.ctlProducts", "TheLicensesKey"
```

The first parameter (Products.ctlProducts in this example) names the component, and the second parameter (TheLicensesKey) is whatever key the component requires. You have to get the correct key from the manufacturer of the component.

7. Press F5.

As shown in Figure 10-8, you see the CtlProducts UserControl, which you created and registered in Step 1.

Or perhaps disaster strikes, and you see the error message displayed in Figure 10-9.

Figure 10-8:
This UserControl has been added to a running VB project, even though it's neither on the form, nor in the Toolbox.

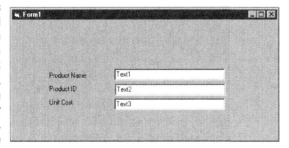

Figure 10-9:
The UserControl has been deleted, moved, or messed up in the Registry.

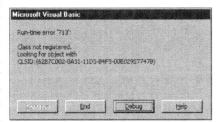

To solve the problem of a missing UserControl (refer to Figure 10-9), follow the steps in the section "Creating a Data-Bound UserControl," earlier in this chapter; however, name the UserControl something other than *ctlProducts* when you open the File Save dialog box in Step 23 (choose File⇨Make ctlProducts.OCX). In this way, you register what is essentially a new UserControl. Then, edit the code so your new UserControl's name appears in this line:

```
Controls.Add("Products.ctlNewName", "MyUserControl")
```

You can't use the VBControlExtender object to dynamically add *intrinsic controls* (those controls that are always on the Toolbox). If you want to add an intrinsic control dynamically during runtime, you can use a control array, or use code like this example, which adds a TextBox:

```
Private Sub Form_Load()
Form1.Controls.Add "VB.TextBox", "cmdObj1"

    With Form1!cmdObj1
        .Visible = True
        .Width = 3000
        .Text = "I popped into existence!"
    End With
End Sub
```

For an explanation of this code, see Step 5 in this section.

Part V
The Internet Connection

The 5th Wave — By Rich Tennant

LET'S JUST KEEP THE CURSOR ON THE COMPUTER SCREEN, YOUNG MAN, AND OFF YOUR BROTHERS FOREHEAD! NOW LOWER HIM GENTLY BACK INTO HIS CRIB.

In this part . . .

1f you're swept up in Internet Madness (and who isn't?), Part V is for you. You find out how to use the ActiveX Document Migration wizard to quickly port your classic Windows utilities and applications (you have written some great ones, haven't you?) into Web pages. You also see the ways to use databases with a Web site, including creating both Active Server Pages and IIS (Internet Information Server) applications.

Chapter 11

Translating Windows Applications to Web Pages: Using the ActiveX Document Migration Wizard

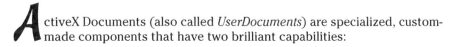

In This Chapter

- ▶ Creating a simple Windows utility
- ▶ Working with the ActiveX Document Migration wizard
- ▶ Testing a new ActiveX Document
- ▶ Building an ActiveX Document by hand
- ▶ Adding your ActiveX Documents to Web pages
- ▶ Blending menus
- ▶ Connecting a database to a UserDocument

A ctiveX Documents (also called *UserDocuments*) are specialized, custom-made components that have two brilliant capabilities:

✔ **You can dump them into Web pages without much fuss.** For example, assume you've written a Visual Basic utility that adds the correct sales tax for each state. You can put this utility right into a Web site without rewriting it in Jscript, VBScript, or other languages, and without adding special browser-compatible components. Automatically (for the most part, anyway), you can migrate an existing VB utility directly into an Internet or intranet Web page, where it can work right along comfortably within the HTML code that makes up the rest of the Web page.

✔ **They make distributing updates or bug fixes a snap.** ActiveX Documents offer an additional benefit if you must frequently upgrade your VB programs: painless bug fixing and version replacement. When providing solutions for a large number of people, consider the advantages of distributing the program from a single copy residing on a server. If you fix bugs or enhance functionality in an ActiveX Document program, you simply replace that single ActiveX Document on the server. Everyone on your intranet gets the upgrade with no further hassles, and without human intervention.

In addition to these benefits, you can easily attach ActiveX Documents to databases. Also, ActiveX Documents can display VB forms in a browser, and they can even add menus to Internet or intranet pages.

This chapter shows you the quickest way to move an existing Visual Basic application from its native Windows environment to an Internet Web page. This method works just fine for small sites or fast solutions to simple situations. However, if you're working with larger-scale, security-sensitive, or complex Web-database applications, you want to go beyond the solutions I present in this chapter. (See Chapters 12 and 13 for more heavy-duty Web database examples.) Nonetheless, this chapter gets you up and running very, very fast. If you're creating a small, local intranet (or a personal Web site), using the ActiveX Document Migration wizard might be just what you're looking for.

You can easily port features and existing code into Internet pages using ActiveX Documents, which makes them useful for working on Internet database jobs. Considering their easy maintenance (you only change the single server instance of the Document), and because they migrate so easily from the traditional Windows operating system to browsers, you'll want to know how to solve programming problems using ActiveX Documents.

Some programmers might argue that many of the capabilities of an ActiveX Document are also features of other kinds of ActiveX UserControls. True. After all, they are all part of the ActiveX component family, and thus naturally share many qualities. However, Microsoft provides a Migration wizard only for the ActiveX Document, intending that you use this style component to port your existing VB applications and utilities into Web pages.

Nevertheless, many experts suggest that for large-scale Web sites, or where database security is an issue, you avoid creating a database connection from a client (user's) machine to your server. Building an ActiveX object that links to a database goes against the WinDNA architecture model and the three-tier philosophy that Microsoft supports. Database connections should usually go from the server-side to the database, not from the client. If you want data-binding on the Web, or in three-tier applications, either use RDS in ADO or create disconnected ADO recordsets on the server-side, send them to the client, and then bind them to controls. This way, you get the advantages of data-binding without forcing a connection from the client-side.

How easy is it to move a traditional Windows-based utility to a browser? Very.

An ActiveX Document is easy to upgrade because, even though it's downloaded to each user's local hard drive, it's only downloaded once. Thereafter, each time any page containing that Document is downloaded to the user's browser, that browser checks the version on the user's hard drive against the version number of the Document residing on the server. Only if the server's

Document is a newer version is it downloaded to the user's hard drive, replacing the older version.

Creating a Simple Windows Utility

Before you can try the ActiveX Document Migration wizard, or otherwise experiment with UserDocuments, you must have some utility that you want to transport from Windows to a browser. In this section, you build a simple Windows program that adds 7 percent tax to whatever the user has typed in as the total order cost. After you finish this project, you can migrate it to a Web page. (I show you how in the section "Working with the ActiveX Document Migration Wizard," a bit later in this chapter.)

To build a Windows utility that you can use for experimenting with the ActiveX Document Migration wizard, follow these steps:

1. **Start a new Visual Basic project by choosing File➪New Project.**

   The New Project dialog box opens.

2. **Double-click the Standard EXE icon in the dialog box.**

   The dialog box closes, and you see the familiar Windows-style programming template, with a blank Form1 ready for you to design.

3. **Put a TextBox and a CommandButton on Form1.**

4. **In the Properties window, change the button's Caption property to** Calculate Tax.

5. **Double-click the CommandButton.**

   You see the code window.

6. **Type this code into Command1's Click event:**

   ```
   Private Sub Command1_Click()
       Text1 = Text1 * 1.07
   End Sub
   ```

7. **In the code window, type this code into the Form_Load event:**

   ```
   Private Sub Form_Load()
       Command1.Left = Text1.Left
   End Sub
   ```

   In a VB project, this Form_Load code aligns the components vertically. However, an ActiveX Document can't have code in a Load or Unload event, because the document will reside in a browser as part of a Web page, and the browser itself is supposed to be the one to deal with creating, or destroying, a page. In the next section of this chapter, I show you how the ActiveX Document Migration wizard handles any code that it finds in a Form_Load or Form_Unload event.

8. Press F5.

The program runs. The CommandButton is lined up vertically with the TextBox.

9. Type 10 **into the TextBox and then click the CommandButton.**

The correct result, 10.7, appears in the TextBox.

Working with the ActiveX Document Migration Wizard

The ActiveX Document Migration wizard can quickly translate your Windows-style VB project into a component that you can drop into a Web page. To see how this translation works, follow these steps:

1. Create a standard VB project and make sure you have that project loaded in VB.

In the preceding section, I show you how to create a little, traditional Windows utility that calculates sales tax. If you want to follow along with the steps I describe in this section, you can use that utility to experiment with the ActiveX Document Migration wizard.

2. Choose Add-Ins⇨Add-In Manager.

The Add-In Manager dialog box opens.

3. In the listbox that's displayed in the Add-In Manager dialog box, double-click VB 6 ActiveX Doc Migration Wizard.

The wizard is loaded into your project.

4. Click OK.

The dialog box closes.

5. Choose Add-Ins⇨ActiveX Document Migration Wizard.

The ActiveX Document Migration Wizard dialog box opens.

6. Click Next.

You see the wizard's Form Selection page, as shown in Figure 11-1.

7. Click Form1.

Form1 is selected, as shown in Figure 11-1.

8. Click Next.

You see the wizard's Options page, as shown in Figure 11-2.

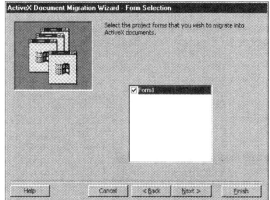

Figure 11-1:
Select the forms in your project that you want to migrate to Web pages.

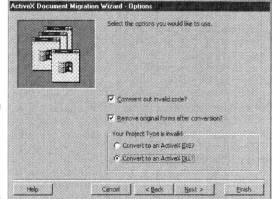

Figure 11-2:
Customize how the wizard behaves.

9. **Click the Comment Out Invalid Code check box.**

By making this selection, you tell the wizard to put a comment symbol (') at the beginning of any line of illegal programming (code that a browser can't execute). These comment lines appear in green (the default color for comments in code). After the wizard finishes its work, you can review the source code and decide what to do with code the wizard has removed from your project. You may need to revise it. Code that a browser won't execute includes End and Form1.Show.

10. **Click the Remove Original Forms After Conversion check box.**

This option specifies that you don't need the forms after the wizard transforms your project into a browser-compatible ActiveX Document. (You can use the forms later if you want; they won't be erased from your hard drive.)

11. Click the Convert To An ActiveX DLL option button.

I compare the two Document flavors — DLL or EXE — and describe their tradeoffs in Chapter 10. See the Technical Stuff icon near the beginning of that chapter.

12. Click Next.

You're in the home stretch now. You see the final page of the wizard, as shown in Figure 11-3.

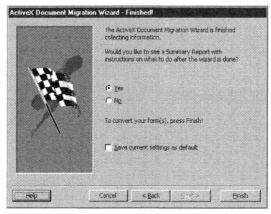

13. Leave the Summary Report option selected.

Many wizards now include the Save Current Settings As Default option. This feature is helpful if you use a wizard over and over. It saves all the choices you made (DLL, remove original forms, and so on) while running the wizard. Then, when you next run the wizard, all your choices are the defaults, and you can keep clicking the Next button to finish the wizard's work more quickly.

14. Click Finish.

You're prompted to save Form1 in case you want to use it later.

15. Go ahead and save Form1.

The File Save dialog box closes, and a message box tells you that your ActiveX Document has, in fact, been created.

16. Click OK.

The message box closes, and the wizard's summary report appears.

17. Look at the report if you want.

It's not specific to your project; it merely describes how to test your new ActiveX Document, and where to find additional information in Help on these components.

18. Click Close.

The Report dialog box closes.

Testing a New Document

You can easily test a new ActiveX Document in your browser. To see how, follow these steps:

1. Load your ActiveX Document in VB.

For all the details on creating a new ActiveX Document, see the preceding section in this chapter.

2. Press F5.

A Properties dialog box appears, as shown in Figure 11-4.

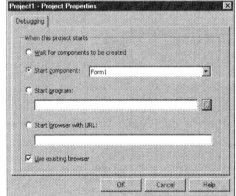

Figure 11-4: Leave the default option selected: *Use existing browser.*

The Properties/Debugging dialog box shown in Figure 11-4 simplifies the process of testing ActiveX components like Documents. Such components run in a host container — for example, Internet Explorer — instead of running as standard, stand-alone Windows applications. The option you select in this step specifies that you want to load the ActiveX Document into Internet Explorer.

3. Click OK.

The Properties dialog box closes, and the File Download dialog box appears, as shown in Figure 11-5.

4. Click the Open This File From Its Current Location option button, as shown in Figure 11-5.

Figure 11-5:
Whether or not you see this warning dialog box depends on your browser's security settings.

5. **Click OK.**

   The File Download security dialog box closes, and your ActiveX Document is displayed, running and ready, in Internet Explorer, as shown in Figure 11-6.

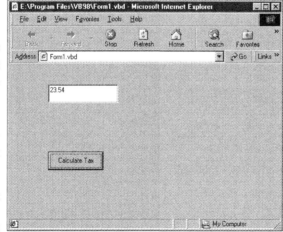

Figure 11-6:
A successful migration: You see your Document loaded and running in Internet Explorer.

Depending on how old your version of Internet Explorer is, and on the version of Windows you're using, you may have difficulty loading an ActiveX Document into Internet Explorer. If you do have problems getting a Document to run in Internet Explorer (IE) when you press F5 to test it (Step 2 in the preceding list), try shutting down Internet Explorer. Then, press F5 to see if VB can start IE. If that doesn't work, try running IE, pressing F5, and then switching to the running IE. Choose File➪Open from IE's menus and browse your hard drive to locate the Document file (its filename extension is .VBD). Click OK to load it into IE.

Quick document debugging

You run a Document in Internet Explorer while simultaneously running VB so you can debug your Document. For example, get this chapter's sample ActiveX Document running in Internet Explorer. Then, type in the word **North** in the TextBox and click the CommandButton captioned Calculate Tax. You see the error message displayed in Figure 11-7.

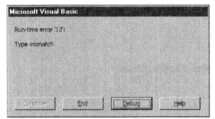

When you see the error message shown in Figure 11-7, click the Debug button, and you return to the VB editor, which highlights the line in your code where the error occurred, as shown in Figure 11-8.

Notice in Figure 11-8 that you can use some of VB's debugging tools. In this example, the Immediate Window is used to query the contents of the TextBox. The Immediate Window reveals that the TextBox contains the word *North* rather than a number, and you shrewdly conclude that there's no way 7 percent can be added to North. You're on your way to fixing the problem.

The mystery of the aligned controls

The name of this section sounds like the title of a Hardy Boys book, right? If you're following along with the example I describe in the previous sections of this chapter, you may wonder how the browser executes the code that aligns the CommandButton with the TextBox. An ActiveX Document doesn't have a Form_Load event, but Form_Load is where you put the code that forces the alignment. What gives?

Take a look at the code window in VB to see what the wizard did to your source code in the process of migrating your Windows application to an ActiveX Document that can work within a browser.

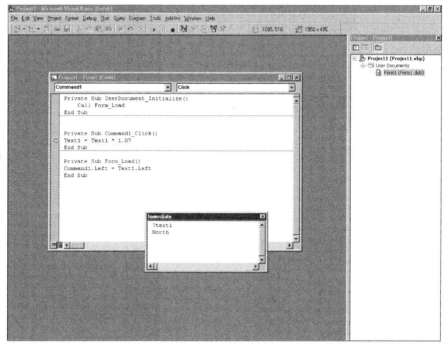

Figure 11-8:
The error
in the
Document's
code is
displayed,
in the
traditional
VB
debugging
window.

The ActiveX Document Migration wizard took it upon itself to leave your Form_Load code alone, but the wizard is smart enough to know that the browser (Internet Explorer) will not execute a Load event. In an ActiveX Document, a subroutine named Form_Load has no special meaning. It's just another subroutine, to the browser. It could just as easily be named Sub Frank or Sub Frank_Ranthid.

To cause this code to execute before Internet Explorer displays the Document, the wizard triggers (calls) Sub Form_Load in the Initialize event of the UserDocument. Here's the revision the wizard made to your original code:

```
Private Sub UserDocument_Initialize()
    Call Form_Load
End Sub
```

The effect is the same: The CommandButton lines up with the TextBox. Only the name of the event has been changed.

Building an ActiveX Document by Hand

In previous sections of this chapter, I show you how the ActiveX Document Migration wizard can simplify your work. Wizards are great, and you should make use of them whenever possible. But what if you want to add a utility to a Web page, and you don't have that utility already built in the form of an existing Windows-style application? In such cases, you can employ the ActiveX Document template and design a new UserDocument from scratch.

To create a new UserDocument, follow these steps:

1. **Start a new VB project by choosing File⇨New Project.**

   The New Project dialog box appears.

2. **Double-click the ActiveX Document DLL icon in the dialog box.**

   The dialog box closes, and you see UserDocument1 listed in the Project Explorer, in a folder named User Documents.

3. **Double-click UserDocument1 in the Project Explorer.**

   An empty UserDocument form appears.

4. **Add any controls that you want to include on the UserDocument.**

   If you want to recreate the example UserDocument that I describe in previous sections of this chapter, put a TextBox and a CommandButton on the UserDocument.

   Remember, you're building a custom control, so it's your choice what you include, and how you design it.

5. **In the Properties window, set the properties you need for the various controls on your UserDocument.**

   For the example UserDocument, change the CommandButton's caption property to **Calculate Tax**.

6. **To open the code window so you can enter programming for a control on your UserDocument, double-click that control.**

   To continue with the example, double-click the CommandButton so you can enter code for that control's Click event.

   You see the code window.

7. **Type in the programming for the selected control.**

   For example, type this code into Command1's Click event:

   ```
   Private Sub Command1_Click()
       Text1 = Text1 * 1.07
   End Sub
   ```

   Of course, to provide features for your own custom control, you write programming under the various components just as you would if you were creating a typical, traditional Windows program.

8. **In the code window, type in any code for the UserDocument's Initialize event.**

For the example ActiveX Document, type this code into your UserDocument's Initialize event:

```
Private Sub UserDocument_Initialize()
    Command1.Left = Text1.Left
End Sub
```

You can use any kind of formatting you want for your project. Note that you need not format programmatically — you can just drag components around to position and size them.

9. **To test this UserDocument, press F5.**

   A Properties dialog box appears (refer to Figure 11-4, earlier in this chapter).

10. **Click OK.**

    The Properties dialog box closes, and the File Download dialog box appears (refer to Figure 11-5).

11. **Click the Open This File From Its Current Location option button.**

12. **Click OK.**

    The File Download security dialog box closes, and your ActiveX Document is displayed, running and ready, in Internet Explorer (refer to Figure 11-6, earlier in this chapter).

Depending on how old your version of Internet Explorer is, and on the version of Windows you're using, you may have difficulty loading an ActiveX Document into Internet Explorer. If you do have problems getting a Document to run in Internet Explorer (IE) when you press F5 to test it, see the warning near the end of the section "Testing a New Document," earlier in this chapter.

Adding Your Documents to Web Pages

After you build ActiveX Documents, you naturally want to know how you can add them to Web pages. You simply compile the UserDocument into a .DLL file.

It's quite easy. Follow these steps:

1. **Create your UserDocument, and make sure you have it loaded in VB.**

   If you're following along with the examples I describe in previous sections of this chapter, you have a little Tax Calculator UserDocument loaded in VB.

2. **Choose Add-Ins⇨Add-In Manager.**

   The Add-In Manager dialog box appears.

3. **Double-click Package and Deployment Wizard.**

   VB loads the Package and Deployment wizard into your project.

4. **Click OK.**

   The Add-In Manager dialog box closes.

5. **Choose Add-Ins⇨Package and Deployment Wizard.**

   The Package and Deployment Wizard dialog box opens.

   You may see a message informing you that you must first save your current project before you can use the wizard. If so, choose File⇨Save Project and save your UserDocument and Project as instructed.

6. **Click the Package button on the first page of the Package and Deployment Wizard dialog box.**

   The wizard does some of its work. If it asks whether you want to recompile, click Yes.

   You see the wizard's Package Type page, as shown in Figure 11-9. The Standard Setup Package option is for traditional Windows applications that you might, for example, package and give to someone else on a diskette. The Internet Package option is the one you use in this section; it creates a .CAB-based package that is downloadable over the Internet. The final option, Dependency File, merely builds a list of the libraries and other runtime components that your application needs in order to work.

   A .CAB file (stands for *cabinet*) is a specialized kind of file that encloses the files necessary to download your component over the Internet. When downloaded, the user's browser is able to extract your component from the .CAB file, expand the component, and insert it into a Web page.

7. **Select Internet Package and then click <u>N</u>ext.**

   You're asked to select the folder where you want to save the package.

8. **Decide where to save the package and click <u>N</u>ext.**

   You see a list of the files that the wizard intends to include in this package. When sending a component over the Internet, you can't assume that people using your component will already have all the dependency files installed. They might need the files. Best to leave this list alone.

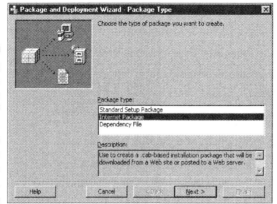

Figure 11-9:
The wizard
offers you
the option of
creating a
.CAB file
that you can
use in Web
pages.

9. **Click Next, accepting the wizard's wise choice of files.**

   You're shown where, on the whole World Wide Web, the included files can be downloaded from.

   If you prefer, you can instruct that some of the files needed by your component *not* be included in the .CAB file that's being built here. Instead, you can specify an alternative Web site — or even the Microsoft site. Components like msvbvm60.dll and many others are in .CAB files digitally signed by Microsoft, and made available on the Microsoft Web site. If you want to reduce the size of your .CAB file, and reduce traffic to your server, tell the wizard that you want some of these files downloaded from Microsoft's site. This also enables you to calm people who feel that digitally signed components are safe (guaranteed virus free).

10. **Again, accept the wizard's choices of file locations and click Next.**

    You see the Safety Settings page, informing you that you haven't authenticated this UserDocument. In my view, this kind of authentication isn't widely used because it can be easily circumvented by people bent on causing trouble. In any case, you can ignore this page.

11. **Click Next.**

    You're shown the final page in the wizard, which suggests the name Internet Package 1 for your .CAB file.

12. **Agree with this name by clicking Finish.**

    The wizard saves your .CAB file to the hard drive and shows you a report, telling you the location of the .CAB file and also a batch file that can rebuild the .CAB file, in case you make some changes to this package.

13. **Open Windows Explorer and locate the folder named Package.**

    The wizard created this folder, which contains your .CAB file, the UserDocument, and associated files.

You see an .HTM file — a file that browsers can display — named Project1.HTM. This file contains a slew of comment HTML code for the benefit of Internet Explorer, but the real meat of the code appears in the following lines:

```
<HTML>
<HEAD>
<TITLE>Project1.CAB</TITLE>
</HEAD>
<BODY>
<a href=UserDocument1.VBD>UserDocument1.VBD</a>

</BODY>
</HTML>
```

This `<a href>` code displays a hyperlink in the browser page. If the user clicks it, your UserDocument is loaded into the browser. (You must keep the UserDocument file in the same folder as this .HTM file.)

By double-clicking Project1.HTM in Windows Explorer, you can load this Web page into Internet Explorer. Then, click the hyperlink in the browser: `UserDocument1.VBD`. Your Interest Calculator utility loads into the browser. You can, of course, put any other content you want into this HTML page.

Your .CAB file should contain all the files and dependencies required by your application. This way, even if it doesn't need to download all of them (because some are already installed on the browser's machine), the browser will know what is needed for your application to run. When you deploy an ActiveX Document or ActiveX Control, the .CAB file needs the .OCX file (the ActiveX Document or Control), the dependency .DLLs, the VB runtime engine, and other dependencies you might need. The user's browser checks its local system and makes sure that all the components required are installed and that the local version is at least equal to, or more recent than, the .CAB versions. If a version is too old locally, or simply missing, the browser downloads the file from the .CAB and installs it. Stated simply: The browser will check, and the runtime will download, any files you include in the .CAB. Lucky for you, the VB Package and Deployment wizard usually handles all of this, so you need not worry about it.

Blending Menus

Here's a neat trick you can try with UserDocuments: You can create menus that will appear in a user's browser — blended in right there on the menu bar with the normal Internet Explorer menus.

To create dynamic menus, follow these steps:

1. **Follow Steps 1 through 7 in the section titled "Building an ActiveX Document by Hand," earlier in this chapter.**

   You have the Tax Calculator utility UserDocument loaded in VB.

2. **Double-click UserDocument1 in the Project Explorer window.**

   UserDocument1 gets the focus.

3. **Press Ctrl+E.**

   The VB Menu Editor opens.

4. **In Menu Editor's Caption field, type** ThisIsNew.

5. **Type** mnuNew **in the Name field.**

6. **Select Right in the NegotiatePosition drop-down list.**

   This choice tells the browser to merge the new menu into the right side, where practical, of the browser's menu bar.

7. **Add a second-level menu.**

   To add a second-level menu in the Menu Editor, click <u>N</u>ext, click the down-arrow button, and then click the right-arrow button.

8. **Type** Microsoft **in the Caption field and** mnuMicrosoft **in the Name field, as shown in Figure 11-10.**

Figure 11-10:
VB's Menu Editor makes short work of designing menus.

9. **Click OK.**

   The Menu Editor dialog box closes.

10. **Double-click the UserDocument1 form.**

    The code window opens.

11. **Use the left drop-down menu in the code window to locate the mnuMicrosoft procedure.**

12. **Type this code into the mnuMicrosoft_Click procedure:**

```
Private Sub mnuMicrosoft_Click()
Hyperlink.NavigateTo "http://www.microsoft.com"
End Sub
```

This code opens the Microsoft Web site if the user clicks the Microsoft submenu you created.

13. **Press F5.**

Your UserDocument is loaded into Internet Explorer with a new menu up on top, as shown in Figure 11-11.

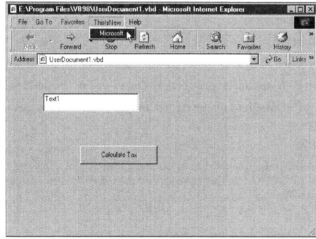

Figure 11-11:
Your new menu item and sub-menu appear on the Internet Explorer menu bar.

If your Internet Explorer browser fails to load the UserDocument, try pressing the browser's Back and Forward keys. If that fails, try restarting Windows and then recreating the UserDocument and menus. Then, press F5, and things should work as expected.

Connecting a Database to a UserDocument

As with other kinds of custom ActiveX components, you can easily attach a database to a UserDocument. Follow these steps:

1. **Complete Steps 1 through 7 in the section "Building an ActiveX Document by Hand," earlier in this chapter.**

   You have the Tax Calculator utility UserDocument loaded in VB.

2. **Click the UserDocument to give it the focus.**

3. **Double-click the Data Control in the Toolbox.**

   A Data Control is added to the UserDocument.

4. **In the Properties window, click the button with the three dots (...) in the Data Control's DatabaseName property.**

   A DatabaseName file-browser dialog box appears.

5. **Locate and then double-click BIBLIO.MDB.**

   This sample database is located in your VB98 folder.

6. **In the Properties window, set the Data Control's RecordSource property to Categories.**

7. **Click Text1.**

   Its properties appear in the Properties window.

8. **Set Text1's DataSource property to Data1 in the Properties window.**

9. **Set Text1's DataField property to CategoryName in the Properties window.**

10. **Press F5.**

    You see the database field in action in the browser. Click the Data Control to see the various category names in Text1, as shown in Figure 11-12.

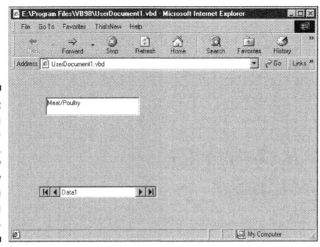

Figure 11-12:
With a User-Document, you easily can display database records in a browser.

Chapter 12

Mixing HTML and VB: Active Server Pages

*Y*ou can use Active Server Pages (ASP) to display data in a Web page. With the ASP technology, you basically blend VBScript with HTML, creating a Web page that runs partly in the user's browser and partly on your server.

In other words, when a Web page is loaded into a browser, the browser handles the typical HTML codes — for example, $<H1>$, which causes the browser to display text as a large headline ($<H1>$ means Heading #1). However, if a Web page contains ASP programming (any code between the special percent symbol codes $<%$ and $%>$), a VBScript engine on the server (where the Web page originated) interprets that programming before the Web page is sent to the user's browser.

The server runs the VBScript code and then sends the result to the user's browser. (You can also use Jscript, which derives from the Java language, but in this book, VBScript is, obviously, the preferred language.)

What use is ASP in a real-world situation? Without ASP, Web pages can be mere exercises in publishing — not all that much more useful or advanced than the traditional advertisement. If you own a bookstore, you can print a flyer or take out an ad in a paper. You can do the same kind of thing with your Web site: List titles and display covers. But adding ASP to your Web pages enables you to let users tap into your databases directly (read-only, of course, unless you specify otherwise). With ASP, you could let a visitor to your bookstore's site see the latest discounts, see *all* the books you offer, compare prices interactively, and even place orders. Users can do things that used to require a phone call to your office, and a person in your office providing assistance. Think of it this way: The ASP technology — to a great extent — lets users be their own customer service department.

If you know VB, you know virtually everything about VBScript, but if you're interested in learning more about HTML or ASP, you may want to take a look at *HTML 4 For Dummies,* by Ed Tittel and Natanya Pitts, or *ASP: The Power Guide to Developing Server-Based Web Applications,* by Andrew M. Fedorchek and David K. Pensin (both books published by IDG Books Worldwide, Inc.).

VBScript is similar to VB, but it's designed to run in browsers so it's missing some commands — notably, commands that may endanger a user's local computer. In other words, VBScript is stripped-down VB. It doesn't have file-renaming, file-deleting, disk-formatting, or similar commands because VBScript can run immediately when a Web page is loaded into a browser. You wouldn't want mindless, nasty people putting the following code in a Web page that you innocently load into your browser while surfing the Web:

```
function BlastIt()
    Format C:\
end function

<body onload="BlastIt()">
```

If VBScript included file-formatting commands, that code would fry your C: drive. Fortunately, VBScript does not include the Format command in its vocabulary, along with other commands that could be dangerous in the wrong hands.

This chapter shows you how to work with ASP — how to connect a user's browser to a database on your server. Of course, many people want to experiment with Internet and client/server technologies, but they want to use their standalone machine at home, or do the testing on their workstation. Do you have to test ASP using two machines — the client machine (the user) that contacts the server (where the database resides that's being exposed to the user with ASP)? Luckily, Microsoft understands that you may need to create a virtual client/server on a standalone machine. Microsoft calls the solution to this need *PWS,* or *Personal Web Server.* With PWS, you can have your computer interact with a "server" that's actually in your desktop computer.

Getting PWS up and running has proven tricky for many people. If you haven't been able to get PWS to work for you, take a look at the sidebar, "Getting your hands on the Personal Web Server."

Getting your hands on the Personal Web Server

ASP can't run without a Microsoft Web server as its host. Even to test ASP pages, you have to install Microsoft Internet Information Server (IIS) or a component of IIS called Personal Web Server (PWS). Windows NT 4 included PWS Version 2, but you want the latest version (Version 4 at the time of this writing).

You have the following options for getting Version 4:

✔ Install it from Visual Basic 6 Enterprise Edition

✔ Download the Windows NT 4 Option Pack

Even if you're using Windows 95 or Windows 98, this Option Pack provides you with what you need: Personal Web Server running on your machine (or full IIS on an NT machine), so you can test ASP pages that you write.

You can download the Option Pack, or parts of it, from the following site:

```
www.microsoft.com/NTServer/nts/
     downloads/recommended/
     NT4OptPk/default.asp
```

When asked which components of the Option Pack you want, specify that you want to download Personal Web Server for Windows or NT 4. If you see a message informing you that PWS requires NT Service Pack, don't be confused. The PWS runs on Windows 95 or 98.

You must use Microsoft Internet Explorer 4.0 or later to run the Personal Web Server.

Setting Up an ASP Test Directory

ASP provides a way for a client browser (located somewhere on the Internet) to ask for information from your database located on your server. Here's the scenario: Someone (anywhere) loads your Web page. That person's browser interprets the page's HTML code and displays the page. Your computer (the server) interprets the page's ASP code, runs it to achieve some result, and then sends the results to the user's browser *as standard HTML*. In other words, the user can employ any browser, even Netscape's Navigator, because the client side of this operation doesn't need any special Microsoft components. All the user's browser sees is ordinary HTML.

How can you test ASP code? Do you have to set up your computer as an NT Server Web site host? Then, do you have to go over to a friend's house and use that person's browser to load your Web page and try to get some data from the server's database? Fortunately, the answer is no. You can use the browser on your computer as the client and, thanks to Personal Web Server, as the server, too.

Some directories on a Web server can be marked executable, but others are not (they do not permit execution of the scripts they contain). In this section, I show you how to create a location on your hard drive where you can save .ASP files and test them.

To set up an alias (a shorthand that represents a path on your hard drive) and create a directory where your .ASP scripts can execute, follow these steps:

1. **Download and install IIS, or at least the PWS component of IIS.**

   If you need help locating PWS, see the sidebar "Getting your hands on the Personal Web Server," in this chapter.

2. **Click the IIS or PWS icon in your system tray (next to the time).**

   If you don't see it in the system tray, click Start➪Programs and then locate and choose Windows NT 4.0 Option Pack➪ Microsoft Personal Web Server.

   The Personal Web Manager appears, as shown in Figure 12-1.

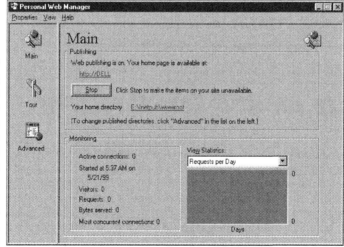

Figure 12-1:
This accessory enables you to create virtual directories and otherwise manage PWS.

3. **Note the name of your computer (displayed in blue).**

   Figure 12-1 shows a computer named `http://DELL`. Of course, you see a different name on your computer. This name is an important part of the URL that you need to type into your browser to test ASP pages.

4. **Click the Advanced icon in the left pane (or choose <u>V</u>iew➪Advanced).**

   You see the Advanced Options page, as shown in Figure 12-2.

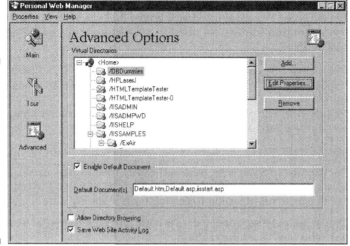

Figure 12-2:
The advanced options include editing existing virtual directories or adding new ones.

5. Click Add.

You see the Edit Directory dialog box shown in Figure 12-3.

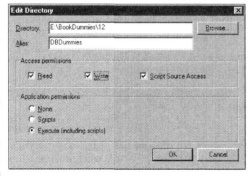

Figure 12-3:
Create a new directory in this dialog box and specify that scripts can be executed within this directory.

Notice that the dialog box shown in Figure 12-3 includes three check boxes and three option buttons. These boxes and buttons enable you to specify the level of access that visitors are permitted when they get to this directory. For example, Read permission allows an .HTM page to be sent to the visitor's browser. However, you would not select Read permission for directories containing applications that visitors shouldn't be able to access directly. The Write option permits visitors to save files into this directory. The Script option permits .ASP scripts to be executed. The Application Permissions section of the dialog box permits you to specify that scripts, but not other applications (or both) can be executed in this directory.

6. **Only you will be using this directory, so go hog-wild and click all three Access Permissions check boxes and the Execute (Including Scripts) option button. No need to protect your computer against your own self!**

If you intend to give other users access to this directory, you should avoid giving both Execute and Write permissions (someone could upload and then run a nasty virus). Also, if you don't want outsiders reading your scripts or peeking at your programs, don't simultaneously permit the Read and Execute options.

7. **Give this directory an alias — for example,** DBDummies.

You use this nickname as part of the URL that you type into your browser to load a page with ASP scripts that you want to test. You use the alias instead of typing in the full path to an .ASP file.

8. **Choose an existing directory on your hard drive where you want to store the .ASP files for testing.**

You can click the Browse button to locate that directory. Remember the name of the directory so you can store your test .ASP files there for the examples later in this chapter.

9. **Click OK.**

A warning message tells you that you're playing with fire by permitting both the Write and Execute options.

10. **Click Yes, admitting that you're a wild one and are willing to take this risk.**

The message and dialog boxes close. Your new virtual directory appears in the list on the Advanced Options page.

11. **Click the Minimize button in the top-right corner of the Personal Web Manager to minimize it.**

The Web Manager appears on the taskbar, but is no longer visible. You need not have this Manager running to use the Personal Web Services. The PWS (or on NT the big brother, IIS) runs automatically.

Writing Your First ASP Script

Now for some fun! In this section, I show you how to write a simple ASP script.

You can do most things in an ASP script that you can do in a traditional VB application, with a few peripheral exceptions. VBScript — the language you use to write these scripts — is a subset of VB. The main things missing involve contacting peripherals, like the printer.

With VBScript, however, you can make calculations, something HTML cannot do. HTML is basically a mindless language; it can't even add 2 + 2. HTML is a page description language that tells the browser how large to make text, what color to display it in, whether it's italic, and so on.

So, when you write ASP, you're able to calculate — add sales tax, check data entry, and so on. Wait a minute. Can't you just insert some VBScript right into HTML and have it execute client-side, in the visitor's browser, without going to the trouble of executing it on the server-side? Yes, but I can think of at least two big reasons why a client-side scripting solution is less than ideal:

✔ Not all browsers (translation: Netscape Navigator) can execute VBScript.

✔ Executing a script on the server enables you to access a database on the server.

Writing a standard (not ASP) script

In this example, you use VBScript, but the script you write isn't an ASP script. Instead, it runs in the client's browser. This example sets the stage for understanding the differences between standard scripting and ASP scripting. To see how to run a standard script, follow these steps:

1. **Choose Start➪Programs➪Accessories➪Notepad.**

   Notepad runs.

2. **Type this HTML page into Notepad:**

   ```
   <HTML>
   <HEAD>

   <SCRIPT LANGUAGE=vbscript>
   a = 2 + 2
   msgbox a
   </SCRIPT>

   </HEAD>

   <BODY>
   The result of 2 + 2.

   </BODY>
   </HTML>
   ```

   When you include a `<SCRIPT>` section in your HTML page like this, it executes as soon as the page is loaded into Internet Explorer (in Navigator, you see the script code instead).

3. **Choose File➪Save As.**

   The Save As dialog box appears.

4. **Browse your hard drive until you locate the special directory that you created in the section "Setting Up an ASP Test Directory," earlier in this chapter.**

5. **In the File Name field in the dialog box, type** SCRIPT.HTM.

6. **Click the Save button.**

   Your file, SCRIPT.HTM, is saved to your special test directory.

7. **Run Windows Explorer. (Choose Start⇨Programs ⇨Windows Explorer.)**

8. **Browse with Explorer until you locate the directory where you stored SCRIPT.HTM.**

9. **Double-click SCRIPT.HTM.**

   Assuming that you have Internet Explorer as your default browser, IE runs and it loads SCRIPT.HTM. As soon as your script is loaded into Internet Explorer, you see the message box shown in Figure 12-4.

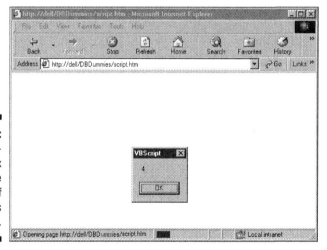

Figure 12-4:
The message box displays the results of the script's calculations.

Writing the same script in ASP

The process of translating the VBScript from the previous example into an ASP page is relatively straightforward. Just remember these points:

- ✔ If you're writing HTML, you use the ordinary HTML tags, such as `<BODY>` or `<H1>`.

- ✔ When you want to signal to the server that some code needs to run on the server (the active server!), you use the percent (%) symbol.

To see how to write an ASP page, follow these steps:

1. **Choose Start⇨Programs⇨Accessories⇨Notepad.**

   Notepad runs.

2. **Type this ASP code into a blank page in Notepad:**

   ```
   <HTML>
   <HEAD>
   </HEAD>

   <BODY>

   AN ASP EXAMPLE
   <BR>

   <%
   a = 2+2
   response.write " The result of 2 + 2: "
   response.write(a) %>

   </BODY>
   </HTML>
   ```

   Notice that the VBScript code is located between the `<%` and `%>` symbols. Everything outside those symbols is HTML code.

3. **Choose File⇨Save As.**

   The Save As dialog box opens.

4. **Browse your hard drive until you locate the special test directory that you created in the section "Setting Up an ASP Test Directory," earlier in this chapter.**

5. **In the File Name field in the dialog box, type TEST1.ASP.**

6. **Click the Save button.**

   Your file, TEST1.ASP, is saved to the test directory.

7. **Run Internet Explorer.**

8. **In the Address field, type the URL for this .ASP file.**

   Remember that this URL points to the location of TEST1.ASP on your hard drive, but it isn't a traditional file path. Instead of including the drive and directory, you substitute the alias that you gave this hard drive location in the section "Setting Up an ASP Test Directory," earlier in this chapter. The alias you used is DBDummies.

   Therefore, the URL you type into Internet Explorer typically looks like this example:

   ```
   http://dell/DBDummies/test1.asp
   ```

However, instead of *dell*, you use the name of your computer. If you don't know the name, follow the instructions in the section "Finding your computer's name," later in this chapter.

When testing .ASP files, you must remember two things:

- **Save the file with an .ASP, *not* .HTM, extension.** Without the .ASP, the browser will not execute any ASP code in the page.

- **You must type the URL into Internet Explorer's Address field.** This URL is the location of the .ASP file on your hard drive, but instead of using the full path, you must use the alias you defined for this drive and directory. In other words, you can't autoload an .ASP file into Internet Explorer by double-clicking its filename within Windows Explorer.

9. **Press F5 while in Internet Explorer.**

Your TEST1.ASP page is loaded, and the ASP code is executed, as shown in Figure 12-5.

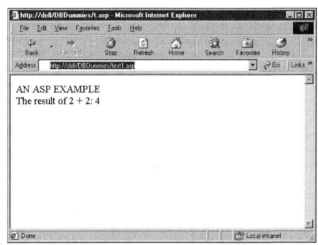

Figure 12-5:
Your first ASP script executes perfectly, displaying the result of a server-side computation

Finding your computer's name

If you don't know what to use for your computer's name in the URL you must type into Internet Express's Address field to test an .ASP Web page, follow these steps:

1. **Right-click the My Computer icon on your desktop.**

A context menu pops out.

2. **Choose Properties from the context menu.**

   The Properties dialog box opens.

3. **Click the Network Identification tab.**

4. **Look at the *Full Computer Name* on the Network Identification page. That's your computer's name. Whatever it is, you should replace *your_computers_name* in the HTTP URL with that name. (The computer name is used as the "server name" by the PWS.)**

   Replace *your_computers_name* in this URL:

   ```
   http://your_computers_name/DBDummies/t.asp
   ```

Client/Server Connecting to a Database

Now for the real meat — the real usefulness of the ASP technology: Accessing a database on the server side and providing controlled access to that database for a *client,* a visitor dialing in via the Internet. In the following example, you extract the 6,246 author names from the BIBLIO sample database located on the server and then "send" them to the user's browser and display them on a Web page.

If you have the proper setup to expose your computer to outside calls (so your computer acts as an Internet server), someone could call and load this page into their browser. That would be a real (versus virtual) client/server test. However, in this example, you use the Personal Web Server to simulate a server relationship with the client (Internet Explorer) also located on your system. It may seem a bit artificial, but it's actually the same process as getting a phone call from a browser in Zanzibar, and feeding the client those 6,246 author names from your database.

To see how to send data from a server and display it on a remote client's browser, follow these steps:

1. **Run Notepad.**

2. **Type this ASP code into a blank page in Notepad, but replace the boldface path with the path to BIBLIO.MDB on your hard drive:**

   ```
   <HTML>
   <HEAD>
   </HEAD>
   <BODY>

   <H2>Authors from the Biblio Database</H2>

   <%
   ```

(continued)

(continued)

```
dim dbconnection
dim rsAuthors

set dbconnection =
        Server.CreateObject("ADODB.Connection")

dbconnection.open "Provider=Microsoft.Jet.OLEDB.4.0;" _
                & "Data Source=C:\Program
        Files\VB98\biblio.mdb"

SQLQuery = "SELECT author FROM authors ORDER BY author"

set rsAuthors = dbconnection.Execute(SQLQuery)

do until rsAuthors.eof

n = n + 1
Response.Write n & ". "

Response.Write rsAuthors("Author")  %>

<BR>
<%
  rsAuthors.movenext
loop

rsAuthors.close
set rsAuthors = nothing
%>

</BODY>
</HTML>
```

When you type in this programming, make sure you replace the path in the following line:

```
"Data Source=C:\Program Files\VB98\biblio.mdb"
```

In place of `C:\Program Files\VB98\biblio.mdb`, that line should list whatever path on your hard drive leads to the BIBLIO.MDB sample database (usually, it's located in your VB98 directory). Also, remember that you should usually avoid using an absolute path like this — it's better to use relative paths whenever possible. But for the purposes of this example, you can go ahead and use a specific path to your .MDB file.

The commands such as CreateObject and MoveNext are ADO database programming. You can find out about ADO in Chapters 14–16. The database-related programming in this code is the same as you would write in an ordinary Windows VB application (with the exception of the Response.Write command).

Notice that this code goes in and out of script and HTML — for example:

```
Response.Write rsAuthors("Author")  %>
<BR>
<%
```

In your script, you want to move to the next line each time you print an author's name. That's the job of the HTML tag `<BR>`. So, you leave scripting for a moment with the `%>` tag, do the `<BR>` line break, and then start scripting again with the `<%` tag. As this example demonstrates, when doing page formatting, you must be in HTML. When doing the actual database access, or any computation, you write your script between the script tags: `<%` and `%>`.

Notice that the VBScript code is located between the `<%` and `%>` symbols. Everything outside those symbols is HTML code.

3. **Choose File⇨Save As.**

   The Save As dialog box appears.

4. **Browse your hard drive until you locate the special test directory that you created in the section "Setting Up an ASP Test Directory," earlier in this chapter.**

5. **In the File Name field in the dialog box, type DATATEST.ASP.**

6. **Click the Save button.**

   Your file, DATATEST.ASP, is saved to the directory.

7. **Run Internet Explorer.**

8. **In the Address field, type the URL for this .ASP file.**

   The URL you type into Internet Explorer looks something like this example, except you must replace *dell* with the name of your computer:

   ```
   http://dell/DBDummies/datatest.asp
   ```

   If you have problems, see Step 8 in the section "Writing the same script in ASP," earlier in this chapter.

9. **Press F5 while in Internet Explorer.**

   Your DATATEST.ASP page is loaded, and the ASP code is executed, as shown in Figure 12-6.

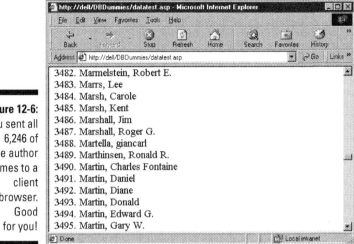

Figure 12-6:
You sent all
6,246 of
these author
names to a
client
browser.
Good
for you!

Chapter 13

IIS Applications: Moving Beyond ASP

*V*isual Basic 6 includes support for *IIS applications,* which execute programming server-side. (*IIS* stands for Internet Information Server.) These applications use a subset of VB. After processing an IIS application, the server sends the results, as HTML, to the user's browser. Because the server sends vanilla HTML across the Internet, any browser can accept and display the results.

But all this is true of ASP (Active Server Pages) as well, so why use IIS applications? (I examine ASP in Chapter 12.)

ASP and IIS applications have some differences, and Microsoft says that IIS applications are designed to enhance and complement ASP, not replace it. The following qualities make IIS applications useful for some Internet database jobs:

- ✔ You can use classes (which have several advantages, including easy reusability), compiled VB code, and ActiveX components. (Currently, drawbacks include restricted scalability and some extra overhead.)

- ✔ You can exploit the IIS object model, thereby gaining considerable control over the contents and behavior of Web pages you send to visitors.

- ✔ Your coding is not mixed right in with the HTML (as it is in scripting), so you can keep it from prying eyes. The code is further concealed because it is compiled and it never leaves your server anyway.

✔ IIS applications also employ the ASP object model, but VB automatically generates the necessary wrappers for you. A *wrapper* provides an interface between code it encloses and some outside caller.

The phrase *object model* means the collective objects (and their features) of a particular technology. Often displayed as a diagram, an object model identifies the hierarchical relationships between various objects (and collections of objects). Put another way, the object model describes dependent objects and where they fit into the overall hierarchy. A hen object, for example, includes a collection of egg objects. Each egg object includes a yolk object. A hen object model would show how some objects and collections are contained within other, higher objects.

To test IIS applications, you must be using Internet Explorer 4 or higher (preferably 5), as well as IIS for NT systems or Personal Web Server (PWS) for Windows 95/98. If you don't have the browser and the IIS or PWS utilities, download them for free from Microsoft's Web site at www.microsoft.com. (For additional information on using and installing IIS and PWS, see Chapter 12.)

Note: Although Visual Basic 6 offers another interesting technique called DHTML applications, I don't explore DHTML applications in this book. For one thing, DHTML only works client-side, so it doesn't offer much in the way of database connectivity. Also, you shouldn't use DHTML on the Internet, only on intranets, because it requires Internet Explorer, and the latest figures indicate that a bit less that 50 percent of browsers currently in use are not Internet Explorer.

Building Your First IIS Application

You can easily get an IIS application up and running because VB 6 provides a Designer for you. To build a simple IIS application, follow these steps:

1. **Choose File⇨New Project.**

   The New Project dialog box appears.

2. **Double-click the IIS Application icon in the New Project dialog box.**

   The dialog box closes, and VB displays the IIS Application template (essentially, a blank, empty VB editor).

3. **Click the small + symbol next to Designers in the Project Explorer.**

   You see WebClass1 in the Project Explorer.

4. **Double-click WebClass1.**

   The WebClass Designer appears, as shown in Figure 13-1.

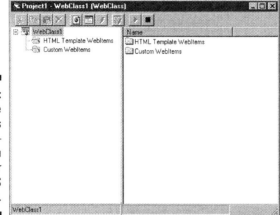

Figure 13-1:
The
WebClass
Designer —
the tool you
use for
creating IIS
application.

5. Double-click WebClass1 in the left pane of the WebClass Designer.

The code window appears, and you see that the Designer has added this code to your IIS application:

```
Option Explicit
Option Compare Text

Private Sub WebClass_Start()
    'Write a reply to the user
    With Response
        .Write "<html>"
        .Write "<body>"
        .Write "<h1><font face=""Arial"">WebClass1's
        Starting Page</font></h1>"
        .Write "<p>This response was created in the Start
        event of WebClass1.</p>"
        .Write "</body>"
        .Write "</html>"
    End With
End Sub
```

What's going on here? It appears that when this WebClass starts, it writes several lines of HTML code, that together make up a complete, if simple, Web page. You have a headline enclosed in the <H1> tags, and a body paragraph <P>.

This VB code *generates* the HTML code, which it sends to a browser by using the familiar With...End With structure and a Response.Write command.

You don't think this code creates a complete Web page? Try the next step.

6. **Press F5.**

   You see the Project Properties dialog box.

7. **Leave the defaults in this dialog box as-is: WebClass1 as the Start Component, and the Use Existing Browser option checked.**

8. **Click OK.**

   The dialog box closes, and Internet Explorer (IE) starts automatically with this page loaded, as you can see in Figure 13-2.

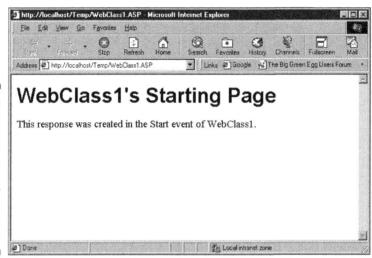

Figure 13-2: Here you see the default IIS template, created entirely by VB's WebClass Designer.

When you run an IIS application while working on it in VB, VB uses a temporary directory to store the necessary files for supporting your application. (See the Address field in Figure 13-2.) However, this temporary location is no longer necessary after you save your IIS application to disk. When you finish work and are ready to save your IIS application, create a separate directory to hold it. Put any future IIS applications in their own directories, so things don't get mixed up. Also notice in Figure 13-2 that an IIS application is defined within an .ASP file (VB automatically does this for you).

Modifying an IIS Application

In this section, I show you how to make a change to an IIS application in VB and then test it by running it in Internet Explorer. Follow these steps:

1. Complete Steps 1 through 5 in the preceding section.

You have the WebClass Designer's code window open and the default WebClass_Start event code displayed.

**2. Change the lines for the headline <H1> and the body paragraph <P> in the source code as follows, and add a line between them that inserts two blank lines

, like this:**

```
.Write "<h1><font face=""Arial"">Changes Can Be
        Made</font></h1>"
.Write "<BR><BR>"
.Write "<p>Please sign up for our trip to South
        Carolina's outer ridges.</p>"
```

Figure 13-3 shows the modified code in the WebClass Designer's code window. You're writing VB source code that generates HTML source code, which the server sends to the user's browser. The Response.Write code and the quotation marks are not sent to the user's browser.

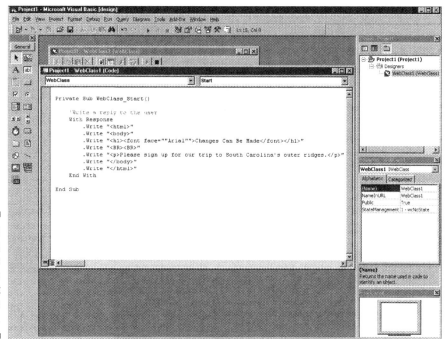

Figure 13-3:
Making some changes to the default source code.

3. Press F5 to test your changes to this program.

If you see a dialog box, click OK, accepting the default settings. (For details about this dialog box, see Steps 7 and 8 in the preceding section.)

You see your changes appear in the displayed Web page in Internet Explorer, as shown in Figure 13-4.

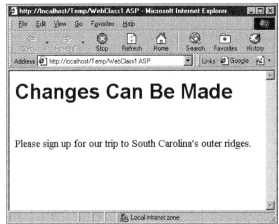

Figure 13-4:
You've
modified this
Web page
within VB.

Adding an HTML Template

The VB editor isn't designed to write and test HTML code. You can do it, as I show you in the preceding section, but if you need to create a Web page of any complexity, you want to use an HTML editor such as FrontPage or Visual InterDev. These dedicated HTML editors have lots of wizards and shortcuts. Also, you don't have to type Response.Write statements and quotation marks for every line of HTML code you want to generate.

How do you add HTML pages created outside VB to an IIS application? You add what are called *HTML templates*. Like WebClasses, they are considered "WebItems" in your project. (WebClasses are standard VB code, or they can be VB class modules.)

HTML templates have a useful feature: You can insert special tags into their HTML code to specify areas in the HTML that you plan to replace. For example, you can surround the text that makes up a headline with these tags: <WC@ and /WC@. Whatever appears between those tags will be replaced by something in the WebClass code. In this way, you can dynamically manipulate the HTML that eventually gets sent to the user's browser.

For example, VB knows today's date; HTML does not. If you want to display the current date in an HTML document, it must be dynamically created and then inserted into existing HTML code.

To see how to add an HTML template to an IIS application, and then replace parts of the HTML using VB code in a WebClass, follow these steps:

1. **Run Windows Notepad.**

2. **Type this simple HTML page into Notepad:**

```
<html>
<body>
<h1>The Happy Day Holiday Travel Agency Page!</h1>
<BR>
Today's Date: <WC@TD>Date</WC@TD>

<WC@mess>message</WC@mess>

</body>
</html>
```

Notice the *TD* and *mess* identifiers added to the WC tags. You can use any name you want for these identifiers. Later (in Step 15), you use the identifiers to — what else? — identify each particular pair of WC tags, and the replacement zone enclosed between that pair. As you see in the code here in Step 2, you can insert as many WC tags as you need, giving each of them a unique identifier.

3. **Choose File⇨Save, and save this Notepad file.**

   For the example, name the file HAPPY.HTM.

4. **Open the WebClass Designer's code window and display the default WebClass_Start event code.**

   (For details about completing this step, see Steps 1 through 5 in the section "Building Your First IIS Application," earlier in this chapter.)

5. **Using Windows Explorer, create a directory for your IIS application.**

   For this example, name the directory **MYIISAPP1**.

6. **In VB, choose File⇨Save Project, and save your project in the directory you just created (MYIISAPP1).**

7. **Right-click HTML Template WebItems in the left pane of the WebClass Designer.**

   A context menu pops out.

8. **Choose Add HTML Template from the context menu.**

   A file-browsing dialog box appears.

9. **Locate and then click the file you saved earlier from Notepad (HAPPY.HTM).**

   A new HTML template is added to your project with the default name *Template1* highlighted.

10. **Change the name from *Template1* to a more descriptive name.**

    For the example, name your HTML template **Happy**.

11. **Double-click WebClass1 in the left pane of the WebClass Designer.**

The code window appears.

12. **Type this code into the Start event (this is the only code you want in this event):**

```
Private Sub WebClass_Start()
happy.WriteTemplate
End Sub
```

In your project, replace the name *happy* that I use here with whatever name you gave your .HTM file in Step 3 in this section.

Running this project triggers the WriteTemplate event of the Happy HTML template. This event handles any substitutions in the HTML code signaled by the special <WC@ tags.

13. **Using the drop-down listbox at the top left of the code window, locate your template, as shown in Figure 13-5.**

In my example, the template is named *Happy*.

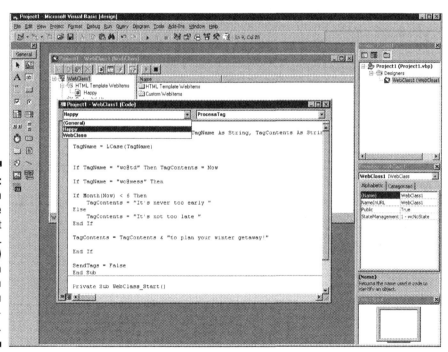

Figure 13-5: Even an HTML page (VB calls it an HTML template) has its own events in which you can put programming.

14. **In the listbox at the top right of the code window, locate the ProcessTag event for the Happy template.**

15. **Type this code into the ProcessTag event:**

```
Private Sub Happy_ProcessTag(ByVal TagName As String,
        TagContents As String, SendTags As Boolean)
TagName = LCase(TagName)
If TagName = "wc@td" Then TagContents = Now
If TagName = "wc@mess" Then
If Month(Now) < 6 Then
    TagContents = "It's never too early "
Else
    TagContents = "It's not too late "
End If
TagContents = TagContents & "to plan your winter getaway!"
End If
SendTags = False
End Sub
```

All tags in a given HTML template page go through this event for processing. That's why you have to use If...Then or a Case structure to test the
incoming TagName. First, you use the LCase command so you can just
use lowercase in all your tests in this procedure and don't have to worry
about cases. Each TagName begins with wc@ followed by whatever name
you used in the HTML code when you first specified a substitution.
Anything you put between the <WC@ and /WC@> tags in the HTML is
thrown out and replaced with what's specified here in this event.

For instance, when the wc@td tag is processed, the entire
<WC@TD>Date</WC@TD> in the original HTML is replaced with whatever
VB calculates is the current date and time (the VB command Now).

This substitution scheme includes a truly terrifying optional feature:
recursive substitution. This nasty house-of-mirrors feature enables you
to include new substitution tags when you make a substitution. In turn,
these new tags are then, themselves, parsed by this same event. Talk
about code that's impossible to debug or maintain (and pretty hard to
explain)! The SendTags = False line in this event prevents new substitution tags from being included back in the HTML. I suggest avoiding
recursive substitution because it's the programming equivalent of run-
away microphone feedback, and just as annoying.

16. **Press F5.**

You see the results of your substitutions, as shown in Figure 13-6.

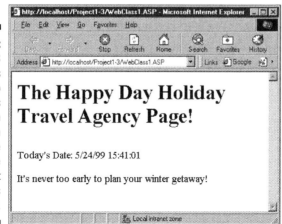

Figure 13-6:
VB
calculates
two
substitutions
and then
inserts them
into the
HTML before
sending it
to this
browser.

No real limit exists to what you can send as a substitution. It can be a huge amount of text (you can use the TagContents argument for that), an expression, the returned argument from a function, or results from a database query. If you want, even an entire large HTML page could be generated and sent from within a single substitution tag.

Attaching Databases to Web Pages

You can attach databases to Web pages in several ways, but using IIS applications ranks among the more straightforward and flexible methods. This approach gives you good debugging, the ability to create WebClasses, and great facilities for working with queries. You can use HTML templates (see the preceding section) to build dynamic substitutions (substituting database fields for tags).

Combining ADO programming (see Part VI) with IIS applications gives you everything you need for doing databases on the Web. You work within the familiar VB environment, but instead of displaying the data on a traditional window (the classic VB form), you pipe it out into the world by sending it as HTML that any browser — even those used in the far reaches of Tibet — can display.

A very interesting technology called DHTML (Dynamic HTML) is similar in some ways to IIS applications. However, DHTML works client-side only, and it requires Internet Explorer, so it isn't suited to helping out with Internet database projects. Half the people in the world, as of this writing, use browsers that cannot read and execute DHTML.

Filling an HTML table with data

This example shows you how to take data from the Publishers table in the BIBLIO.MDB sample database and then fill HTML tables with the data. To see how to make an easy, yet powerful, database connection to the Internet, follow these steps:

1. **Choose File⇨New Project in VB.**

   The New Project dialog box appears.

2. **Double-click the IIS Application icon in the New Project dialog box.**

   The dialog box closes, and VB displays the IIS Application template.

3. **Using Windows Explorer, create a directory for this IIS application.**

   For the example that I'm describing, name the directory **IISDATAB**.

4. **Choose File⇨Save Project.**

   A File Save dialog box appears.

5. **Save your project in the folder you created in Step 3 (IISDATAB).**

6. **Run Notepad.**

7. **Type this code into Notepad:**

```
<html>
<body>
<BR><BR>
<h1 ALIGN=CENTER>PUBLISHERS</h1>
<BR>
<WC@Pubs></WC@Pubs>

</body>
</html>
```

   You're going to replace that pair of WC@ tags with a table. For information about substitution tags like these, see the section "Adding an HTML Template," earlier in this chapter.

8. **Choose File⇨Save in Notepad.**

   A file-saving dialog box opens.

9. **Save the file as** PUBS.HTM.

10. **Click the small + symbol next to Designers in the Project Explorer.**

    You see WebClass1 in the Project Explorer. In the next few steps, you add your HTML template to your project.

11. **Double-click WebClass1.**

    The WebClass Designer appears.

12. Right-click HTML Template WebItems in the Designer.

A context menu appears.

13. Choose Add HTML Template from the context menu.

A file-browser dialog box opens.

14. Find PUBS.HTM on your hard drive and double-click it.

The file-browser dialog box closes, and a new HTML Template appears in your project. By default, the WebClass Designer names it Template1.

15. Leave it named Template1.

16. Right-click Custom WebItems in the Designer's left pane.

A context menu appears.

17. Choose Add Custom WebItem.

The menu closes, and a new WebItem named WebItem1 appears.

18. Leave it with the default name, WebItem1.

19. Double-click WebItem1 in the left pane of the WebClass Designer.

The code window opens, showing you default code in the Start event of this WebClass.

20. Erase the default source code in the Start event and replace it with this code:

```
Private Sub WebClass_Start()
    Template1.WriteTemplate
End Sub
```

When this WebClass starts executing, the first event to trigger is the well-named Start event. In this example, you simply pass execution to the Template1_ProcessTag event (that's what happens when you use the WriteTemplate method — it triggers the ProcessTag event).

21. From the drop-down listbox at the top left of the code window, select Template1.

22. In the listbox at the top right of the code window, select the ProcessTag event for Template1.

23. Type this code into the ProcessTag event:

```
Private Sub Template1_ProcessTag(ByVal TagName As String,
        TagContents As String, SendTags As Boolean)
TagName = LCase(TagName)
If TagName = "wc@pubs" Then
TagContents = fnShowData
End If
SendTags = False
End Sub
```

The section "Adding an HTML Template,"" earlier in this chapter, shows how you can use several substitution tags in an HTML template. It's not necessary, though, because as this example demonstrates, you can use just one substitution: WC@PUBS. In the preceding code, the tag causes the function fnShowData to execute.

24. **Move your cursor down (press and hold the down-arrow key) until you're below the last End Sub at the bottom of the code window.**

You want the cursor on a blank line in the code window. This way, you can create a new function in the code window.

25. **Type in this new function:**

```
Private Function fnShowData()
Dim cBiblio As ADODB.Connection
Dim rsPubs As ADODB.Recordset
Dim SQLQuery As String
Dim strData As String
Dim r As String

r = "Provider=microsoft.jet.OLEDB.3.51;" & "Data
        Source=C:\Program Files\Microsoft Visual
        Studio\VB98\biblio.mdb"

'make the connect to the biblio database
Set cBiblio = New ADODB.Connection
cBiblio.ConnectionString = r
cBiblio.Open

SQLQuery = "SELECT * FROM Publishers ORDER BY Name"
Set rsPubs = New ADODB.Recordset
rsPubs.Open SQLQuery, cBiblio

strData = "<TABLE BORDER=1 CELLPADDING=3>"

Do While Not rsPubs.EOF
strData = strData & "<TR><TD>" & rsPubs("Company Name") &
        "</TD><TD>" & rsPubs("Telephone") & "</TR>"
rsPubs.movenext
Loop

strData = strData & "</TABLE>"

fnShowData = strData

rsPubs.Close
Set rsPubs = Nothing
cBiblio.Close
Set cBiblio = Nothing

End Function
```

This fnShowData function builds a recordset named rsPubs that contains the Publishers table from the sample BIBLIO database. After the recordset exists, the HTML source code is created by combining HTML tags for a table — `<TR>` and `<TD>` — with data from the recordset: `rsPubs("Company Name")`. Each time this Do While loop executes, the string containing the data (strData) grows bigger and bigger.

I explain the details of using ADO programming in Part VI, "Hands-On Programming."

You use ADO programming in Step 25, and ADO isn't automatically made a part of a VB project. Instead, you must explicitly reference it.

26. **Choose Project⇨References.**

The References dialog box opens.

27. **In the Available References listbox, click the check box next to Microsoft ActiveX Data Objects 2.1 Library.**

You can also use the 2.0 Library, if that's what you see in the listbox. These are merely different versions of the same library. Which one you have depends on what Service Packs you might have uploaded from Microsoft, or what versions of Visual Basic or Visual Studio you're using. Use whatever version you see in this listbox.

A check appears in the box.

28. **Click OK.**

The References dialog box closes, and this library is added to your project. The ADO technology isn't, by default, part of VB. Adding this library adds it, making it possible for VB to understand such source code as `ADODB.Connection`.

29. **Press F5.**

Your project runs, and you see the results shown in Figure 13-7.

If pressing F5 does not result in your seeing the table loaded into your browser, try stopping this VB program and then shutting down Internet Explorer (or whatever browser you may be using). Then press F5 again. This time (after a brief pause), the browser should automatically start running and display the table.

If you make changes to the HTML code in Notepad, or whatever HTML editor you use, how can you update these changes in the IIS application? If you right-click the name of the HTML template (in the left pane of the WebClass Designer), you see a context menu with a Refresh HTML Template option. However, this option does not work at the time of this writing. To really make a change in the template, you must right-click its name to see the context menu and then choose Delete to remove it entirely from this project. Then, right-click HTML Template WebItems (in that same left pane of the Designer), choose Add HTML Template from the context menu, and locate your .HTM file to add it, once again, to the project.

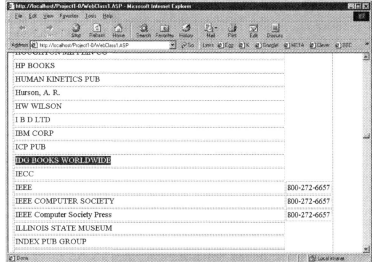

Figure 13-7:
A
dynamically
generated
table is filled
with
database
records.
That wasn't
hard,
was it?

Letting the user get data from the server

Client/server communication over the Internet has traditionally been a buga-boo to programmers — hard to code and harder to debug. As I explain in this section, however, you can easily enable a user to click some displayed data and then see more information from the database. (In this example, the user clicks a company name and then sees more information about that particular company.)

In the following steps, I show you how to use two HTML templates in a single project. You also see how to use the URLFor command to create hyperlinks on a Web page that are funneled back to your server if the user clicks them. You can then handle any of these clicks in your WebClass. To see how all this works, follow these steps:

1. **Load into VB an IIS application with a single HTML template that displays a table.**

   To use my example, follow the steps in the preceding section, "Filling an HTML table with data."

   You have an IIS application with a single HTML template that displays a table of publishers' names and phone numbers.

   If you're following along with the examples I present in this chapter, and you want to reload this IIS application into VB, choose File⇨New Project and then locate the IISDATAB directory that you created to hold this project (see Step 3 in the previous section).

2. **Run Notepad and type in this code:**

```
<html>
<body>
<BR>
<h3>You asked for further information about
        <WC@Co></WC@Co>:</h3>
<BR>
<WC@Info></WC@Info>
</body>
</html>
```

In this step, you're creating a second HTML template for use in this project. You can use multiple HTML templates in a project. The purpose of this template is to provide a separate Web page from the one that holds your table. When the user clicks a cell in the table, the user's browser displays this new Web page, with the requested additional information about the item the user clicked.

3. **Choose File⇨Save in Notepad.**

You see the File Save dialog box.

4. **Save this file in a directory as** INFO.HTM. **Don't use the same directory (IISDATAB) that you're using for the rest of this project.**

5. **Right-click HTML Template WebItems in the left pane of the WebClass Designer.**

A context menu pops out.

6. **Choose Add HTML Template from the context menu.**

The context menu closes, and a file-browser dialog box appears.

7. **Locate the file INFO.HTM that you created in Step 4 on your hard drive and double-click it.**

A new template appears in the WebClass Designer named Template2. Leave it named Template 2. This template contains INFO.HTM. Now you've added this second Web page to your project.

8. **Double-click WebClass1 in the Designer.**

The code window opens.

9. **Move your cursor (using the up-arrow key) to the very top of the code window (the listboxes at the top of the code window should say** General Declarations**) and insert these lines:**

```
Dim strName As String
Dim strInfo As String
```

These two variables — strName and strInfo — are now global, meaning that all the procedures (Subs and Functions) in this WebClass can access them.

10. **Move your cursor down a few lines from the top of the code window so you're on a blank line just above the first Sub, and type in these lines:**

```
Private Sub Template2_ProcessTag(ByVal TagName As String,
        TagContents As String, SendTags As Boolean)
TagName = LCase(TagName)
If TagName = "wc@co" Then
TagContents = strName
End If
If TagName = "wc@info" Then
TagContents = strInfo
End If
SendTags = False
End Sub
```

This source code makes substitutions necessary to display the information the user requested. The *strName* variable contains the name of whatever table item the user clicks, and the *strInfo* variable contains data from a different field in the database that provides additional information about this item. In my example, the additional information is the telephone number of a publisher the user clicked.

11. **Locate the fnShowData function in the code window and change this line:**

```
strData = strData & "<TR><TD>" & rsPubs("Company Name") &
        "</TD><TD>" & rsPubs("Telephone") & "</TR>"
```

Insert the following code in place of that line:

```
strData = strData & "<TR><TD><A HREF=" & URLFor(WebItem1,
        n) & ">" & rsPubs("Company Name") &
        "</A></TD><TD></TR>"
```

The URLFor command will trigger the WebItem1 UserEvent and will send the information back to this event in the variable *n*. This variable holds the name of the company that the user clicks in the browser. You add *n* to the code in the next step.

12. **In that same fnShowData function, add a line after the following Do While line:**

```
Do While Not rsPubs.EOF
```

Here's the new line of code that you need to add (shown in bold):

```
Do While Not rsPubs.EOF
n = rsPubs("Company Name")
```

13. **At the top of the fnShowData function, add a line to declare the new variable *n*. Add the new line immediately after this one:**

```
Dim r As String
```

The following code shows both declarations:

```
Dim r As String
Dim n As String
```

14. **In the drop-down list in the top left corner of the code window, locate WebItem1, and in the drop-down list at the top right of the code window locate UserEvent.**

15. **Type this code into WebItem1_UserEvent:**

```
Private Sub WebItem1_UserEvent(ByVal EventName As String)
Dim cBiblio As ADODB.Connection
Dim rsPubs As ADODB.Recordset
Dim SQLqry As String
Dim r As String

r = "Provider=microsoft.jet.OLEDB.3.51;" & "Data
        Source=C:\Program Files\Microsoft Visual
        Studio\VB98\biblio.mdb"

Set cBiblio = New ADODB.Connection
cBiblio.ConnectionString = r
cBiblio.Open

SQLqry = "SELECT * FROM Publishers WHERE [Company Name] =
        '" & EventName & "'"

Set rsPubs = New ADODB.Recordset
rsPubs.Open SQLqry, cBiblio

strName = rsPubs("Company Name")
If IsNull(rsPubs("Telephone")) Then
strInfo = "There is no telephone number provided for this
        company in the database."
Else
strInfo = "Their telephone number is: " &
        rsPubs("Telephone")
End If

Template2.WriteTemplate

rsPubs.Close
Set rsPubs = Nothing
cBiblio.Close
Set cBiblio = Nothing

End Sub
```

This code is similar to the code in the fnShowData function (see the previous section). It opens the database. Then, it builds a recordset containing information in which the company name clicked by the user (held in the EventName parameter that's passed back from the browser) is the same as the company name in the database. Then, it looks in the recordset for that company's telephone number and sets the global variables strName and strInfo to the company name and phone number (or the apology that the phone number is NULL). Template2 is then triggered, and it replaces the substitution tags with the values in those two global variables.

16. **Press F5.**

    You see a list of company names in Internet Explorer.

17. **Click one of those company names.**

    A new page is loaded into the browser, showing the telephone number, as shown in Figure 13-8. Isn't technology great?

Figure 13-8:
Here's the information the user requested, zapped to the user's browser from your server.

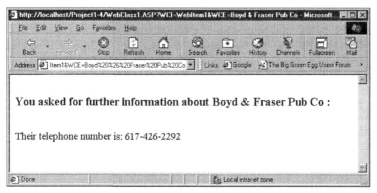

Consider what you've accomplished in this section: A user clicks your table of publishers (or whatever list your table displays) in a Web browser. This user might be located in, for example, Taiwan. A message is immediately sent back to your server. Then, your server looks up the correct additional data from your database (in this example, a phone number), and a second HTML page is sent back to Taiwan with that phone number. Talk about *distributed* computing!

Debugging IIS Applications

You're probably used to the classic debugging tools and techniques available in VB. You press F5, and your project runs in the VB editor just as it would in the real world of Windows. You can use the Immediate Window, single-stepping, and the rest of the powerful suite of testing implements in Visual Basic.

But can you use VB to debug IIS applications, given that they actually run within Internet Explorer when you press F5? Lucky you — you can. For the most part, before VB 6, you couldn't systematically and intelligently debug Web-based applications. With the IIS Application feature in VB 6, however, it's now an option — a welcome option.

Don't kid yourself, though. Browser error messages and database error messages are often cryptic and uninformative — their biggest weakness is they often don't tell you *where* in your code the error occurred. Sometimes, Internet Explorer tells you a problem exists in "Line 38" in your source code. (So you have to count by hand because the lines are not numbered in the VB editor.) That's better than nothing, though. Database programming error messages are notoriously obscure.

Did you know you can still number your lines in VB — a direct descendent of BASIC? You can simply add line numbers just like the good old days (the early '80s), and the Err object's LineNumber property (or some similar name) can return the exact line number where the error occurred. That line must be numbered, though, for this trick to work. I don't recommend coding your applications with line numbers, but it's a neat trick to debug a thorny problem. You'll probably want to remove those line numbers after you solve your problem, though.

The second biggest shortcoming of database and Internet error messages is that the message is either too general to be helpful (`Invalid procedure call or syntax error`) or simply incomprehensible (`Error in rollback wrapper server interlude #4226`).

Despite these difficulties, you can often isolate problems using VB's single-stepping, breakpoints, and other debugging tools — even when working with databases, the Internet, or both in combination.

For a detailed look at debugging in VB, see Chapter 17.

Part VI
Hands-On Programming

The 5th Wave — By Rich Tennant

Get the Huggies, hon— she's reaching for the Diaper icon.

In this part . . .

Programmers only allowed in this section of the book. Well, everyone is welcome, actually — at least, all programmers who want to get some hands-on database programming under their belts. Sure, there's lots of programming in other parts of this book, but Part VI is the fun zone for writing and testing database application source code without relying too much on assistants (like wizards and templates). Sometimes, if you want something done right, you've just got to do it yourself — right?

The chapters in this part explain the best, tested database programming strategies. You also discover how to cross the bridge from the older (but sturdy and time-proven) DAO technology to the new, exciting ADO and OLE DB strategies. When you try examples in these chapters, you get a good idea what's best for each database programming job you're doing.

At the end of this part, Chapter 17 gives you a list of the more common (and more mystifying) database programming errors. If you look over this chapter, you'll avoid puzzling over some real head-scratchers. And if you enjoy a challenge, you'll find a nice, perplexing example in which you're asked whether you can figure out the solution (I provide the solution elsewhere in that chapter).

Chapter 14

Doing It Yourself: Data Access Programming

*T*hroughout this book, you see how to let VB do the database programming for you. Wizards, templates, and designers can provide a quite useful starting point for anyone getting started with database programming. They can often handle tedious grunt-work details for you, such as the highly repetitive code necessary to add property procedures to a class. Often, you can just fire up one of these assistants and let it do part of the programming. That frees you to concentrate on customizing and improving the overall effectiveness of the application you're building.

When you take the bus to Chicago, you get to relax and let the driver deal with the hassles of driving. However, you do pay a price when you turn a job over to someone else — you lose flexibility and freedom. So, riding on the back of a wizard is fine for some tasks, but you certainly also need to know how to take the wheel yourself. In this chapter, you get down and do some programming of your own.

This chapter introduces you to the world's most popular desktop database programming technology, Data Access Objects (DAO). After you understand how to open and manipulate databases using DAO, you're well on your way to using other techniques, such as ADO (ActiveX Data Objects, the subject of Chapter 16). To explore the comparative virtues of DAO versus ADO, see Chapter 15.

When you work with DAO or ADO, you're working with objects. In this chapter, I assume you have some experience with objects and their features: collections (sets of objects) and members (properties, methods, and events).

Anyone who has used Visual Basic is already fairly well-grounded in objects. A TextBox, for example, is an object and it has properties (like FontSize), methods (like Move), and events (like Click). Similarly, when you program with a DAO object, you employ its properties and methods, and you can write code in its events. However, with DAO, you must first *instantiate* (bring into existence) an object. The object doesn't exist until you program it into existence (unlike a TextBox that's already there waiting for you to use it on the VB Toolbox).

Opening a Database Connection

Opening a connection to a database means first creating a database object. That process involves two steps:

1. Create an object variable to hold the database object.

You can use Visual Basic's Dim command to create the variable.

2. Use the Set command to assign a particular database to this object variable.

To open a database connection using VB's DAO code, follow these steps:

1. Choose File⇨New Project.

The New Project dialog box appears.

2. Double-click the Standard EXE icon in the New Project dialog box.

The dialog box closes, and the Standard VB Form is displayed.

3. Double-click Form1.

You see the VB code window.

4. Move your cursor up (press and hold the up-arrow key) until you're at the very top of the code window, and then press the Enter key to create a blank line.

The listboxes at the top of the code window say General
Declarations. This section in the code window is outside of all events
(procedures). By using the Dim command here, you make your database
object available to all the events and procedures in the entire module
(Form1, in this case).

5. **Type this code into the General Declarations section of Form1:**

```
Dim dbBiblio As Database
```

In place of dbBiblio, type whatever name you want to use for the database object. With this declaration, all the events, subroutines, and
functions in Form1 can use this database object.

6. **Move your cursor to the Form_Load event, and type in this code:**

```
Private Sub Form_Load()
Set dbBiblio = opendatabase("C:\PROGRAM
        FILES\VB98\BIBLIO.MDB")
Show
Print dbBiblio.Name & " has been opened " & Error(Err)
End Sub
```

For the examples that I describe throughout this chapter, I use the
BIBLIO.MDB sample database, so in place of C:\PROGRAM
FILES\VB98\BIBLIO.MDB in this code, substitute the path leading to
the database file you're using. And as in the General Declarations,
replace dbBiblio with the name of your database object.

7. **Press F5.**

You get the following error message: User Defined Type Not
Defined. This message means the database object doesn't exist as a
type of object you can declare (Dim). Before you can use DAO (or ADO),
you must first *reference it* (add its library of capabilities to the VB
project).

Failing to reference the Object Library is a common mistake when working
with database objects. Remember that any failure to reference a library
can cause the error message I mention in the preceding paragraph.

8. **Choose Project⇨References.**

The References dialog box opens.

9. **Locate Microsoft DAO 3.51 Object Library in the listbox (you can use
   DAO 3.6 instead if it appears in the list) and click the box next to it in
   the listbox titled Available References.**

A check appears in the box. (The actual version of DAO in your computer depends on what software you've installed on your system, and
when. For the jobs involved in this chapter, the version you use doesn't
matter.)

10. **Click OK.**

    The References dialog closes, and VB adds the DAO library to your project.

11. **Press F5.**

    Your form displays the message that the database has been successfully opened and is ready for business.

Working with the Mighty Recordset Object

After you open a connection to a database (see the preceding section), the next step when accessing data under DAO is to create a recordset object.

A recordset is a temporary container that you fill with a group of records, based on criteria that you specify. A recordset is similar to an array. The criteria you use for filling a recordset may be a table, a stored query definition, or a SQL SELECT statement.

 A SQL statement requests data in a manner similar to this example: From the table named Authors, give me all the records in which the last name begins with the letter *S*. A *stored procedure* is a special kind of SQL statement that is stored right there in the database (instead of being part of your application, as the SQL statement in the next example). For in-depth discussions of SQL, see Chapters 18 and 19.

Creating a recordset filled with a table

Here's how you use the OpenRecordset command to load an entire table into your recordset:

1. **Open an active connection to the database you want to use.**

    For details about this step, see the section "Opening a Database Connection," earlier in this chapter.

2. **Double-click Form1.**

    You see the code window.

3. **Erase the source code in the Form_Load event (from the previous example) and replace it with this code:**

```
Dim dbBiblio As Database
Private Sub Form_Load()
Dim rsTitles As Recordset
Set dbBiblio = opendatabase("C:\PROGRAM
       FILES\VB98\BIBLIO.MDB")
Set rsTitles = dbBiblio.OpenRecordset("Titles")
MsgBox rsTitles.Fields("Title")
End Sub
```

In place of `C:\PROGRAM FILES\VB98\BIBLIO.MDB` in this code, substitute the path leading to the desired database file on your hard drive. Also, if you're not following my example and using BIBLIO.MDB, change `Titles` to a table in your database, and change `Title` to a field in your database.

What's new in this code (compared to the previous example) is that you've defined a recordset object variable (the line that begins with `Dim rsTitles`). Then, you use the Set rsTitles command, which pours data from the database table named Titles into your recordset object variable. Finally, just to prove to yourself that you are, in fact, extracting data from this table, you use a message box to display the "current record" in the field named Title.

The term *current record* simply means that a pointer in the recordset gets incremented or decremented, as appropriate, each time you use such commands as MoveNext or MovePrevious. The pointer goes all the way to the final record when you use the MoveLast command. In other words, only one record at a time is the current record. When you first create a recordset (prior to any move commands), the pointer is located at the first record. Always remember, though, that an ordinary table in a relational database isn't necessarily in alphabetic order (or any other order). As I explain in Chapter 18, however, you can create an alphabetized *recordset* with SQL statements like this one: ORDER BY LastName.

When creating the recordset in this step, how do you know that Titles is a table in this database and Title is a field within that table? You just know. Somehow, you get a list of the tables and their fields. In this case, you can choose Add-Ins⇨Visual Data Manager and then, in the VDM, choose File⇨Open Database⇨Microsoft Access. Locate the database on your hard drive (BIBLIO.MDB, in this example), and the VDM's Database Window displays the tables. Click the small + symbol next to each table to see its fields. (You can query databases in code to get their structure, but examining them using tools like the VDM or just getting the information from the database's documentation is easier.)

4. **Press F5.**

   The program runs, and you see a message box displaying the name of the Title of the first record in the Titles table, as shown in Figure 14-1.

Figure 14-1:
Aha! You've extracted data from a database and displayed it. Nothing can stop you now.

5. **Click OK.**

   The message box closes.

6. **Choose Run⇨End.**

   Your program stops running, and VB returns to editing mode.

7. **Type this additional code just above the End Sub in the Form_Load event:**

   ```
   rsTitles.MoveNext
   MsgBox rsTitles.Fields("Title")
   ```

   By using the MoveNext command, you cause the pointer in the record-set to move up one record in the recordset. If you're not following my example and using BIBLIO.MDB, change Title to a field in the database you're working with.

8. **Press F5.**

   You see message boxes displaying the title of the first record in the recordset, followed by the title of the second record.

Creating a recordset based on a SQL statement

Specifying that you want to see only a part of the data in a table is often useful (and more efficient, after you create a recordset). For example, rather than loading the entire Titles table as you do in the previous section, you can be picky and ask to see only those titles that begin with the letters *NO*.

Why not just make your life easier and import an entire table, rather than going to the trouble of specifying a subset of data from that table? After all, once the table is loaded into a recordset, you can use various techniques (such as the Find command) to specify that you want to display only particular pieces of data from that table. True enough. But the smaller the recordset, the less computing that's required to move through it, search it, or send it over the Internet or an intranet. And remember, some fields (notably the memo type) can be gargantuan. Also, a table may contain too many records — terabytes of data, millions of records — to hold in memory.

To create a recordset that's based on a SQL query, follow these steps:

1. **Follow the steps I describe in the section "Opening a Database Connection," earlier in this chapter.**

   You have a project that references the DAO Object Library.

2. **Replace all the source code in that example with this code:**

```
Dim dbBiblio As Database
Private Sub Form_Load()
Dim rsTitles As Recordset
Set dbBiblio = opendatabase("C:\PROGRAM
        FILES\VB98\BIBLIO.MDB")
SQLQuery = "SELECT * FROM Titles WHERE Title LIKE 'NO*'"
Set rsTitles = dbBiblio.OpenRecordset(SQLQuery)
MsgBox rsTitles.Fields("Title")
End Sub
```

In place of `C:\PROGRAM FILES\VB98\BIBLIO.MDB` in this code, substitute the path leading to the BIBLIO.MDB sample database file on your hard drive. Or, if you aren't following along with my example, substitute the full path for the database you're using. Also, in the SQLQuery, replace `Titles` with a table in your database, and `Title` with a field in your table.

In the preceding lines, I use boldface to highlight the new code. After you create the object variables with the two Dim commands, and open the database with the OpenDatabase command, you define a variable by creating a string that begins with the SQL command SELECT. In effect, this string says, "Choose all records (the first * means *all*) in the database if (WHERE) their Title field begins with the letters *no* (LIKE 'NO*')."

Notice that you must use single quotes surrounding the NO* — you can't use double quotes inside a VB string. Also, the * following the NO is a wildcard symbol meaning any characters after the NO are fine.

I prefer to define a variable (SQLQuery) that defines the SQL statement and then use that variable for the OpenRecordset command. However, some programmers use the SQL statement directly in the OpenRecordset line, like this example:

```
Set rsTitles = dbBiblio.OpenRecordset("SELECT * FROM
            Titles WHERE Title LIKE 'NO*'")
```

I find the SQL statement easier to read and work with when you break the process down into two lines.

For additional information on SQL, see Chapters 18 and 19.

3. Press F5.

You see the book titled No Bugs! (dream on) displayed in a message box.

Recordsets are remarkably flexible beasts. They can cater to nearly your every whim. For instance, they can contain partial content from multiple tables joined together. For additional information on the many ways you can use SQL to produce all kinds of recordsets, see Chapter 19.

Filling a ListBox with Data

In previous sections of this chapter, my examples use message boxes to display part of a record. This cunning technique enables you to prove to yourself that you have, in fact, opened a database and extracted some of its data. Although cheap and simple, message boxes aren't the most elegant tools, particularly if you're trying to display many records at a time, or you want the user to be able to edit the data.

The ListBox offers a more effective way to display data. To fill a ListBox with every title in the BIBLIO.MDB database, and the date each title was published, follow these steps:

1. Choose File➪New Project.

The New Project dialog box appears.

2. Double-click the Standard EXE icon in the New Project dialog box.

The dialog box closes, and the Standard VB Form is displayed.

3. Double-click the ListBox icon in the Toolbox.

VB adds a ListBox to Form1.

4. Choose Project➪References.

The References dialog box opens. Before doing any database-related programming, you must first add a reference to a database technology library (DAO or ADO, for example).

5. In the Available References listbox, locate Microsoft DAO 3.51 Object Library (you can use DAO 3.6 instead if it appears in the list) and then click its check box.

A check appears in the box.

6. **Click OK.**

The References dialog box closes, and VB adds the DAO library to your project.

7. **Double-click Form1.**

You see the VB code window.

8. **Move your cursor up (press and hold the up-arrow key) until you're at the very top of the code window, and then press the Enter key to create a blank line.**

The listboxes at the top of the code window say General Declarations. This section in the code window is outside of all events (procedures). By using the Dim command here, you make your database object available to all the events and procedures in the entire module (Form1, in this case).

9. **Type this code into the General Declarations section of Form1:**

```
Dim dbBiblio As Database
```

Now all the events, subroutines, and functions in Form1 can use this database object.

10. **Move your cursor to the Form_Load event, and type in this code:**

```
Private Sub Form_Load()
Dim rsTitles As Recordset
Set dbBiblio = opendatabase("C:\PROGRAM
        FILES\VB98\BIBLIO.MDB")
Set rsTitles = dbBiblio.OpenRecordset("Titles")

Do Until rsTitles.EOF = True
    List1.AddItem rsTitles.Fields("Title") & " (" &
        rsTitles.Fields("[Year Published]") & ")"
    rsTitles.MoveNext
Loop

End Sub
```

In place of C:\PROGRAM FILES\VB98\BIBLIO.MDB in this code, substitute the path leading to the BIBLIO.MDB sample database file on your hard drive. Also, if you're not following my example and using BIBLIO.MDB, change Titles to the name of a table in your database, and change Title and Year Published to the names of fields in your database.

This code fills the ListBox by using the AddItem command. When you have a field name that's two words (for example, Year Published), you need to enclose it in brackets. The EOF (end-of-file) property tells you when you've reached the last record in the recordset after all the MoveNext commands have iterated through the whole set of records.

11. **Press F5.**

Your program runs, and the ListBox fills with data, as shown in Figure 14-2.

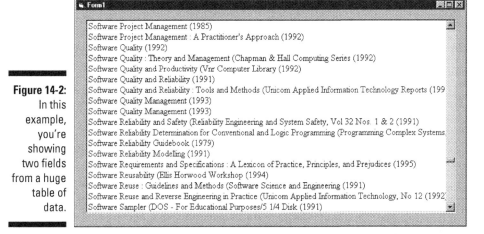

Figure 14-2:
In this
example,
you're
showing
two fields
from a huge
table of
data.

The BIBLIO.MDB database contains many records, so it takes a few seconds before this program displays the ListBox full of data. Oddly, though, setting the ListBox's Sorted property to True doesn't slow things down very much, and the titles are alphabetized for you. Note, though, that sorting data at the database, using the SQL clause ORDER BY is generally better than in a ListBox or other approach. Database engines have much more powerful sorting algorithms than you'll find elsewhere. Also, a database engine can sort while retrieving records. One final reason, if you're still not convinced: A database server (in the case of an RDBMS) is often the most powerful hardware. To find out how to use ORDER BY, see Chapter 19.

How Many Records Are There?

Sometimes, you want to know the total number of records in a recordset. In some cases, a user may be interested *only* in the total. For example, perhaps a user wants to know how many books in the BIBLIO.MDB sample database have the term *C++* in their titles. The user doesn't want to see the list of titles, just how many C++ books the database lists.

This example demonstrates how you display the total number of records in a recordset:

1. **Follow the steps in the previous section, "Filling a ListBox with Data."**

   You have a form with a ListBox on it, and you've written code that displays all the titles and publication dates of the books in the Titles table of the BIBLIO.MDB database.

2. **Add three new lines (shown here in boldface) to the code in the previous example, creating the following listing in the code window:**

```
Dim dbBiblio As Database

Private Sub Form_Load()
Dim rsTitles As Recordset
Set dbBiblio = opendatabase("C:\PROGRAM
        FILES\VB98\BIBLIO.MDB")

SQLQuery = "SELECT * FROM Titles WHERE Title LIKE
        '*C++*'"

Set rsTitles = dbBiblio.OpenRecordset(SQLQuery)

Do Until rsTitles.EOF = True
    List1.AddItem rsTitles.Fields("Title") & " (" &
        rsTitles.Fields("[Year Published]") & ")"
    rsTitles.MoveNext
Loop

MsgBox rsTitles.recordcount

End Sub
```

In place of `C:\PROGRAM FILES\VB98\BIBLIO.MDB` in this code, substitute the path leading to the BIBLIO.MDB sample database file on your hard drive.

In this example, you fill the ListBox with the records in the recordset. This process has the effect of moving the pointer in the recordset all the way to the last record. Therefore, when you display the RecordCount property in a message box at the end, you get the correct count.

The RecordCount property does not, by itself, contain the total number of records unless you first move to the end of the recordset. You can make that move, as in this example, by filling a component with all the records, or you can use this code to move to the end of the recordset:

```
RsTitles.MoveLast
MsgBox rsTitles.recordcount
```

Strangely enough, you have to "physically" move to the last record, one way or another, before you get an accurate answer from the RecordCount property. Doesn't make sense, but it's one of those quirks you have to remember.

3. **Press F5.**

You see the correct number of records in your recordset.

Experience has shown me that customers often request the feature of seeing the total number of records, but most of them don't use it. A good programmer should make sure this feature is really needed. Often, just getting this count requires that you open a recordset, execute the MoveLast command to read the recordcount, and then use MoveFirst to move back and display the first record (or use a bookmark to maintain the display of the current record). In any case, these are time-consuming operations if you have lots of records or if there's network traffic. A good application implements only what is needed and doesn't contain time-consuming, needless operations.

Figuring Out Whether You're Dealing with an Empty Recordset

When working with recordsets, your application can easily cause errors by trying to move past the last record, or before the first record. If you use one of the move commands, such as MoveNext or MoveFirst, but you have no records in the recordset, you get the infamous No current record error message, as shown in Figure 14-3. (I mention this error in Chapters 7, 8, and 17 as well as here — the error is that important and that confusing to beginning database programmers who perhaps justifiably expect VB or the database engine to prevent this error from shutting down a VB application.)

Figure 14-3:
This error
message
can mystify
users —
just before
shutting
down your
application!

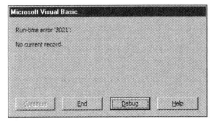

Microsoft Visual Basic

Run-time error '3021':

No current record.

| Continue | End | Debug | Help |

Unfortunately, several errors can cause this message: The user deletes records from the recordset until none are left; the user clicks your Next button (with a MoveNext command in that button's code) until going right past the last record; the MoveFirst command is executed against an empty recordset; and so on.

You must ensure that this error doesn't happen. It can crash your application unless you insert `On Error Resume Next` at the beginning of any Sub or Function in which this error may occur.

But the best solution is to prevent the problem in the first place. Here's how you can prevent one of the causes of this error by checking to see if a recordset is empty:

1. **Follow the steps in the "How Many Records Are There?" section earlier in this chapter.**

   You have a listbox and the code necessary to fill it with a recordset.

2. **Modify the code from the previous example to include the changes shown here in boldface:**

   ```
   Dim dbBiblio As Database

   Private Sub Form_Load()
   Dim rsTitles As Recordset
   Set dbBiblio = opendatabase("C:\PROGRAM
           FILES\VB98\BIBLIO.MDB")

   SQLQuery = "SELECT * FROM Titles WHERE Title LIKE
           '*CZX*'"

   Set rsTitles = dbBiblio.OpenRecordset(SQLQuery)

   Do Until rsTitles.EOF = True
       List1.AddItem rsTitles.Fields("Title") & " (" &
           rsTitles.Fields("[Year Published]") & ")"
       rsTitles.MoveNext
   Loop

   rsTitles.MoveFirst
   End Sub
   ```

   In place of `C:\PROGRAM FILES\VB98\BIBLIO.MDB` in this code, substitute the path that leads to the BIBLIO.MDB sample database file on your hard drive.

   The SQLQuery in this example looks for any titles with the letters *czx* in them (an impossibility in all Earth languages other than Welsh). Therefore, your recordset contains no records.

3. **Press F5.**

The error message displayed in Figure 14-3 appears because the MoveFirst command can't move to the first record in a recordset that has no records.

4. **Add this code (in boldface) just above the line with the MoveFirst command:**

```
If rsTitles.EOF = True And rsTitles.BOF = True Then Exit
        Sub
rsTitles.MoveFirst
```

If the recordset's EOF (end of file) and BOF (beginning of file) properties both are True, you know you have an empty recordset.

You may wonder why the rsTitles.MoveNext command in the Do...Until Loop doesn't trigger the No current record error message. The reason: That loop never executes in this example because it first tests if EOF is true (and EOF is true of this recordset because it's empty).

Some programmers like to handle the No current record error by referring it to an error handler in the same procedure. Here's an example showing how you code an alternative way to handle this error:

```
Private Sub Form_Load()
On Error GoTo ErrorHandler
Dim rsTitles As Recordset
Set dbBiblio = opendatabase("C:\PROGRAM
            FILES\VB98\BIBLIO.MDB")

SQLQuery = "SELECT * FROM Titles WHERE Title LIKE '*CZX*'"

Set rsTitles = dbBiblio.OpenRecordset(SQLQuery)

rsTitles.MovePrevious

Exit Sub
ErrorHandler:
    If Err = 3021 Then
        Exit Sub
    Else
        Msgbox Error(Err)
    End If

End Sub
```

At the top of the procedure, you insert an On Error command, sending execution to your error handler routine at the end of the procedure (should any error occur while this procedure runs). The Exit Sub is inserted so the error handler isn't executed every time this procedure runs. If an error 3021 (no current record) *does* occur, you don't inform the user and shut down the application — you just exit the subroutine and ignore it. Otherwise, display an error message for any other kind of error.

In place of C:\PROGRAM FILES\VB98\BIBLIO.MDB in this code, substitute the path leading to the BIBLIO.MDB sample database file on your hard drive.

Searching Recordsets

After you create a recordset — whether a whole table, or the part of a table specified by a SQL query — you sometimes need to search that recordset. You don't always display *every* record in a recordset.

To search a recordset, you use the Find and Seek commands. The Find commands work with ordinary recordsets generated by SQL queries, and the Seek command works with complete tables that have an index. (Put another way, you use Find with Dynasets and Snapshots, and you use Seek with tables.) See "Editing Records" later in this chapter for more information on Dynasets and Snapshots.

Seek is harder to program, but runs faster because it uses an index. In this section, I show you how to use the more common Find commands. If you're dealing with a program in which speed of searching is important, create a table-type recordset and investigate the Seek command.

You use a WHERE clause in a SQL statement along with the database Find command. (When you actually *create* a recordset with a SQL statement, you use both SELECT and WHERE clauses, and possibly other clauses.)

You may be thinking, "If I *create* a recordset with a SQL statement, why do I then need to use a second SQL statement with the Find command?" Good question.

Even though your original SQL statement narrows the field (by creating a recordset that includes only some of the records in a table), a user may want to see a subset of that recordset. (A subset of the subset, to be accurate.)

For example, assume you've created a recordset of books whose titles include the word *data*. However, your application provides a TextBox with which users can further limit the number of displayed records. If they type in *Jet* and click a CommandButton labeled Find, you then display only those titles that include the words *data* and *Jet*.

The following example shows you how to use the Find command. Complete these steps:

1. **Choose File⇨New Project.**

   The New Project dialog box opens.

2. **Double-click the Standard EXE icon in the New Project dialog box.**

   The dialog box closes, and the Standard VB Form is displayed.

3. **Double-click the ListBox icon in the Toolbox.**

   VB adds a ListBox to Form1.

4. **Double-click the TextBox icon in the Toolbox.**

   VB adds a TextBox to Form1.

5. **Double-click the CommandButton icon in the Toolbox.**

   Form1 now includes a CommandButton.

6. **Choose Project⇨References.**

   The References dialog box opens.

7. **In the Available References listbox, locate Microsoft DAO 3.51 Object Library (you can use DAO 3.6 instead, if it appears in the list) and click its check box.**

   A check appears in the box. You may have different versions of DAO, depending on the software installed in your system.

8. **Click OK.**

   The References dialog box closes, and VB adds the DAO library to your project.

9. **Double-click Form1.**

   You see the VB code window.

10. **Move your cursor up (press and hold the up-arrow key) until you're at the very top of the code window, and then press the Enter key to create a blank line.**

    The listboxes at the top of the code window indicate that you're in the General Declarations section.

11. **Type this code into the General Declarations section of Form1:**

    ```
    Dim dbBiblio As Database
    Dim rsTitles As Recordset
    ```

Remember that by creating the database and recordset object variables in the General Declarations section, all the events, subroutines, and functions in Form1 can use these objects. This feature is important in this example because the CommandButton's Click event needs the recordset created in the Form_Load event.

12. **Type in the code shown here for both the Command1_Click and Form_Load events.**

Here's the complete source code for this example:

```
Dim dbBiblio As Database
Dim rsTitles As Recordset

Private Sub Command1_Click()
List1.Clear
SQLQuery = "Title LIKE '*" & Text1 & "*'"
rsTitles.FindFirst SQLQuery
If rsTitles.NoMatch = True Then Exit Sub
List1.AddItem rsTitles.Fields("Title")
Do Until rsTitles.NoMatch = True
    rsTitles.FindNext SQLQuery
    List1.AddItem rsTitles.Fields("Title")
Loop
End Sub

Private Sub Form_Load()
Set dbBiblio = opendatabase("C:\PROGRAM
        FILES\VB98\BIBLIO.MDB")
SQLQuery = "SELECT * FROM Titles WHERE Title LIKE
        '*data*'"
Set rsTitles = dbBiblio.OpenRecordset(SQLQuery)
Do Until rsTitles.EOF = True
    List1.AddItem rsTitles.Fields("Title") & " (" &
        rsTitles.Fields("[Year Published]") & ")"
    rsTitles.MoveNext
Loop
End Sub
```

In place of C:\PROGRAM FILES\VB98\BIBLIO.MDB in this example code, substitute the path leading to the BIBLIO.MDB sample database file on your hard drive.

The code you're interested in for this example takes place in the Command1_Click event. First, you clear the recordset from the listbox so you can display only a subset. Then, you define the SQL WHERE clause (without actually using the word WHERE). In this example, you add the contents of the TextBox to the query by using the & text concatenation operator. If you type the word *jet* into the TextBox, then click this CommandButton, this code translates from this line:

```
SQLQuery = "Title LIKE '*" & Text1 & "*'"
```

To this one:

```
SQLQuery = "Title LIKE '*jet*'"
```

When you're concatenating a SQL argument like this, remember to use single quotes inside. A VB text variable can have only one pair of double quotes, and they must be at the start and end only, as this example illustrates.

Following the creation of that SQLQuery, you use the FindFirst command to locate the first record that matches and then you test the recordset's NoMatch property. If NoMatch is set to True, no record was found that matched your query, so you exit this subroutine and do nothing further:

```
rsTitles.FindFirst SQLQuery
If rsTitles.NoMatch = True Then Exit Sub
```

If a match is found, add it (the current record's Title field) to the listbox:

```
List1.AddItem rsTitles.Fields("Title")
```

Then, loop through the rest of the recordset, using the FindNext command to locate any additional matches:

```
Do Until rsTitles.NoMatch = True
    rsTitles.FindNext SQLQuery
    List1.AddItem rsTitles.Fields("Title")
Loop
```

Notice that you want to use the FindFirst command before you start looping with the FindNext command. FindFirst resets the pointer to the beginning of the recordset, so using FindFirst ensures that you start from the start and indeed locate all matches.

In addition to the FindFirst and FindNext commands illustrated in this example, VB also has FindPrevious and FindLast commands.

13. Press F5 and type the word Jet **into the TextBox. Click the CommandButton.**

You see only those records that contain the word *Jet* in the title, as shown in Figure 14-4.

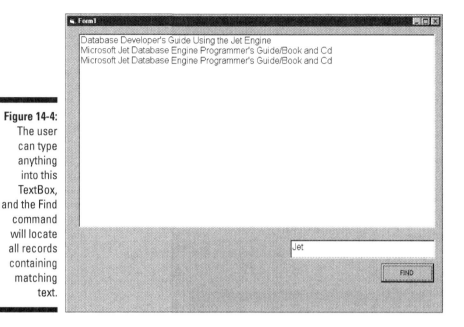

Figure 14-4:
The user
can type
anything
into this
TextBox,
and the Find
command
will locate
all records
containing
matching
text.

Marking Your Place with a Bookmark

If you've tried some of the examples in this chapter, you may be wondering how to mark a particular record so you can return to it later. You can remember a location within the recordset by putting that location into a *bookmark*.

For example, assume you're displaying the total number of records to the user. To use the RecordCount feature properly, you must first use the MoveLast command. However, you may want the currently displayed record to remain stable — not to suddenly display the last record simply because you must use MoveLast to count the records. The solution is to bookmark the current record, move to the last record, check the RecordCount, and then return to the bookmarked record.

You can save as many bookmarks as you want; just save each one in a different string variable.

To see how to use the bookmark feature, follow these steps:

1. **Choose File⇨New Project.**

   The New Project dialog box appears.

2. **Double-click the Standard EXE icon in the New Project dialog box.**

The dialog box closes, and you see the Standard VB form.

3. **Double-click the TextBox icon in the Toolbox.**

VB adds a TextBox to Form1.

4. **Add four CommandButtons to Form1.**

5. **In the Properties window, change each CommandButton's Caption property, according to the following list:**

   - Command1.Caption = Save Bookmark

   - Command2.Caption = Return to Bookmark

   - Command3.Caption = Previous

   - Command4.Caption = Next

The project should look something like Figure 14-5.

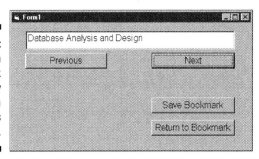

Figure 14-5:
You can bookmark as many records in a recordset as you want.

6. **Choose Project⇨References.**

The References dialog box opens.

7. **In the Available References listbox, locate Microsoft DAO 3.51 Object Library (you can use DAO 3.6 instead, if it appears in the list) and click its check box.**

A check appears in the box.

8. **Click OK.**

The References dialog box closes, and VB adds the DAO library to your project.

9. **Double-click Form1.**

You see the VB code window.

10. **Type this code into the code window, placing those three Dim commands at the top in the General Declarations section of the code window:**

```
Dim dbBiblio As Database
Dim rsTitles As Recordset
Dim rsBookmark As String

Private Sub Command3_Click()
If rsTitles.BOF = True Then Exit Sub
rsTitles.MovePrevious
If rsTitles.BOF = True Then Exit Sub
Text1 = rsTitles.Fields("Title")
End Sub

Private Sub Command4_Click()
If rsTitles.EOF = True Then Exit Sub
rsTitles.MoveNext
If rsTitles.EOF = True Then Exit Sub
Text1 = rsTitles.Fields("Title")
End Sub

Private Sub Form_Load()
Set dbBiblio = opendatabase("C:\PROGRAM
        FILES\VB98\BIBLIO.MDB")
Set rsTitles = dbBiblio.OpenRecordset("Titles")
Text1 = rsTitles.Fields("Title")
End Sub

Private Sub Command1_Click()
rsBookmark = rsTitles.Bookmark
End Sub

Private Sub Command2_Click()
rsTitles.Bookmark = rsBookmark
Text1 = rsTitles.Fields("Title")
End Sub
```

In place of C:\PROGRAM FILES\VB98\BIBLIO.MDB in this code, substitute the path that leads to the BIBLIO.MDB sample database file on your hard drive.

If you're using a different database from the BIBLIO.MDB database I'm using in this example, change C:\PROGRAM FILES\VB98\BIBLIO.MDB to the path that points to your database. Also, change Titles to the name of a table in your database, and change Title to the name of a field in that table.

As this example's code demonstrates, you set a bookmark by assigning the recordset's Bookmark property to a string variable (rsBookmark = rsTitles.Bookmark). To return the recordset pointer to the book-marked record, you set the Bookmark property to the previously saved string variable, like this:

```
rsTitles.Bookmark = rsBookmark
```

If you plan to use the bookmark in more than one procedure, declare (Dim) the bookmark's string variable in the General Declarations section of your form (as in this example). If you declare it in one of the proce-dures, it works only in that procedure. Put another way, the scope of the variable will be *local* to that procedure.

11. **Press F5.**

The project runs. Click the Next button to move forward a few records; then click the Save Bookmark button. Click the Next button to move for-ward further, then click the Return to Bookmark button, and you're back to the record you bookmarked.

Editing Records

In previous sections in this chapter, I show you how to open a database and how to search for and display data. In some cases, however, you may want to permit a user to *change* data in a database — that is, to edit, add, or delete individual records.

You can work with three primary types of recordsets: Table, Dynaset, and Snapshot. You can optionally specify which kind you want to use when you use the OpenRecordset command. If you don't specify which type you want, you get the default recordset type — the Dynaset.

Each style of recordset specializes in a different kind of data manipulation:

- ✓ The fastest type, the Table-type recordset can read or write to a particu-lar table within a database. (You cannot use a SQL statement to open a Table recordset.)

- ✓ Offering greater flexibility, a Dynaset-type recordset can read or write to all (or just parts) of various tables, even from various databases. (A Dynaset is sometimes the product of a query across several tables, known as a *join*. You can find out much more about doing joins in Chapter 18.)

- ✓ A Snapshot-type recordset is like a Dynaset-type, but is read-only; no data can be edited, added, or deleted in the actual databases of which the snapshot is taken. Another distinction between Dynaset and

Snapshot is that a Snapshot is a view of the data as it existed when the query was executed. Its static nature means that updates that might have occurred in the background from other users will not be visible unless you refresh the Snapshot. Dynasets would actually reflect such background changes.

In most cases, you do just fine using the default Dynaset type. But if you want to use a different type of recordset, use this syntax:

```
Set recordsetname =
            databasename.OpenRecordset("tablename",dbOpenTable)
```

For example, to open the Titles table in the BIBLIO database, you could use this code:

```
Set rsTitles = dbBiblio.OpenRecordset("Titles",dbOpenTable)
```

Or, to open a Snapshot-type recordset:

```
Set recordsetname =
            databasename.OpenRecordset("tablename",dbOpenSnapshot)
```

For example, to open a snapshot of the Titles table in the BIBLIO database, you could use this code:

```
Set rsTitles =
            dbBiblio.OpenRecordset("Titles",dbOpenSnapshot)
```

Or, if you're using a SQL query variable, use this style of code:

```
Set rsTitles = dbBiblio.OpenRecordset(SQLQuery,dbOpenTable)
```

Editing an existing record

Editing data is a two-step process:

1. **Execute the recordset's Edit method and then assign values to the current record's fields.**

2. **When you're sure you want to commit (save) the replacement record to the database on the hard drive, execute the recordset's Update method.**

To see how to edit and update an existing record, follow these steps:

1. **Follow Steps 1 through 8 in the section "Marking Your Place with a Bookmark," earlier in this chapter.**

2. **Change the Caption properties of two of the CommandButtons, assigning the following captions:**

   - Command1.Caption = Edit
   - Command2.Caption = Update

3. **Double-click Form1.**

   You see the VB code window.

4. **Type the following code into the code window, placing those two Dim commands at the top in the General Declarations section of the code window.**

   This code is identical to the previous example, with the exception of a missing Dim command at the top and new code located in the Command1 and Command2 Click events (highlighted in boldface in the following code):

```
Dim dbBiblio As Database
Dim rsTitles As Recordset

Private Sub Command3_Click()
If rsTitles.BOF = True Then Exit Sub
rsTitles.MovePrevious
If rsTitles.BOF = True Then Exit Sub
Text1 = rsTitles.Fields("Title")
End Sub

Private Sub Command4_Click()
If rsTitles.EOF = True Then Exit Sub
rsTitles.MoveNext
If rsTitles.EOF = True Then Exit Sub
Text1 = rsTitles.Fields("Title")
End Sub

Private Sub Form_Load()
Set dbBiblio = opendatabase("C:\PROGRAM
        FILES\VB98\BIBLIO.MDB")
Set rsTitles = dbBiblio.OpenRecordset("Titles")
Text1 = rsTitles.Fields("Title")
End Sub

Private Sub Command1_Click()
rsTitles.Edit
rsTitles.Fields("Title") = Text1
End Sub

Private Sub Command2_Click()
rsTitles.Update
MsgBox "The change has been made."
End Sub
```

Note that if users click the Edit button twice in a row without clicking Update an error will occur. You should trap this error and tell the users that they must first click the Update button to save the current record before clicking the Edit button.

If you're using a different database from the BIBLIO.MDB database I'm using in this example, change C:\PROGRAM FILES\VB98\BIBLIO.MDB to the path that points to your database. Also, change TITLES to the name of a table in your database, and change TITLE to the name of a field in that table.

5. **Press F5.**

   The program runs.

6. **When the first record appears in the TextBox, change it by typing in some new data.**

7. **Click the Edit button.**

   The Edit command is executed, which makes it possible to change this field in the recordset. The field is then changed in the recordset by assigning the contents of Text1 to rsTitles.Fields("Title").

8. **Click the Update button.**

   The changed record is now stored in the database on the hard drive.

9. **Choose Run⇨End in VB.**

   The program stops running.

10. **Press F5.**

    The program runs, and the first record appears, modified as you had changed it in Step 6. In this way, you confirm that you did, in fact, modify the database and not just the recordset.

A recordset exists only while your application runs or until you close the recordset (Recordsetname.Close) and then set its object variable to Nothing (rsTitles = Nothing). In either case, the recordset disappears, and no changes are saved to the database unless you have successfully executed the Edit, followed by the Update methods.

You have two ways to reference a field in a recordset, as shown in the following examples:

```
✔ rsTitles.Fields("Title") = Text1
✔ rsTitles!Title = Text1
```

This second version takes advantage of the fact that the Fields "collection" is the default for a recordset, so you can just omit it. The ! (called a *bang*) is an alternative punctuation.

Adding new records

Permitting users to add new records isn't always easy. It *can* be easy, if you're dealing with an extremely simple database — no relationships, no shared indexes, no required fields. But you don't find many databases like that.

Adding a new record to a database involves two fundamental steps:

1. **Execute the AddNew method, which creates a new but empty record (located at the "end" of the recordset).**

2. **Assign a value (some text, a number) to a field or fields in this new record and execute the Update method to commit this new record into the database.**

In the following example, you see several error messages you can get if you try to add new records without covering all the bases. (You can fill in all the fields for a new record in a table and *still* get an error message saying that a particular field cannot be *Null,* or empty.) And, of course, in addition to seeing all these possible error messages, you see the solutions.

To see how to add a new record to a database, follow these steps:

1. **Follow Steps 1–8 in the section "Marking Your Place with a Bookmark," earlier in this chapter.**

2. **Change the Caption properties of two of the CommandButtons, assigning the following captions:**

    • Command1.Caption = Add New Record

    • Command2.Caption = Update

3. **Double-click Form1.**

    You see the VB code window.

4. **Type this code into the code window, placing those two Dim commands at the top of the General Declarations section in the code window:**

    ```
    Dim dbBiblio As Database
    Dim rsTitles As Recordset

    Private Sub Command3_Click()
    If rsTitles.BOF = True Then Exit Sub
    rsTitles.MovePrevious
    If rsTitles.BOF = True Then Exit Sub
    Text1 = rsTitles.Fields("Title")
    End Sub
    ```

```
Private Sub Command4_Click()
If rsTitles.EOF = True Then Exit Sub
rsTitles.MoveNext
If rsTitles.EOF = True Then Exit Sub
Text1 = rsTitles.Fields("Title")
End Sub

Private Sub Form_Load()
Set dbBiblio = opendatabase("C:\PROGRAM
        FILES\VB98\BIBLIO.MDB")

SQLQuery = "SELECT * FROM Titles WHERE Title LIKE '*Zen*'
        ORDER BY Title"

Set rsTitles = dbBiblio.OpenRecordset(SQLQuery)
Text1 = rsTitles.Fields("Title")
End Sub

Private Sub Command1_Click()
rsTitles.AddNew
Text1 = ""
MsgBox "Please type in the new record, then click the
        Update button"
End Sub

Private Sub Command2_Click()
rsTitles.Update
MsgBox "The new record has been added to the " &
        dbBiblio.Name & " database."
End Sub
```

In this example, I use boldface text to highlight the lines of code of special interest.

For the purposes of this example, you want to have a small recordset. That way, you can see if your new record was added to the recordset without having to navigate through hundreds of records. Therefore, you create a recordset based on the criterion *Zen*, which limits the record-set to only those books with *Zen* in their titles.

In place of C:\PROGRAM FILES\VB98\BIBLIO.MDB in this code, substitute the path that leads to the BIBLIO.MDB sample database file on your hard drive.

5. **Press F5.**

6. **Click the Add New Record button.**

   A message box that you created in code tells you to type in the new record and then press the Update button.

7. **Type this title into the TextBox:** *The Zen of VB.*

   You want to use the word *Zen* in your new title so it will appear in the recordset the next time you run this program.

8. **Click the Update button.**

   Whoops! You see the error message shown in Figure 14-6.

Figure 14-6:
This error tells you that you must also fill in the PubID field in this table (it can't be *Null,* or empty).

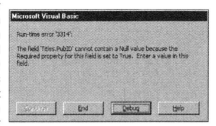

The cure is to make sure that you fill in the PubID field in this new record.

9. **Click Debug. To fix this, and other errors the code in Step 4 causes, you should replace the entire source code with this code:**

```
Dim dbBiblio As Database
Dim rsTitles As Recordset
Dim rsPublishers As Recordset

Private Sub Command3_Click()
If rsTitles.BOF = True Then Exit Sub
rsTitles.MovePrevious
If rsTitles.BOF = True Then Exit Sub
Text1 = rsTitles.Fields("Title")
Text2 = rsTitles.Fields("ISBN")
End Sub

Private Sub Command4_Click()
If rsTitles.EOF = True Then Exit Sub
rsTitles.MoveNext
If rsTitles.EOF = True Then Exit Sub
Text1 = rsTitles.Fields("Title")
Text2 = rsTitles.Fields("ISBN")
End Sub
```

```
Private Sub Form_Load()
Set dbBiblio = OpenDatabase("C:\PROGRAM
        FILES\VB98\BIBLIO.MDB")
SQLQuery = "SELECT * FROM Titles WHERE Title LIKE '*Zen*'
        ORDER BY Title"
Set rsTitles = dbBiblio.OpenRecordset(SQLQuery)
SQLQuery = "SELECT * FROM Publishers ORDER BY PubID"
Set rsPublishers = dbBiblio.OpenRecordset(SQLQuery)
Text1 = rsTitles.Fields("Title")
Text2 = rsTitles.Fields("ISBN")
End Sub


Private Sub Command1_Click()
Text1 = ""
Text2 = ""
Label3 = "Please type in the new record, then click the
        Update button"
End Sub


Private Sub Command2_Click()
On Error GoTo ErrorHandler
Dim n As Long
rsPublishers.MoveLast
n = rsPublishers.Fields("PubID")
n = n + 1
rsPublishers.AddNew
rsPublishers.Fields("PubID") = n 'a required field
rsPublishers.Update
Label3 = "A publisher's ID (PubID) field has been
        generated: " & n

With rsTitles
    .AddNew
    !Title = Text1
    !ISBN = Text2 'a required field (and must be unique)
    !PubID = n
    .Update
End With

MsgBox "Your new record has been added to the " &
        dbBiblio.Name & " database."
Exit Sub
ErrorHandler:
If Err Then MsgBox Error(Err)
End Sub
```

In place of C:\PROGRAM FILES\VB98\BIBLIO.MDB in this code, substitute the path that leads to the BIBLIO.MDB sample database file on your hard drive.

To accommodate this source code, add a second TextBox, named Text2, to hold the ISBN number (a required field). Also, add three Labels: Labels 1 and 2 identify TextBoxes 1 and 2, and Label 3 sits below them to display messages to the user. The final setup should look like Figure 14-7.

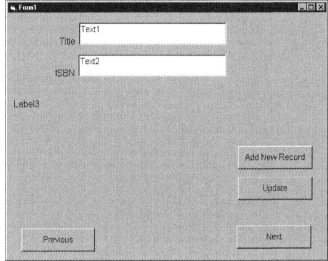

Figure 14-7:
The completed Add New Record user interface.

Notice that this new code defines a second recordset to hold the Publishers table (Dim rsPublishers As Recordset). You need to define this second recordset because adding a new record to the Titles table also requires adding a new record to the Publishers table.

The PubID field (a primary index) links both recordsets. This index consists of sequential numbers from 0 on up — each new record added to this database needs to have a unique PubID, one higher than the highest previous PubID. So you must calculate the PubID in your code by moving to the last (highest) record in the Publishers table and then adding one to that record's PubID:

```
Dim n As Long
rsPublishers.MoveLast
n = rsPublishers.Fields("PubID")
n = n + 1

rsPublishers.AddNew
rsPublishers.Fields("PubID") = n 'a required field

rsPublishers.Update
```

This code generates a unique PubID, adds a new record to the Publishers table, fills in that necessary PubID field, and updates (saves) the Publishers table. This step enables you to add a new record and update it to the Titles table.

Creating a unique ID field is usually accomplished by using an identity column or AutoNumber field. The code in the preceding example isn't very efficient in larger scale scenarios. To see how to use AutoNumber fields, see Chapter 2.

Notice the alternative syntax you can use, employing the With...End With structure:

```
With rsTitles
    .AddNew
    !Title = Text1
    !ISBN = Text2 'a required field (and must be unique)
    !PubID = n
    .Update
End With
```

This way, you don't have to keep typing in **rsTitles** on each line. And you also get to use the always exciting bang (!) symbol.

A period separates a method (like AddNew and Update) from the object, hence:

```
.Update
```

A bang symbol can separate a property from its object. Here are equivalent lines to a couple of the lines in the preceding code:

```
rsTitles.AddNew
rsTitles.Fields("ISBN") = Text2
```

10. **Press F5.**

   The new, revised program runs. You see the first title in the database that contains the word Zen.

11. **Click the Add New Record button.**

   A message tells you to type in the new record.

12. **Type in a title such as** *The Zen Master* **and an ISBN number like 5252252232 (it can be pretty much any number).**

13. **Click the Update button.**

   Label3 shows you the new (program-generated) PubID serial number assigned to this record, and a message box tells you that the record has been successfully added to the database.

14. **Click OK.**

   The message box closes.

15. **Choose Run⇨End.**

The program stops running.

Handling common errors when adding a new record

In the following sections, I explain some of the error messages you may see if you fail to provide all the necessary fields when adding a new record.

Failing to add a required record to a related table

Sometimes, you add what seems to be a complete record (all its fields are filled with data, for instance), but you get a message that a *related* record is incomplete. For example, if you fail to add a new record (with the PubID filled in) to the Publishers table, you get the error message shown in Figure 14-8.

Figure 14-8:
This database includes a table, other than the one you're updating, that contains a related — and required — field.

This code solves the problem shown in Figure 14-8:

```
rsPublishers.AddNew
rsPublishers.Fields("PubID") = n 'a required field
rsPublishers.Update
```

Failing to add data to an index or key field in the same table

If you don't provide new data (the field remains *Null*, or empty) for a field in the table that's used as a primary key or an index, you get the error message shown in Figure 14-9.

Figure 14-9:
All primary
key and
index fields
must con-
tain data, or
the Update
command
fails and you
see this
message.

This code solves the problem shown in Figure 14-9:

```
!ISBN = Text2 'a required field (and must be unique)
```

You must assign a value to the ISBN field in this table. That field must contain data, and data that is not repeated in any other record.

Entering a duplicate value in a field requiring a unique value for each record

In the example I describe in previous sections, both the PubID and ISBN fields must contain a unique value (contents) for each record in the database you're using. If you provide a duplicate ISBN for your new record, for example, you get the error message shown in Figure 14-10.

Figure 14-10:
This helpful
message
warns you
that you
can't enter a
duplicate
value in a
field that
prohibits
them.

You can solve this problem by searching a recordset (with the Find command) to see if the ISBN number the user entered duplicates one already in the records. Because your recordset in this example is limited to records with titles that contain the word *Zen*, you would have to open a different recordset containing the entire Titles table:

```
Dim rsCheckISBNs As Recordset
Set rsCheckISBNs = dbBiblio.OpenRecordset("Titles")
```

This example demonstrates that trapping this error when duplicates are found (error messages generated) is generally preferable, rather than slowing down every update to make sure no duplicates are introduced (by using validation techniques). Deciding whether to prevent errors or to take action when an error happens is always a matter or identifying which scenarios are more likely to occur. If you expect that a particular error will be quite rare, use error trapping rather than preemptively checking for potential errors during user-entry. If an error will likely be common, simply prevent it by using safety code like the programming demonstrated here.

If you run into any of the preceding error messages (or similar ones) when trying to add a new record, you can use the VisData utility that comes with VB 6 to track down the problem. Choose <u>A</u>dd-Ins➪<u>V</u>isual Data Manager (VisData). Then, in VisData, choose <u>F</u>ile➪<u>O</u>pen Database➪<u>M</u>icrosoft Access, and locate the database on the hard drive. Use the Database Window to click the small + symbols next to the tables and fields. You can double-click any field's name to display all the properties of that field, including whether the Required property is set to True or False. You can also see each table's index(es).

Removing Records

Fortunately, removing records from a database is usually a simple matter — much simpler than adding a new record. You use the Edit method to make the current record susceptible to change (including being removed from the database) and then you remove it with the Delete method. The Update method makes the deletion official by deleting the record from the disk file, but ending your application also forces an update without your having to put the command explicitly in your programming.

The following example shows you how to delete records. Follow these steps:

1. **Choose <u>F</u>ile➪<u>N</u>ew Project.**

   The New Project dialog box appears.

2. **Double-click the Standard EXE icon in the New Project dialog box.**

   The dialog box closes, and the Standard VB Form is displayed.

3. **Double-click the TextBox icon in the Toolbox.**

   VB adds a TextBox to Form1.

4. **Add three CommandButtons to Form1.**

5. **In the Properties window, change each CommandButton's Caption property, according to the following list:**

   - Command1.Caption = Delete

   - Command2.Caption = Next

   - Command3.Caption = Previous

6. **Choose Project⇨References.**

   The References dialog box opens.

7. **In the Available References listbox, locate Microsoft DAO 3.51 Object Library (or use DAO 3.6 if it appears in the list) and click its check box.**

   A check appears in the box.

8. **Click OK.**

   The References dialog box closes and VB adds the DAO library to your project.

9. **Double-click Form1.**

   You see the VB code window.

10. **Type this code into the code window, placing those two Dim commands at the top of the General Declarations section in the code window:**

```
Dim dbBiblio As Database
Dim rsTitles As Recordset

Private Sub Command3_Click()
If rsTitles.BOF = True Then Exit Sub
rsTitles.MovePrevious
If rsTitles.BOF = True Then Exit Sub
Text1 = rsTitles.Fields("Title")
End Sub

Private Sub Command2_Click()
If rsTitles.EOF = True Then Exit Sub
rsTitles.MoveNext
If rsTitles.EOF = True Then Exit Sub
Text1 = rsTitles.Fields("Title")
End Sub

 Private Sub Form_Load()
Set dbBiblio = OpenDatabase("C:\program
        files\vb98\biblio.mdb")
SQLQuery = "SELECT * FROM Titles WHERE Title LIKE '*Zen*'
        ORDER BY Title"
```

(continued)

(continued)

```
Set rsTitles = dbBiblio.OpenRecordset(SQLQuery)
Text1 = rsTitles.Fields("Title")
End Sub

Private Sub Command1_Click()
rsTitles.Edit
rsTitles.Delete
If rsTitles.EOF = True Then Exit Sub
rsTitles.MoveNext
Text1 = rsTitles!Title
End Sub
```

In place of `C:\PROGRAM FILES\VB98\BIBLIO.MDB` in this code, substitute the path leading to the BIBLIO.MDB sample database file on your hard drive. Also, if you're not following my example and using BIBLIO.MDB, change `Titles` to the name of a table in your database, and change `Title` and `Year Published` to the names of fields in your database.

11. **Change the Caption property of Command1 (in the Properties window) to** Delete.

12. **Press F5.**

   You see the first title in the database containing the word *Zen*.

13. **Click the Delete button.**

   The currently displayed record is deleted, and the MoveNext command moves you to the next record and displays its title.

Manipulating a Database's Structure

With programming, you can get into a database and find out what tables it has and what fields those tables contain. What's more, you can actually create new tables, fields, indexes, relationships, and stored queries — even create entire databases — just from code.

Creating a well-designed database using a tool like VisData (Add-Ins⇨ Visual Data Manager) or Microsoft Access is easier, of course. But in some cases, you may want to access or otherwise manipulate the structure of a database. If you want to know how, follow these steps:

1. **Choose File⇨New Project.**

   The New Project dialog box opens.

2. **Double-click the Standard EXE icon in the New Project dialog box.**

   The dialog box closes, and the Standard VB Form is displayed.

3. **Choose Project⇨References.**

The References dialog box opens.

4. **In the Available References listbox, locate Microsoft DAO 3.51 Object Library and click the box next to it (don't use DAO 3.60 for this example).**

A check appears in the box.

5. **Click OK.**

The References dialog box closes, and VB adds the DAO library to your project.

6. **Double-click Form1.**

You see the VB code window.

7. **Type this programming into the code window:**

```
Dim dbNewDB As Database
Dim tdNewTable As TableDef
Dim fld As Field
Private Sub Form_Load()

Set dbNewDB = CreateDatabase("C:\MyNewDB.mdb",
        dbLangGeneral)
Set tdNewTable = New TableDef

Set fld = tdNewTable.CreateField("Country", dbText, 75)
tdNewTable.Fields.Append fld

Set fld = tdNewTable.CreateField("ContactName", dbText,
        50)
tdNewTable.Fields.Append fld

Set fld = tdNewTable.CreateField("IndexNum", dbDouble)
tdNewTable.Fields.Append fld

tdNewTable.Name = "Overseas"
dbNewDB.TableDefs.Append tdNewTable

Set dbNewDB = Nothing

End Sub
```

In place of the database name (MyNewDB.mdb) and the various table and field names, feel free to substitute your own names.

The CreateDatabase method of the Database object enables you to bring a new database into existence, via programming, as this example illustrates. After you create a new (but structurally empty) database, you then define its structure by adding tables and fields. You add a table to your database with a TableDef object and then populate the table using a field object and the CreateField method, followed by the Append method to add each new field to the Fields collection of the table. After you add all the fields you want in a table, add the table to the database's TableDefs collection by using the TableDefs Append method.

8. **Press F5.**

Your program runs and a new database named MyNewDB is created.

9. **Choose Run➪End.**

The application stops running.

10. **Choose Add-Ins➪Visual Data Manager.**

The VisData utility runs.

11. **From the VisData menus, choose File➪Open Database➪Microsoft Access.**

A file-browser dialog box opens.

12. **Locate the new database you created — MyNewDB.MDB — on your hard drive and double-click its name in the file-browser dialog box.**

The browser dialog box closes, and your database is loaded into VisData, as shown in Figure 14-11.

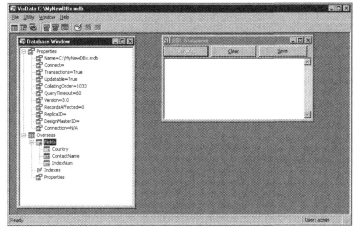

Figure 14-11:
Here's your brand-new, program-generated database, all ready to accept data.

You may have been using DAO 3.6 Library if you've been trying out some of the examples in this chapter, and version 3.6 is available to you. That's just fine, but if you try to use DAO 3.6 Library in this example, you get an unrecognized database format error when loading the example into VisData. VisData doesn't know how to handle DAO 3.6. So repeat Step 4 in this procedure, deselecting the Microsoft DAO 3.6 Object Library and instead selecting the Microsoft DAO 3.51 Object Library.

Chapter 15

Acronym Soup: ADO, DAO, RDO, UDA

*C*hapter 14 describes DAO (Data Access Objects), and Chapter 16 examines ADO (ActiveX Data Objects). In this chapter, you find a bridge — an explanation of what these terms mean, how they're connected, and what happened to RDO (Remote Data Objects) in the shuffle. Oh yes, I also describe UDA (Universal Data Access) — the buried treasure toward which all the other roads — DAO, ADO, RDO — supposedly lead.

But don't run for the exits, just because the subject of database programming is scattered with acronyms. Understanding these acronyms is important. They represent the yesterday, today, and tomorrow of database management — if Microsoft has anything to say about it. And in all likelihood, for the foreseeable future, Microsoft *will* have something to say about it.

Getting a Handle on Database Technologies

Hundreds of ways exist for storing data in databases. Most useful computer applications store data, but they often do it in peculiar, proprietary ways. Can you use Access — Microsoft's popular database application — to search the e-mail messages in your Outlook Express Inbox? Nope.

But you *should* be able to search those messages. You should be able to add some of those messages to your company's customer-service database if you want, for example. You should be able to store or copy e-mail anywhere, but you can't. Access saves data in files with an .MDB extension; the latest version of Outlook Express stores e-mail in files with an .MBX extension. And the twain do not meet.

And how about simple, plain .TXT files produced by Notepad or other simple, but often quite useful, text editors? Why can't a database application retrieve data from these kinds of files? Or from any and all kinds of files?

Various current trends hamper data universality, not least of which is the increasing importance of distributed computing and client/server computing. A primary trend today involves working harmoniously with applications and data spread across two or more machines. (In other words, the Internet and intranets divide data from the database application — and cause other divisions.)

Increasingly, businesspeople are realizing that lots of important information remains unused or unintegrated because it's not in the "proper" format. Companies set up on the Internet and ask for feedback on their products. More and more, that feedback comes in the form of e-mail. How many companies can make wide use of the information in that e-mail? Can they sort it, search it, and otherwise exploit it in an organized fashion? In other words, can they manage the data and store it for efficient integration into other data? Very few companies can do so. And even fewer can make efficient use of HTML-based data such as the Web-based catalogs of their competitors.

Considering the twilight of the RDO technology

You may want to know something about Remote Data Objects (RDO), even though it's being replaced by the newer ADO technology. RDO was designed to handle data management for large or complex installations — SQLServer, Oracle, and the like.

Unlike DAO, RDO doesn't work well with data in Jet (VB and Access) databases. However, RDO offers an object model that opens the innards of nearly all low-level behaviors of ODBC. For this reason, developers have used it when they needed to deal with sophisticated queries and highly complex stored procedures. Technically, RDO is a COM wrapper around the ODBC API. *Low-level behaviors* refer to the individual steps necessary to accomplish a larger job. For instance, when you use a *high-level* language, you can simply request that a recordset be closed by issuing a single command: `recordsetname.Close`. On the low level, though, many individual steps are taken to accomplish this job. It's similar to the captain of a ship crying out "full steam ahead," but down in the engine room they're running around doing all kinds of things to make this command actually work.

Think of RDO as the traditional workhorse for client/server database programming (VB 5 and VB 6 have virtually identical implementations of RDO). And think of DAO as the workhorse for desktop database programming for smaller-scale situations.

RDO first appeared in VB 4 and grew to be the most useful way for VB programmers to deal with client/server database programming. RDO's properties and methods are quite similar in most respects to those of DAO, so if you've worked with the DAO object model, you have little trouble using the RDO object model.

As you can see in the following example, the RemoteData control works very much like its cousins — the ADO and DAO Data Controls. In this example, you don't connect to a database on a server. You simulate it by using an ODBC data source.

To complete this example, you need to have an ODBC connection defined. To create the ODBC connection that you use in the following example, complete the example I describe in the section "Creating an ODBC file data source," in Chapter 5.

To see what RDO looks like, follow these steps:

1. **Choose File➪New Project.**

   The New Project dialog box opens.

2. **Double-click the Standard EXE icon in the New Project dialog box.**

   The dialog box closes, and the Standard VB Form is displayed.

3. **Press Ctrl+T.**

   The Components dialog box opens.

4. **Locate Microsoft RemoteData Control 6.0 and click its check box.**

5. **Click OK.**

The dialog box closes, and VB adds the RemoteData control (MSRDC) to your Toolbox.

6. **Double-click the MSRDC icon in the Toolbox.**

VB adds a RemoteData control to your project.

7. **In the Properties window, double-click the (Custom) property.**

You see the Property Pages dialog box for the RemoteData control, as shown in Figure 15-1.

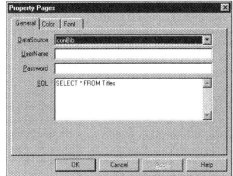

Figure 15-1:
The
Property
Pages for an
RDO data
control.

8. **Click the down-arrow symbol to the right of the DataSource listbox.**

The listbox drops down and displays ODBC connections you've previously defined.

9. **Select the connection you want to use.**

For this example, use the conBib connection, which I show you how to create in Chapter 5. If you don't see this connection, follow the steps in Chapter 5 in the section "Creating an ODBC file data source."

You need to define a SQL statement that brings in (from the data source) whatever data you want to use.

10. **In the SQL text box, type in** SELECT * FROM Titles, **as shown in Figure 15-1.**

11. **Click OK.**

The dialog box closes. You've connected your RDO data control to the Biblio database (via the conBib connection), and you've pointed to the Titles table in that database (via the SQL statement you entered in Step 10).

12. **Double-click the TextBox icon on the Toolbox.**

VB adds a TextBox to your project.

13. **In the Properties window for TextBox1, click the DataSource property.**

14. **Click the down-arrow icon next to this property's text box in the Properties window.**

    You see MSRDC1 (the RDO RemoteData control) listed as an available data source.

15. **Select MSRDC1.**

    The drop-down list closes, and MSRDC1 becomes the DataSource property for this TextBox.

16. **In the Properties window for TextBox1, click the DataField property.**

17. **Click the down-arrow icon next to this property's text box in the Properties window.**

    You see a list of all the tables in the Biblio database (Title, Year Published, ISBN, and the five other tables).

18. **Click Title in the drop-down list.**

    The drop-down list closes, and Title becomes the DataField property for this TextBox.

19. **Press F5.**

    Your project runs and it makes the RDO connection. The TextBox displays data from the database, as shown in Figure 15-2.

Figure 15-2:
Your
RemoteData
control dis-
plays data
from a data-
base.

Understanding Open Database Connectivity (ODBC)

You should understand the meaning of the still widely used Microsoft database standard, ODBC (Open Database Connectivity). ODBC takes on the burden of translating databases into formats that database applications can understand. Simply put, ODBC sits on your machine or a user's computer (the client) and translates any remote (server) relational database into data packages that your client application can handle. On a fundamental level, your application can use SQL to query (or modify) the data held in a remote database without worrying about the details of the remote database's methods for storing that data.

The same ODBC technology that supports RDO also supports ADO, so you don't need to modify databases used with RDO when you move to the new ADO technology. You do need, however, an OLE DB provider for ODBC (included with ADO) to use ODBC drivers in ADO.

One useful feature of ODBC is that you can specify ODBC *connections* (technically, they're called *Data Source Names,* or *DSN*) and give them names. Then the next time you want to connect to that database, you already have all the necessary information (password, log-on information, type of database, and so on) filled in and you can use the DSN itself. (Chapter 5 describes the process for creating an ODBC DSN. See the section "Creating an ODBC file data source.")

However, like many other acronyms you've gotten used to over the years, ODBC is now in the twilight of its useful life. Microsoft has announced its successor: OLE DB. ODBC enables you to get relational data into a client computer. OLE DB enables you to get *any* data source's data into a client computer. At least, that's the promise. You use ADO as the programmer's gateway to OLE DB.

Currently, in VB 6, OLE DB has facilities that enable you to access Jet (VB and Access-style databases, with .MDB extensions), SQLServer, and Oracle. However, the data sources that OLE DB can work with cover the waterfront, including structured, semistructured, and unstructured data; relational and nonrelational data; SQL-based and non-SQL data. Examples include desktop databases, flat-files, mail stores, directory services, personal information managers (PIMs), multidimensional stores, and even those elusive OLAP cubes (don't ask).

Working with Data Access Objects (DAO)

No database technology can currently compare to the popularity of DAO, Data Access Objects. DAO is robust, well-tested, and used by most database programmers today. They understand its object-model (all those collections and their methods and properties), which I describe in Chapter 14.

Recognizing DAO's weaknesses

DAO has several weaknesses, and that's why it's being superceded. DAO is best at desktop (rather than client/server, Internet, or intranet) database management. It doesn't like old database formats (yet lots of businesses have stuff stored in legacy formats), and it doesn't like new data formats: HTML,

DHTML, e-mail, plain text, and various oddities. It wants relational data — data organized into tables, fields, indices, and relations. You can't blame DAO for these things — it was never designed to do anything other than what it does, and does splendidly. Nevertheless, the time has come to phase DAO out and raise the curtain on the next star of the database world.

The solution: UDA

What solution does Microsoft propose for addressing DAO's shortcomings? UDA — Universal Data Access. This plan doesn't require that you massage data. You don't have to pour an e-mail .DBX file, a bunch of old .DBF dBase files, and a Notepad .TXT file through filters until they end up in an .MDB file. Tools that support the UDA strategy are designed to extract data from its current format, interpret it, and let you, the programmer, work with it without worrying about its native format. Doesn't matter whether you have .TXT, .MDB, or .DBF files — forgetaboutit.

Technically, UDA isn't an actual product you can buy. Instead, it's the name of Microsoft's strategy for accessing data, wherever that data lies. UDA is the strategy; the set of tools that implements that strategy is called MDAC (Microsoft Data Access Components). The technologies that collectively constitute MDAC are ADO and OLE DB (the flagships), but still included are DAO, RDO, and ODBC.

Now, you may be asking, "Isn't this the same promise that we've been offered before?" What about all the previous attempts to resolve the Babylon problem, such as the Symphony application suite (why can't we all work together in harmony?) offered up in the mid-80s as the solution to the confusion of file types and data storage schemes?

Sure, for nearly two decades now, developers have been playing the universal data access tune. XML is another recent attempt to offer everything to everybody in the Web-development crowd.

So, do I believe that UDA is a step in the right direction? Yes.

And to move toward UDA, you must discover ADO. You may not want to rewrite your existing database applications (or even create new ones) in ADO just yet. For one thing, DAO and RDO are proven, well-established technologies. They work, and work well. For another thing, ADO isn't finished yet in its VB6 version. It doesn't yet support DDL (data definition language). The latest version of ADO, 2.1, ships with Microsoft Office 2000 and Internet Explorer 5. It will include all the features of ADO 2.0, as well as support for DDL.

You should know how to program ADO. In all likelihood, it will become the technology of choice for database programming during the next year and beyond.

Understanding ADO

With ADO, ActiveX Data Objects, you can use Microsoft's new Universal Data Access strategy. ADO does what DAO and RDO could do, but it sometimes simplifies the job of programming — and ADO adds new capabilities of its own.

Consider just a couple of intriguing features of ADO: building recordsets from scratch (*without* any database connection) and disconnecting recordsets from the server. When disconnected, they continue to work fine in your workstation computer. Just like a worm chopped in half, they behave normally. And later, you can rejoin these recordsets to their database. Obviously, this can greatly improve the scalability of an application because lots of people aren't jamming the traffic on the server. Instead they are all working independently with their disconnected recordsets.

In addition to other features, if you know how to use ADO, you can use it to get virtually *any kind of data*: HTML, e-mail, plain text, as well as traditional relational data, and even legacy data sources.

ADO offers (or soon will offer) all the features of DAO and RDO, but it requires some changes in the programming (see Chapter 16 for migration tips and examples). For one thing, ADO is said to "flatten" the object model of DAO and RDO. *Flattening* means streamlining the model by reducing the number of objects, but increasing the number of properties and methods of the objects that remain. Flattening also generally lessens the emphasis on the object hierarchy. Put simply, you can create objects without having to create other, higher objects. You can create a recordset without first having to create a connection object for it. These, and other facets of ADO, are the subject of Chapter 16.

Chapter 16

Focus on ADO

* * *

In This Chapter

▶ Using an ADO Data Control

▶ Understanding ADO programming

▶ Using the ADO Find method

▶ Editing records the ADO way

▶ Viewing a database's organization with Schemas

▶ Understanding Cursors and LockTypes

▶ Working with disconnected recordsets

* * *

*I*n one sense, ADO is a little database-manipulation language nestled within the larger VB language. In another sense, however, ADO is more than a language. If you're interested in the technical details, ADO is a data-access library, part of the Microsoft Data Access Components, and one of the key mechanisms in Microsoft's Universal Data Access (UDA) strategy. ADO can be used by all the Microsoft Visual Studio applications, as well as any non-Microsoft development packages that support COM components and libraries.

But enough techie details. You could write a book about ADO, and someone surely will. This chapter doesn't pretend to tell you every last option and all the commands available to the ADO programmer. Instead, you experiment with the main points: opening a database, building a recordset, using SQL statements, editing records, and so on.

This chapter also explains the main ways that ADO differs from its parent database technology: DAO. That way, you can get an idea about how to translate existing DAO programming to ADO and how to create new programs in ADO based on your knowledge of DAO.

Dropping in a Data Control

To understand how to use ADO, you can either drop an ADO Data Control into a VB Form, or you can write ADO programming. In this chapter, I show you how to do both, starting with the easy way: dropping a control.

To see how to access a database using the ADO Data Control, follow these steps:

1. **Choose File⊅New Project.**

   The New Project dialog box opens.

2. **Double-click the Standard EXE icon in the New Project dialog box.**

   The dialog box closes, and the Standard VB Form is displayed.

3. **Choose Project⊅References.**

   The References dialog box opens.

4. **Click the check boxes next to both Microsoft ActiveX Data Objects Recordset 2.0 Library and Microsoft ActiveX Data Objects 2.0 Library (or use the 2.1 Library, if you have it).**

   Technically, you don't really need both of these libraries for this example, but no harm done if you add them both at this point. You need the Recordset Library if you intend to build recordsets from scratch or make extensive use of disconnected recordsets on a layer that doesn't communicate directly with the database. And if you're doing *those* things, you don't need the main ADO library (Microsoft ActiveX Data Objects 2.0). But why not put them all in when you're working with ADO? That way, you won't get mysterious error messages if a routine you need is missing.

5. **Click OK.**

   The dialog box closes, and VB adds these libraries to your project. By adding those libraries to your project, you can now write ADO programming code and VB will know what you mean by it.

6. **Press Ctrl+T.**

   The Components dialog box appears.

7. **Click the check box next to Microsoft ADO Data Control 6.0 (OLEDB).**

   The DAO Data Control is always on the VB Toolbox, but you must manually add the ADO Data Control to the Toolbox.

8. **Click OK.**

   The dialog box closes, and VB adds the ADO Data Control icon to your Toolbox.

9. **Double-click the ADO Data Control (Adodc) icon in the Toolbox.**

   VB adds an ADO Data Control to Form1.

10. **Double-click the Custom property in the Properties window.**

    The Property Pages dialog box opens.

11. **Click the option button next to Use ODBC Data Source Name.**

    I explain the Use Data Link File option in Chapter 5. Chapter 7 examines the other option, Use Connection String.

12. **In the listbox for the Use ODBC Data Source Name option, click the name of whatever DSN you want to use to connect your application to a database.**

    To follow along with the example I present in this section, click the DSN named *conBib*. If conBib isn't listed, create it by following the steps in Chapter 5, in the section titled "Creating an ODBC file data source." There are various ways to connect to a database; for this example, you can use an ODBC data source name (DSN).

13. **Click the RecordSource tab in the Property Pages dialog box.**

    On this tab, you specify the source of your records (a table, a stored procedure, and so on) within the database you specified in the preceding steps.

14. **In the Command Type listbox, select the type of recordsource you want to use.**

    To follow my example, choose 2 - adCmdTable.

15. **In the Table or Stored Procedure Name listbox, select the particular recordset or table you're interested in.**

    To follow my example, select the table named Titles.

16. **Click OK.**

    The dialog box closes.

17. **Double-click the TextBox icon on the Toolbar.**

    VB adds a TextBox to Form1.

18. **In the Properties window for Text1, click the arrow icon in the DataSource property.**

    A list of all available data sources drops down.

19. **Select Adodc1 (the ADO Data Control) from the list.**

20. **Double-click Text1's DataField property in the Properties window.**

    A list of the available fields appears. Select whatever field you want to display. To follow my example, select the field named Title. If you don't see that field, open the DataField list (by clicking the arrow next to its textbox) in the Properties window and click Title.

21. **Press F5.**

The project runs, and you can navigate through the data in the database by clicking the arrow icons in the ADO Data Control, as shown in Figure 16-1.

Figure 16-1:
The ADO
Data Control
in action.

Note that using an ADO Data Control in this example is similar to using an RDO Data Control (see Chapter 15) and functionally identical to using a DAO Data Control (the default data control that always appears in the VB 6 Toolbox). To decide whether you want to use a DAO or an ADO Data Control, see Chapter 15.

Programming ADO

Although using the ADO Data Control is quite similar to using RDO and DAO Data Controls, writing ADO programming involves numerous differences. The ADO object model (the objects available for your use) differs from the DAO object model. For one thing, ADO has no database object. So, you don't use this kind of programming to create a database object variable:

```
Dim dbBiblio As Database
```

You'll also find differences in the ADO programming commands. In particular, some of the methods used with DAO are no longer available in ADO. For example, instead of the DAO FindNext, FindPrevious, FindFirst, and FindLast methods, ADO folds them all into a single Find method. You use parameters to specify what you want from the Find method, as in this example:

```
ADOrecordset.Find SQLQuery, adSearchForward
```

The adSearchForward parameter is a built-in constant that represents the number 1. This parameter causes the Find method to conduct a forward search from the current record. Find, with adSearchForward, replaces the older DAO FindNext method. This collapse of four methods into one method (with parameters) is part of what's called *flattening* the object model.

The Seek method (not available in ADO Version 2.0, which shipped with Visual Basic 6) is now also available in ADO Version 2.1. You can download it by getting the latest Visual Basic Service Pack at msdn.microsoft.com/vstudio/sp/vbfixes.asp.

The transition from DAO to ADO isn't epic, so you don't have to be the King or Queen of Programmers. This chapter shows you the main points when making the transition.

Opening a database and a recordset using ADO

Because no database object exists in ADO, you open a database in ADO by using a *connection object*. And to get a recordset, you can use the Open method of the recordset object (alternative ways exist). For the most part, these differences amount to different names for the same old jobs, although these new names do reflect underlying differences in the structure of the ADO object model.

The primary difference is that DAO, like most object-oriented technologies, is very hierarchical. For example, in DAO, you can't obtain lower objects (like a recordset) before you create and initialize the higher objects (like the database that contains the data for that recordset). ADO isn't bound by those rules. You can create a recordset before even obtaining a connection. The same goes with fields and other objects.

Objects in ADO are, as they say, *loosely coupled,* and the object model is *flattened.* Sounds like a train wreck, doesn't it? But in practice, it can save both programming time (fewer lines need be written in some situations) and memory (fewer people need be taking up resources on a server).

To see one way to open a database in ADO and then extract a recordset, follow these steps:

1. **Choose File⇨New Project.**

   The New Project dialog box opens.

2. **Double-click the Standard EXE icon in the New Project dialog box.**

   The dialog box closes, and the Standard VB Form is displayed.

3. **Choose Project⇨References.**

   The References dialog box opens.

4. **Click the check box next to both Microsoft ActiveX Data Objects Recordset 2.0 Library and Microsoft ActiveX Data Objects 2.1 Library. (If you don't have the 2.1 version, you can use the Microsoft ActiveX Data Objects 2.0 or 2.5 Library — whatever version you have.)**

5. **Click OK.**

The dialog box closes, and VB adds these libraries to your project, which means that you can write ADO programming code and VB will know what you mean by it.

6. **Double-click Form1.**

You see the code window.

7. **Move your cursor to the very top of the code window and press Enter to create a blank line above the Sub Form_Load.**

The two list boxes at the top of the code window now say General Declarations. You use the General Declarations section for defining variables that you plan to use throughout a Form.

8. **Type this code into the General Declarations section of Form1:**

```
Dim cnBiblio As ADODB.connection
Dim rsTitles As ADODB.Recordset
Dim SQLQuery As String
```

With these declarations, you define three variables that you can use in the events (procedures) anywhere in Form1's code. They have Form-wide scope. The connection object variable holds the equivalent of the database object used in DAO. The Recordset variable holds a recordset object, similar to the DAO recordset. The SQLQuery holds a SQL statement. If you're following my example, this SQL query specifies that you want the recordset ordered alphabetically, based on the title of each book in the Titles table.

9. **In the Form_Load event, type this code (the boldface text simply highlights code that differs from the DAO version of this same programming):**

```
Private Sub Form_Load()
Set cnBiblio = New ADODB.connection
Set rsTitles = New ADODB.Recordset
cnBiblio.ConnectionString =
        "Provider=Microsoft.Jet.OLEDB.3.51; Data
        Source=C:\PROGRAM FILES\VB98\BIBLIO.MDB"
cnBiblio.open
SQLQuery = "SELECT * FROM Titles ORDER BY Title"
rsTitles.open SQLQuery, cnBiblio
MsgBox rsTitles!Title
End Sub
```

In place of C:\PROGRAM FILES\VB98\BIBLIO.MDB in this code, substitute the path that leads to the BIBLIO.MDB sample database file on your hard drive.

Looking at the highlighted code in this example, you see the following differences between this code and DAO programming:

- The ADO connection object replaces the DAO database object.

- The more flexible ADO ConnectionString property, in combination with the ADO connection object's Open method, replaces the DAO OpenDatabase command.

- The ADO recordset object's Open method replaces the DAO database object's OpenRecordset method.

As in DAO, you can access a field in a record by using syntax similar to either of these examples:

- `MsgBox rsTitles.Fields("Title")`

- `MsgBox rsTitles!Title`

If you want to open the entire Titles table and not use a SQL statement, use syntax like this example:

```
rsTitles.open "Titles", cnBiblio
```

You don't need to define the ConnectionString property separately from the Open command. As an alternative to the use of the ConnectionString in the preceding example, simply put the literal string on the same line as the Open command, like this:

```
cnBiblio.open "Provider=Microsoft.Jet.OLEDB.3.51;
        Data Source=C:\PROGRAM FILES\VB98\BIBLIO.MDB"
```

10. **Press F5.**

The database opens, the recordset is filled, and the message box displays the title located first in the alphabetically ordered Title field, as shown in Figure 16-2.

Figure 16-2:
ADO
works —
here's the
first record
in the
recordset.

With the change in terminology from the DAO *database* object to the ADO *connection* object, Microsoft reinforces the notion that ADO can get its data from sources other than the classic database. ADO is supposed to be able to read any data in its native format — such as the HTML of a Web page, or an e-mail file. However, this technology is in only limited use today. I'm unable to find any current examples of source code that demonstrate ADO extracting data from unusual sources such as HTML or the Outlook Express Inbox collection of messages. Undoubtedly, these sources will become accessible over time.

ADO includes a *command object*. You don't need to use the command object to access or manipulate data with ADO. As the previous example illustrates, you can use the connection and recordset objects instead. The command object is usually employed to execute stored or parameterized queries.

Experiencing flatness: Using the ADO Find method

The ADO version of the recordset Find method resembles the DAO version, but thanks to the "flattening" of the object model (rearranging how you write the code), you don't use several Find commands. Gone are DAO's FindFirst, FindNext, and the others. Instead, you use the single ADO Find method, but specify the type of search with *parameters*, such as Find adSearchForward.

Oddly, ADO doesn't flatten the set of methods most similar to DAO's FindNext, FindPrevious, FindFirst, and FindLast commands. ADO still uses MoveNext, MovePrevious, MoveFirst, and MoveLast.

Editing records

As you may recall, before you can use the Update method, DAO requires that you first use the Edit method. Thanks to another instance of the flattening effects that I mention in the preceding section, ADO doesn't need that extra step. Now, when you make a change to a record, ADO sensibly assumes that you are in fact attempting to edit that record. So, ADO doesn't use the Edit command — you just need the Update command to confirm that you want to save the edit.

However, be sure to check out the section "A Cursory Look at Cursors," later in this chapter. By default, when you open a recordset, you can't edit it. To edit records, you must specifically "unlock" the recordset when you open it by using a parameter such as adLockPessimistic or adLockOptimistic with the Open command. By default, the adLockReadOnly lock type is in effect when you open a recordset.

To see how to use the new ADO Find *parameter* programming style, follow these steps:

1. **Choose File⇨New Project.**

   The New Project dialog box opens.

2. **Double-click the Standard EXE icon in the New Project dialog box.**

   The dialog box closes, and the Standard VB Form is displayed.

3. **Add a ListBox, a TextBox, and a CommandButton to Form1.**

4. **Choose Project➪Refere<u>n</u>ces.**

   The References dialog box opens.

5. **Click the check boxes next to both Microsoft ActiveX Data Objects Recordset 2.0 Library and Microsoft ActiveX Data Objects 2.5 Library. (You can use Microsoft ActiveX Data Objects 2.0 Library if you don't have the 2.5 version. Use whatever version of these libraries that you have.)**

6. **Click OK.**

   The dialog box closes, and VB adds these ADO libraries to your project.

7. **Double-click Form1.**

   You see the VB code window.

8. **Move your cursor up (press and hold the up-arrow key) until you're at the very top of the code window, and then press the Enter key to create a blank line.**

   The listboxes at the top of the code window say `General Declarations`. Variables declared in this area of a code window have form-wide scope (they can be accessed from any procedure in the form).

9. **Type these two variable declarations into the General Declarations section of Form1:**

   ```
   Dim cnBiblio As ADODB.connection
   Dim rsTitles As ADODB.Recordset
   ```

   Or use different names for these two variables, if you want.

10. **In the Form_Load event, type this code:**

    ```
    Private Sub Form_Load()
    Set cnBiblio = New ADODB.connection
    Set rsTitles = New ADODB.Recordset
    cnBiblio.ConnectionString =
            "Provider=Microsoft.Jet.OLEDB.3.51; Data
            Source=C:\PROGRAM FILES\VB98\BIBLIO.MDB"
    cnBiblio.open
    SQLQuery = "SELECT * FROM Titles ORDER BY Title"
    rsTitles.open SQLQuery, cnBiblio
    End Sub
    ```

In place of `C:\PROGRAM FILES\VB98\BIBLIO.MDB` in this code, substitute the path that leads to the database you're interested in using. (To follow my example, use the BIBLIO.MDB sample database file on your hard drive.) If you're not following my example but instead are using a different database, change `Titles` to a table in your database, and change `Title` to a field in that table.

11. **Type this code in the Command1_Click event:**

```
Private Sub Command1_Click()
On Error Resume Next
List1.Clear
SQLQuery = "Title LIKE '*" & Text1 & "*'"
Do Until rsTitles.EOF = True
    rsTitles.Find SQLQuery, adSearchForward
    List1.AddItem rsTitles!Title
    rsTitles.MoveNext
Loop
End Sub
```

(If you're not following my example, change Title to a field you're using in your database, and use whatever variable name you're using instead of rsTitles.)

Note the difference between the Find command used in this ADO code and the DAO version. Here's the DAO version:

```
rsTitles.FindNext SQLQuery 'DAO
```

And here's the ADO version:

```
rsTitles.Find SQLQuery, adSearchForward 'ADO
```

Instead of FindNext, ADO uses adSearchForward to modify the behavior of its Find method.

12. **Press F5.**

The program runs.

13. **Type a word into the TextBox and click the CommandButton.**

The ListBox fills with all records containing the word you typed. If you're following my example, type the word *zen*, and you see all titles containing the word *zen*.

Avoiding the notorious "No current record" error

Sooner or later, the loop in the preceding code will trigger the notorious "No current record" error message, which can shut down an application. To avoid this error, I inserted On Error Resume Next at the top of the procedure. In these brief examples, I don't attempt to construct error-handling routines. However, you must add these routines to applications you write. (Chapter 14 describes techniques for handling these errors.)

Schemas: Seeing a Database's Structure

Your VB database programming can automatically generate input forms. By using ADO, you can ask a database what tables and fields it contains, and even what data types it uses in each of those fields. Then you can generate TextBoxes, CheckBoxes, and other display or input devices based on the information you get back about the *scheme* — that is, the structure of the database. (DAO code also can perform these tasks.) To find out how you dynamically populate a form with components during runtime, see Chapter 10.

Displaying the organization scheme using OpenSchema (adSchemaColumns)

You use the OpenSchema method of the connection object to extract information about the structure of a data source. (Remember to say *data source* rather than *database*, because ADO is designed to make it possible to extract data from lots of sources, such as e-mail, not just formal databases.)

To see how you can use ADO code to find out about a database's structure, follow these steps:

1. **Start a new Standard EXE project in VB and add a ListBox to Form1.**

2. **Choose Project⇨References.**

   The References dialog box opens.

3. **Click the check boxes next to both Microsoft ActiveX Data Objects Recordset 2.0 Library and Microsoft ActiveX Data Objects 2.5 Library. (You can use Microsoft ActiveX Data Objects 2.0 Library if you don't have the 2.5 version. Use whatever version of these libraries that you have.)**

4. **Click OK.**

   The dialog box closes, and VB adds these ADO libraries to your project.

5. **Double-click Form1.**

   You see the VB code window.

6. **Move your cursor up (press and hold the up-arrow key) until you're at the very top of the code window, and then press the Enter key to create a blank line.**

7. **Type these two variable declarations into the General Declarations section of Form1:**

```
Dim cnBiblio As ADODB.connection
Dim rsFields As ADODB.Recordset
```

If you're not following my example, replace these variable names with your choice of names.

8. **In the Form_Load event, type this code:**

```
Private Sub Form_Load()
Dim sTable As String
Dim sNewTable As String
Set cnBiblio = New ADODB.connection
cnBiblio.ConnectionString =
        "Provider=Microsoft.Jet.OLEDB.3.51; Data
        Source=C:\PROGRAM FILES\VB98\BIBLIO.MDB"
cnBiblio.open
Set rsSchema = cnBiblio.OpenSchema(adSchemaColumns)
Do Until rsSchema.EOF = True
    sTable = rsSchema!Table_Name
    If Left(sTable, 4) = "MSys" Then GoTo KeepMoving
    If (sTable <> sNewTable) Then
        List1.AddItem "" 'Insert blank line
        sNewTable = rsSchema!Table_Name
        List1.AddItem "            TABLE: " & sNewTable
    End If
    List1.AddItem rsSchema!Column_Name
KeepMoving:
    rsSchema.MoveNext
Loop
CnBiblio.Close
End Sub
```

(If you're not following my example, replace the connection string with a database engine and database of your choosing.)

I use boldface to highlight the key lines in this source code. This code opens an ordinary ADO recordset using the OpenSchema method and the adSchemaColumns parameter, filling the recordset with the names of the tables and fields in the database. Then the ListBox displays the rsSchema!Table_Name and rsSchema!Column_Name (field name).

In this code, note that you don't display any information about any "tables" that begin with the prefix *MSys*. These are not true tables; instead, they contain information about the database and are used by the Jet engine. You don't need to see them, so this line of code skips them:

```
If Left(sTable, 4) = "MSys" Then GoTo KeepMoving
```

9. **Press F5.**

The ListBox fills with the tables and fields in the database, as shown in Figure 16-3.

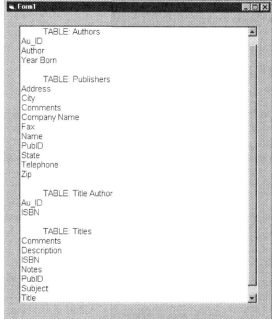

Figure 16-3:
Using the
Open-
Schema
method, you
can see a
data
source's
internal
organi-
zation.

Displaying the data types using OpenSchema (adSchemaProvider Types)

Different databases contain various kinds of data, such as text, small numbers (integers), large numbers, binary numbers. A Jet-engine-based database may include a really huge text data type called a *memo* data type. The Jet data types are fairly similar to the VB variable types. In other kinds of databases, or data sources, other kinds of data types exist. For some applications, you need to know what kind of data a data source contains.

For example, if a field contains binary data (the data can be only true or false, such as whether or not a book is still in print), you may prefer to use a CheckBox as an entry device for that field. This way, the data entry person simply checks, or unchecks, the box. However, if another field's data type is a long number, you need a TextBox long enough to hold the maximum number of digits that a long number data type can potentially require. In the previous section, I show you how to find out the various fields and tables in a database. In this section, you see how to find out what kind of data those fields hold.

To use the OpenSchema method for finding out what data types a data source uses, follow these steps:

1. **Start a new Standard EXE project in VB and add a ListBox to Form1.**

2. **Choose Project⇨References.**

   VB opens the References dialog box.

3. **Click the check boxes next to both Microsoft ActiveX Data Objects Recordset 2.0 Library and Microsoft ActiveX Data Objects 2.5 Library. (You can use Microsoft ActiveX Data Objects 2.0 Library if you don't have the 2.5 version. Use whatever version of these libraries that you have.)**

4. **Click OK.**

   The dialog box closes, and VB adds these ADO libraries to your project.

5. **Double-click Form1.**

   You see the VB code window.

6. **Type these two variable declarations into the General Declarations section of Form1:**

   ```
   Dim cnBiblio As ADODB.connection
   Dim rsFields As ADODB.Recordset
   ```

7. **Type this code into the Form_Load event:**

   ```
   Private Sub Form_Load()
   On Error Resume Next

   Dim sTable As String
   Dim sNewTable As String

   Set cnBiblio = New ADODB.connection
   cnBiblio.ConnectionString =
           "Provider=Microsoft.Jet.OLEDB.3.51; Data
           Source=E:\PROGRAM FILES\VB98\BIBLIO.MDB"
   cnBiblio.open
   Set rsSchema = cnBiblio.OpenSchema(adSchemaProviderTypes)
   Do Until rsSchema.EOF = True
       dt = rsSchema!Type_Name
       cs = rsSchema!Column_Size
       List1.AddItem "Data Type: " & dt & "       Column Size:
           " & cs
       rsSchema.MoveNext
   Loop
   CnBiblio.Close
   End Sub
   ```

(If you're not following my example, replace the BIBLIO.MDB database used in the source code in this step with a database of your choosing.)

I use boldface to highlight the essential differences between this example's code and the code in the previous section. You open the Schema using the (adSchemaProviderTypes) parameter. Then you use the Type_Name and Column_Size arguments to provide the data type and data size for each field.

8. **Press F5.**

The program runs, and you see the data types and sizes for the elements, as shown in Figure 16-4.

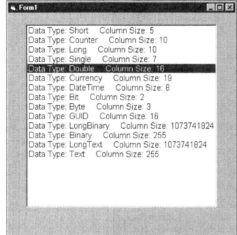

Data Type: Short   Column Size: 5
Data Type: Counter   Column Size: 10
Data Type: Long   Column Size: 10
Data Type: Single   Column Size: 7
Data Type: Double   Column Size: 16
Data Type: Currency   Column Size: 19
Data Type: DateTime   Column Size: 8
Data Type: Bit   Column Size: 2
Data Type: Byte   Column Size: 3
Data Type: GUID   Column Size: 16
Data Type: LongBinary   Column Size: 1073741824
Data Type: Binary   Column Size: 255
Data Type: LongText   Column Size: 1073741824
Data Type: Text   Column Size: 255

Figure 16-4: The Open-Schema method can tell you the data type and its size.

A Cursory Look at Cursors

When you open a recordset, you get a *cursor.* To oversimplify a bit, think of the cursor as a kind of pointer to the data, but an intelligent pointer. For example, when you use the MoveNext method to get to the next higher record in your recordset, you can thank the cursor for making this move possible. In ADO, the type of cursor you use can be rather more important than it ever was in DAO.

Technically, the cursor is more than just a pointer; it's the list of index tables, reference pointers, or static data returned to the client (or kept on the server). A separate pointer is then used to actually navigate through the data.

Examining ADO's cursor types

To understand what cursors are and why they've become an issue you must consider in ADO programming, consider the types of cursors you can specify, as listed in Table 16-1.

Table 16-1	The Four ADO Cursor Types
Cursor Type	*Constant*
Forward-only (usually the default)	adOpenForwardOnly
Keyset-driven	adOpenKeyset
Dynamic	adOpenDynamic
Static	adOpenStatic

In most cases, when you use the Open method to create a standard record-set, you get Forward-only as the default cursor. It's a good choice when you simply want to display a list of data and then close the recordset. However, it isn't the default cursor for all types of recordsets. For example, if you're checking the structure of a database using the OpenSchema command (as in the previous section), the recordset is, by default, a Static type.

When deciding which cursor type to use for a particular recordset, keep the following points in mind:

✔ The Static cursor type doesn't show any changes being made to the records by other people attached to your network. This cursor type is useful for searching through data and generating reports. It's a fast cursor type, but it isn't recommended when large amounts of data need to be returned because it gobbles up a lot of resources. It's very similar to the Snapshot in DAO and Jet.

✔ The default — and the fastest — cursor type, Forward-only, is precisely the same as the Static cursor type, except that you can only move (scroll) forward through the records in the recordset. You can MoveNext, but not MovePrevious, for example. It should be your choice when you're just filling a Listbox or Combobox with read-only data.

✔ The Dynamic cursor type displays editing by other people to the data, including changes made to existing records, as well as any newly added or deleted records. With this type, you can move in all directions through the recordset. It's the best choice for situations in which you always must see the latest version of the data.

✔ The Keyset-driven cursor type is nearly the same as the Dynamic type, but it is somewhat faster because you see only the latest editing of existing records by others. You don't see any new records they have added to the database or deleted from it.

The Keyset and Dynamic cursors are quick to return data when a query is fired because the whole set of data is not immediately returned. However, they are slower to navigate than the other two cursor types. A Keyset cursor is simply a table of keys — or pointers — that references actual data in the database. The cursor does not contain the actual data — only references to it. Consequently, every time you access data in a Keyset cursor, the ADO library fetches the latest data from the database fields and returns it. The advantage is that you always get the latest updated values for your fields, and retrieval is faster initially because only the keyset is returned, not the whole set of data. This approach is also memory efficient when dealing with large recordsets because the whole set of data isn't loaded in memory. The drawback is that *navigating* through the data (Find, for example) is a bit slower because every time you look up a record, the library needs to make a round trip to the server to fetch the data. (Also, although you do see any updates made by other users to *existing* records, the keyset is fixed so that you don't see any newly added or deleted records.)

A Dynamic cursor is the same as a Keyset-type cursor, except that a Dynamic cursor's keyset is dynamically rebuilt every time you navigate through it. The result is that you *can* see any records newly added or deleted by other users. The only drawback to a Dynamic cursor is speed. Because everything is dynamic (both the field content and the list of pointers), many round trips to the server are necessary, and the query engine of the database is always working. Despite this overhead, the Dynamic cursor is the best cursor for ensuring that you always have access to the latest version of the data. It is the ideal cursor to use for mission-critical applications in which many users update data frequently.

In any event, be aware that the Open method of recordsets can take several parameters, one of which is the CursorType. Here's the complete syntax for Open:

```
YourRecordsetsName.Open DataSource, ActiveConnection,
        Cursortype, LockType, Options
```

Here's a typical use of the Open method and its parameters to permit editing records:

```
YourRecordsetsName.Open "SELECT * FROM TITLES,
        YourDataConnectionsName, adOpenDynamic,
        adLockOptimistic
```

If you intend to do batch updating, you should use either the Keyset-driven or Static cursor type.

Setting the LockType to permit editing

If you want to permit editing of the records in a recordset, you need to specify the correct LockType parameter. If you don't specify the LockType when you use the Open command to create a recordset, it defaults to the adLockReadOnly option, which prohibits editing. Table 16-2 describes the LockTypes in ADO.

Table 16-2	ADO Lock Types	
Lock Type	*Constant*	*Description*
Read-only	adLockReadOnly	No editing allowed (the default)
Pessimistic	adLockPessimistic	Locks records at once during editing
Optimistic	adLockOptimistic	Locks records only when you use the Update command
	AdLockBatchOptimistic	Defers all updates until you complete a batch update

Usually, the adLockOptimistic LockType should be your choice if you expect to update records. Not only do all data providers support this kind of locking, but the record is only locked for as long as ADO takes to physically update the record on the hard drive.

The adLockBatchOptimistic LockType lets ADO know that you're going to treat records as a group (a batch) — downloading multiple records in the batch, updating them, and then sending them back to the data provider as a group. You'll find that many data providers simply don't support adLockBatchOptimistic.

The adLockPessimistic LockType keeps a record locked throughout the process of editing the record. Not all data providers support this type of locking.

Working with Disconnected Recordsets

With ADO, you can do some interesting things with recordsets. For example, you can *detach* them from their database — that is, work on them locally — and then add the result back to the database. Of course, working with disconnected recordsets conserves resources and takes a load off the server.

What's more, you can even create a recordset independently and just use it as a way to store temporary data without involving a database at all! Assume that you want to use data binding (attaching a control, such as a TextBox, to a Data Control). Normally, you attach the TextBox to a Data Control that is, itself, connected to a database, as I describe in Chapter 3. However, you can now use ADO to create a brand new, independent recordset. You just define the fields you want in the recordset and then use the Open command.

To use ADO to create a new, independent recordset, follow this example:

1. **Choose File⇨New to start a new VB project.**

2. **Put a ListBox on Form1.**

3. **Choose Project⇨References.**

4. **In the References dialog box, click the check boxes next to both Microsoft ActiveX Data Objects Recordset 2.0 Library and Microsoft ActiveX Data Objects 2.0 Library (or use the 2.1 Library, if you have it).**

5. **Type this code into the Form_Load event:**

```
Private Sub Form_Load()
Dim rs As New ADODB.Recordset
rs.CursorLocation = adUseClient

'Define three new fields and then open the recordset
    rs.Fields.Append "key", adInteger
    rs.Fields.Append "Name", adVarChar, 40,
        adFldIsNullable
    rs.Fields.Append "Address", adVarChar, 40,
        adFldIsNullable

    rs.Open , , adOpenStatic, adLockBatchOptimistic

'Fill in some records
rs.AddNew Array("key", "Name", "Address"), Array(1,
        "Rec1Name", "Rec1Address")
rs.AddNew Array("key", "Name", "Address"), Array(2,
        "Rec2Name", "Rec2Address")

rs.MoveFirst

List1.AddItem "Key      Name        Address"
```

(continued)

(continued)

```
List1.AddItem " "

'Show the original records
While rs.EOF <> True
List1.AddItem rs!Key & "          " & rs!Name & "        " &
        rs!Address
rs.MoveNext
Wend

'"Save" the records
rs.UpdateBatch adAffectAll

'Edit the first record
rs.MoveFirst
rs!Name = "New Name"
rs.MoveFirst

List1.AddItem " "
List1.AddItem " "

'Show the new, and previous, contents of both records
While rs.EOF <> True
List1.AddItem " "
List1.AddItem rs!Key & "          " & rs!Name & "      " &
        rs!Address
List1.AddItem rs!Key.OriginalValue & "          " &
        rs!Name.OriginalValue & "        " &
        rs!Address.OriginalValue
rs.MoveNext
Wend

End Sub
```

A couple of notes about this source code: The adVarChar and adInteger are ADO constants representing data types. The adVarChar constant signifies a string variable type (like the alternative adChar type), but adVarChar is used with the parameter object. The OriginalValue property is good to use if you want to add an Undo feature to your application. For example, rs!Name.OriginalValue returns the data that was previously in the Name field before that field was edited. The Array command is Visual Basic's answer to the Data command in previous editions of Basic. It's a good way to insert small amounts of data into your source code.

When you press F5 and run this example, you first see the two records:

Key	Name	Address
1	Rec1Name	Rec1Address
2	Rec2Name	Rec2Address

Then, you see that the Name field of the first record has been edited
(you see the new, then the OriginalValue version, of record 1):

1	**New Name**	Rec1Address
1	Rec1Name	Rec1Address

However, no changes have occurred in the second record:

2	Rec2Name	Rec2Address
2	Rec2Name	Rec2Address

Chapter 17

Killing Bugs

* *

* *

*N*o programming project of any significance simply rolls out of your fin-gertips error free. You always have to test your application and then track down the inevitable problems that pop up during the testing. And fix them. Bugs usually aren't a result of negligence — it's just that any sizable application has an enormous number of interacting behaviors.

Database programmers face some additional debugging challenges. For one thing, when you're working with databases, errors can be generated in the database engine, in your VB application, or, in some cases, in code residing on a server in another part of the building, or, indeed, in another part of the world. Increasingly, database applications are *distributed*, as they call it. Gone are the days when you could count on everything residing right there on your personal hard drive.

Beyond that, the browser container is increasingly replacing the standard, traditional window model as the host for applications. This is not to say that browsers are full-fledged operating systems (not yet, anyway). But VB code, VB-created components, and VBScript code can be mixed in with HTML browser code. And you may work with such hybrid environments as Active Server Pages and DHTML.

The old days, when you only had to worry about errors generated within the comfy world of the VB editor and the Windows operating system, are pretty much history. Today, errors can jump up at you from several, interacting locations: UserControls (see Chapter 10), HTML, browser script, ASP code, server-side classes, and many other components and objects, some of them even running on (relatively) alien engines like Java.

This chapter explores the more common errors you're likely to encounter when programming in today's object-oriented, database-driven, browser-friendly world. Check out various section headings in this chapter for common error messages you're likely to see, and then read on for a solution to each of those problems.

But first, you may want to explore DAO and ADO error systems and some ways to trap database-programming errors.

What's a Poor Debugger to Do?

VB offers an unquestionably excellent, powerful suite of debugging tools. But what do you do when you get an error message that comes from Internet Explorer? Or from JavaScript? Or from an Active Server Page connection?

You can sit around and mope, or you can *take steps*.

I suggest taking steps.

If the error is generated within traditional VB code, you can use the famous VB debugging facilities: the Immediate Window, watches, breakpoints, single-stepping, and other debugging features. VB's Help feature explains the regular debugging tools quite well. In this chapter, you find out how to deal with various common error messages.

Start by finding out where the error happened

Debugging starts by finding out *where* the bug occurs. As your first step in debugging, you need to locate the line of code where the error occurs. This isn't always a straightforward process, particularly when you're dealing with errors that occur outside traditional VB code.

If VB code causes an error, a message box pops up with a (sometimes) helpful error message and (also sometimes) a button labeled Debug, as shown in Figure 17-1.

Figure 17-1: Clicking the Debug button takes you directly to the location of an error in VB source code.

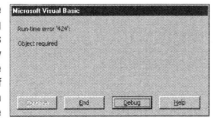

Click the Debug button, and you see the line in the source code (or, some-times, the one immediately following it) where the error occurs. By default, VB highlights this line in yellow. (Many programmers reconfigure all the colors in VB's editor, so if you've changed the default debug highlight from yellow to some other color — well, you know what you've done.)

If an error occurs outside traditional VB code (if the error is generated server-side in script, for example), you often have to resort to inelegant methods for tracking it down. One of the more popular of these inelegant methods involves planting message box commands here and there in your source code, displaying the current state of variables. Then, periodically, the code halts and displays the message box.

You can use the msgbox command in VBScript and in such objects as UserDocuments embedded in an HTML page (see Chapter 12). If a message box appears before the error is generated, the line that contains the error is likely to follow the line with the message box in the source code, and vice versa. Note, however, that the msgbox technique is often undesirable. It stops execution each time, and it can only be used in user services. Server-side components, more often than not, are compiled for unattended execution, which means msgboxes won't be displayed at all.

Make use of the Source property

Many programmers use the error(err) or error.description commands in their source code to display error messages while the program runs. However, these same programmers often overlook the sometimes valuable Source property of the error message. In a client/server or otherwise distributed application, you may have trouble precisely locating the code that's causing trouble. As I explain in the following sections, the Source property can be invaluable for tracking down these types of errors.

Seeing DAO errors

To see how to get the full error report for a DAO error, follow these steps:

1. **Choose File⇨New Project in VB.**

   The New Project dialog box opens.

2. **Double-click the Standard EXE icon in the New Project dialog box.**

   The dialog box closes, and the Standard VB Form is displayed.

3. **Double-click Form1.**

   You see the VB code window.

4. **Move your cursor to the Form_Load event, and type in this code. This code attempts to open a database named** *ZZTop,* **which should generate an error:**

```
Private Sub Form_Load()
    Dim db As Database
    On Error GoTo ErrorHandler
    Set db = OpenDatabase("ZZTop")
    Exit Sub

ErrorHandler:
    Dim E As Error
    For Each E In Errors
        z = z + 1
        With E
            strError = _
                "Error #" & .Number & vbCr
            strError = strError & _
                "Description: " & .Description & vbCr
            strError = strError & _
                "Source: " & .Source & vbCr
            strError = strError & _
                "HelpContext " & .HelpContext & vbCr
            strError = strError & _
                "HelpFile " & .HelpFile & "."
        End With
        MsgBox "Problem #" & z & vbCr & "  " & strError
    Next
    Resume Next
End Sub
```

If you have a database named ZZTop, change the preceding code so it tries to reference a database you don't have.

5. **Choose Project⇨References.**

The References dialog box opens.

6. **In the Available Reference listbox, locate Microsoft DAO 3.51 Object Library and click its CheckBox. (You can use DAO 3.6 instead, or whatever version of DAO you have, if a different version number appears in the list.)**

A check appears in the box.

7. **Click OK.**

The References dialog box closes, and VB adds the DAO library to your project.

8. **Press F5.**

You see a message box like the one shown in Figure 17-2. You're told that the database you're trying to open cannot be found. To fix this error, you need to check the spelling of the database's name, or provide an accurate file path to it.

Figure 17-2:
Don't
neglect the
Source
property of
the error
object when
tracking
down
database
programming
errors.

 The error object is part of an *errors collection*. In this example, you look for each *E* (defined as an error object) in Errors (the collection). Any single DAO or ADO operation can trigger more than one error. That's why the example uses an error collection. In the sample code, you identify each error as Problem #1, Problem #2, and so on.

As soon as a different operation generates another error, the Errors collection is emptied, and the new error replaces the error(s) from the previous problem code.

Seeing ADO errors

The process for getting information on ADO errors differs little from the DAO error-displaying code in the previous example. To see how to get an ADO error report, follow these steps:

1. Start a new Standard EXE project, and double-click Form1.

You see the code window, where you can type in source code.

2. Move your cursor to the Form_Load event, and type in this code:

```
Private Sub Form_Load()
    Dim cn As ADODB.Connection
    On Error GoTo ErrorHandler
    Set cn = New ADODB.Connection
    cn.ConnectionString =
        "Provider=Microsoft.Jet.OLEDB.3.51; Data
        Source=C:\MysteryFolder\VB98\Biblio.mdb"
    cn.open
    Exit Sub

ErrorHandler:
    'Dim ECollection As Variant
    Dim E As Error
```

(continued)

(continued)

```
    Set ECollection = cn.Errors

    For Each E In ECollection
        z = z + 1
        With E
            strError = _
                "Error #" & .Number & vbCr
            strError = strError & _
                "Description: " & .Description & vbCr
            strError = strError & _
                "Source: " & .Source & vbCr
            strError = strError & _
                "HelpContext " & .HelpContext & vbCr
            strError = strError & _
                "HelpFile " & .HelpFile & "."
        End With
        MsgBox "Problem #" & z & vbCr & "   " & strError

    Next
    Resume Next
End Sub
```

If, by some bizarre coincidence, you *do* store your BIBLIO.MDB sample database file in a folder named MysteryFolder, change the path in this code. You want this code to generate an error, and the example assumes you have no folder by that name.

This code displays the error number (which you can sometimes use with VB's Help feature) to look up additional information on the problem. Then, the code displays a brief description of the error (.Description), followed by the Source (in this case, it's the Jet engine), and finally a Helpcontext and Helpfile variable, if any exists.

3. Choose Project⇨References.

The References dialog box opens.

4. Click the CheckBoxes next to both Microsoft ActiveX Data Objects Recordset 2.0 Library and Microsoft ActiveX Data Objects 2.5 Library. (You can use Microsoft ActiveX Data Objects 2.0 or 2.1 Library, if you don't have the 2.5 version.)

5. Click OK.

The dialog box closes, and VB adds these libraries to your project.

6. Press F5.

You see a message box like the one shown in Figure 17-3.

Figure 17-3:
This ADO
error
contains a
highly
accurate
problem
description,
but no
help file.

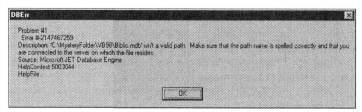

In this example, you are told that the file path to the database you're trying to open isn't correct. To solve this problem, change the file path in the code to the correct one.

Common Programming Error Messages

In this section, I cover some of the more notorious errors you may trigger when writing VB programs. Some of these errors relate to database programming; some are generic. Most of the error messages featured throughout the rest of this chapter are hard to figure out.

Unfortunately, the science of error messages is still in the dark ages. All too often, error messages leave you confused about the true nature of your blunder. With a clear error message, you can solve your problem easily because the message describes the problem and offers a solution. I don't discuss those kinds of error messages in this chapter. To be fair, error messages are sometimes cryptic because many causes may be triggering a particular result. We'll have to wait for more artificial intelligence to provide greater clarity in certain kinds of error messages.

Alas, even after you locate the source of an error, you may still be in trouble. If you want to try your hand at solving a real headbanger, try figuring out the puzzle in the section "The Type Mismatch mystery," later in this chapter.

User-defined type not defined

Assume you're trying to run a VB program that contains this line:

```
Dim cn As ADODB.Connection
```

You get the following error message: User-defined type not defined. That's not the actual problem. However, if you click the Help button on the error message, you get a list of various causes for this error, including this description of the true problem:

> The type is a valid type, *but the object library or type library in which it is defined isn't registered in Visual Basic.* Display the References dialog box, and then select the appropriate object library or type library. For example, if you don't check the Data Access Object in the References dialog box, types like Database, Recordset, and TableDef aren't recognized and references to them in code cause this error.

This is good help. As this passage suggests, choose Project⇨References. In the resulting dialog box, locate the Microsoft ActiveX Data Objects libraries and add them to this project by clicking the CheckBox next to each library's name.

No current record

More than once in their careers, database programmers using the Jet engine are likely to see an error message that says No current record. (VB and Access both base most of their database programming on the Jet engine.) Does this message mean the current record holds no data? Does it mean the table has no records? No, it means the user or some other event caused the pointer to move below the lowest or above the highest record in a recordset. (The MoveNext command, among others, can move the pointer in this way. Or, perhaps the current record just no longer exists for some reason.)

One solution to the No Current Record error is to add a line similar to this example (shown in boldface) prior to any code (such as MovePrevious) that could drop you off the end of a recordset:

```
If rsTitles.EOF = True And rsTitles.BOF = True Then Exit Sub
rsTitles.MovePrevious
```

Another solution to the No Current Record error is to use an ErrorHandler section in a procedure and then just ignore any No Current Record error. (This way, your application won't shut itself down as VB applications do when an error occurs.) Here's an example showing how to use this solution:

```
Private Sub Form_Load()
On Error GoTo ErrorHandler
Dim rsTitles As Recordset
Set dbBiblio = opendatabase("C:\program
          files\vb98\biblio.mdb")
SQLQuery = "SELECT * FROM Titles WHERE Title LIKE '*CZX*'"
Set rsTitles = dbBiblio.OpenRecordset(SQLQuery)
```

```
rsTitles.MovePrevious
Exit Sub
ErrorHandler:
    If Err = 3021 Then
        Exit Sub
    Else
        Msgbox Error(Err)
    End If
End Sub
```

The No Current Record error is error number 3021. The error handler is executed if any error occurs because this line says so: On Error GoTo ErrorHandler. After the error handler executes, it sees if the No Current Record error is the problem and, if so, just ignores it and exits the subroutine. If it's another error, though, the error message is displayed.

Object required

The Object Required error message can be a pain because you may have multiple objects in a single line of code. Clicking the Debug button in the error message box highlights the line of source code that triggered the error, but it doesn't, unhappy you, highlight which object is "missing."

Probably the most common cause of this error message is that you misspelled the name of an object, or you failed to use SET to assign a valid object reference. Check your SET statement (and the earlier DIM or PUBLIC or PRIVATE statements) to verify the spelling, and to ensure that the SET exists.

The cause of this error that's most difficult to figure out involves using the object incorrectly (trying to assign a value to a read-only property), or, even more sinister, a line like this example:

```
List1.AddItem rsState.Fields("State")
```

Getting an Object Required error on this line, you immediately suspect that the rsState recordset object is somehow at fault. However, the true problem may be that you accidentally put a TextBox on the form, instead of a ListBox. In other words, you have no List1 and *that's* the object that's required.

Technically, the preceding line of code actually returns an object instance, not a string. What object? An ADO Field object. If you assign this object to a string (or a ListBox, as is done here) the default property of that object (the value) is then used and this little shortcut coding works. But if you were to assign this expression, not to a ListBox, but to an object collection, it is the object reference that is added to the collection (because a collection can hold objects). Many programmers have become confused by this distinction.

Invalid procedure call or argument

This example isn't a database error, but it is quite common:

```
a = Mid("Saer", 0, 1)
```

This line results in an error message that you've erred in the procedure call or argument. Your argument (the stuff in the parentheses, also sometimes called the *parameters*) is the problem. You're telling VB to start looking in the text "Saer" at the 0th character, and a string cannot have a 0th character. So replace the zero with a 1 and all will be well.

The Type Mismatch mystery

You might think you've seen Type Mismatch errors a time or two in your programming. This sometimes maddening error can apply to various kinds of problems, and it does not tell you which line in your program caused the error. To see what I mean, type this subroutine into VB's code window:

```
Sub LockControls()
    a = InStr("Saer", 0, 1)
End Sub
```

Then, add this code in the Form_Load event:

```
Private Sub Form_Load()
    m = 12.56
End Sub
```

Press F5 to run this code.

You get a Type Mismatch error. Is the error in the Form Load event? In the LockControls event?

If you think a problem exists with the InStr command, you're partly right. This InStr error *should* result in an Invalid Argument error message (see the preceding section). The InStr command has an invalid argument. You're telling VB to look for the number 0 within the text *Saer,* and that's impossible. The 0 here is not a character (a digit); it's a true computable number and cannot occur within a text string. Therefore, you've provided an invalid argument.

VB's error message tells you that you've made a type mismatch, which is true. Type this code in to replace the erroneous InStr command:

```
a = InStr("Saer", "aer")
```

This example demonstrates a correct use of InStr; it asks VB to locate the text *aer* within the text *Saer.* Now that you've made this change, press F5 again. Wow. VB still accuses you of Type Mismatch.

Try changing the code so the entire code window looks like this:

```
Sub LockControls()
    a = 1 + 1
End Sub

Private Sub Form_Load()
    b = 1 + 1
End Sub
```

What could be simpler? Press F5. Haaaaa! You're *still* getting a Type Mismatch error. What gives? Stop reading at this point if you want to ponder the solution to this mystery.

Where's this error? There's nothing wrong with adding 1 + 1 and assigning the result to a variable. The secret answer is that you've used the word *LockControls* as the title of a subroutine. If you title a sub with a reserved word (a word used as a VB command, like Stop), the line turns red the minute you type it in — indicating that you cannot use that word. Type this line in and see:

```
Sub Stop
```

When you press the Enter key, the line turns bright red.

This color change does not happen when you use the term *LockControls.* Don't ask me why. It's not a VB command.

Object variable or With block variable not set

Like the often-seen Type Mismatch error, VB often throws you the error message `Object variable or With block variable not set.` You often see this message when you're working with objects, and it's not too helpful or specific, is it? This error has several possible causes.

Cause #1: You failed to reference an object library

The Object Variable Or With Block Variable Not Set error message can occur for the same reason that you get a User Defined Type Not Defined error:

You're trying to use an object that is not part of VB's intrinsic object set, but you haven't yet set a reference to the object's library. Therefore, VB doesn't know about this object.

The cure for this version of the Object Variable Or With Block Variable Not Set error is to choose Project➪References, locate the proper library, and click the CheckBox next to that library's name. This way, the library (and its objects) becomes part of the current VB project.

Cause #2: You failed to assign an object to an object variable

The Object Variable Or With Block Variable Not Set error also often happens because you've failed to assign an object to an object variable correctly. The following example shows this type of error in action:

1. **Choose File➪New Project in VB.**

   The New Project dialog box opens.

2. **Double-click the Standard EXE icon in the New Project dialog box.**

   The dialog box closes, and the Standard VB Form is displayed.

3. **Double-click the TextBox icon on the VB Toolbox.**

   VB adds a new TextBox named Text1 to your project.

4. **Double-click Form1.**

   You see the VB code window.

5. **In the Form_Click event, type this code:**

   ```
   Private Sub Form_Click()
       Dim textObj As TextBox
       textObj.Text = "Changed!"
   End Sub
   ```

6. **Press F5.**

   The project runs.

7. **Click the form with your mouse.**

   The Form_Click event is triggered, but an error message pops up saying `Object variable or With block variable not set`.

   The Solution: You must use the Set command to assign an object to the object variable you created (textObj).

8. **Change the code to this programming, adding a new line to put a TextBox into the object variable textObj:**

```
Private Sub Form_Click()
    Dim textObj As TextBox
    Set textObj = Text1
    textObj.Text = "Changed!"
End Sub
```

Now when you test this project, it works correctly.

A related error involves trying to access an object that is no longer in existence. Objects can go out of existence because they were declared within a no-longer-active procedure or form.

The Solution: Declare the object with the Public command in the General Declarations section of a form.

Or, an object can be destroyed with this code: myObj = Nothing. If the object is missing, the error is generated when you try to manipulate that missing object.

Cause #3: You put object-related code into the Form_Load event

You can trigger the promiscuous Object Variable Or With Block Variable Not Set error message by trying to access an object that's not yet completely "there" because you're trying to access it from within the Form_Load event. Form_Load executes code *before* such objects as a Data Control (located on that form) are actually brought into existence.

To see how to generate and fix the Form_Load version of the Object Variable Or With Block Variable Not Set error, follow these steps:

1. **Choose File⇨New Project in VB.**

   The New Project dialog box opens.

2. **Double-click the Standard EXE icon in the New Project dialog box.**

   The dialog box closes, and the Standard VB Form is displayed.

3. **Double-click the Data Control icon on the VB Toolbox (the intrinsic Data Control that always appears on the Toolbox, not a newer version that you have to reference).**

   A Data Control appears on Form1.

4. **In the Properties window for the Data Control, click the button with the three dots (...) next to the DatabaseName property.**

   A file-browser dialog box opens.

5. **Locate the BIBLIO.MDB sample database (or any other .MDB database) and double-click it.**

The dialog box closes, and your Data Control is now attached to the database you selected.

6. **Click the down-arrow symbol in the RecordSource property for the Data Control (in the Properties window).**

You see a list of the available tables in your database.

7. **Click one of the table names.**

That table is now opened to your Data Control.

8. **Double-click Form1.**

You see the VB code window.

9. **In the Form_Load event, type this code:**

```
Private Sub Form_Load()
    Data1.Recordset.MoveNext
End Sub
```

10. **Press F5.**

The project runs, and there it is again: The error message pops up saying `Object variable or With block variable not set.`

The Solution: You must move this code to the Form_Activate event (or some other event, such as Form_Click) that triggers *after* the Data Control has actually come into existence. The Form is in existence during Form_Load, but not the controls located on the Form. The Form_Activate event triggers only after everything on the form is ready to go to work. So, move the code into the Form_Activate event, like this, and then rerun this project:

```
Private Sub Form_Activate()
    Data1.Recordset.MoveNext
End Sub
```

Invalid use of NULL

The infamous Invalid Use Of NULL error results from an incompatibility between the types of data that VB deals with and understands, and a type of data commonly found in databases. An empty VB TextBox contains an *empty string*, as it's called. An empty field in a database usually contains *Null*. These are not the same things. If you try to put a Null into a VB ListBox or TextBox, you trigger an Invalid Use Of NULL error.

To reproduce this error, put a TextBox on a VB Form, set a reference to the Microsoft DAO 3.51 Object Library, and type this code into the code window of Form1:

```
Dim dbBiblio As Database
Private Sub Form_Load()
Set dbBiblio = opendatabase("C:\PROGRAM
            FILES\VB98\BIBLIO.MDB")
Set rsTitles = dbBiblio.OpenRecordset("Publishers")
Text1 = rsTitles.Fields("Comments")
End Sub
```

In place of `C:\PROGRAM FILES\VB98\BIBLIO.MDB` in this code, substitute the path that leads to the BIBLIO.MDB sample database file on your hard drive. (If you need more details about constructing this example, see the section "Opening a Database Connection," in Chapter 14.)

In the BIBLIO.MDB database, the Publishers table's Comments field is usually empty (Null). When you run this program, VB attempts, and fails, to assign the Null from the first record to Text1, generating the Invalid Use Of NULL error.

The Solution: Protect yourself with a trick in your code. Adding an empty string to the Fields property creates an empty string that deceives the TextBox into thinking that it's getting something it can use. In other words, the Null is transformed into an empty string by changing this original code that triggers the error:

```
Text1 = rsTitles.Fields("Comments")
```

Replace this line with the following code, which does not trigger the error:

```
Text1 = rsTitles.Fields("Comments") & ""
```

What happens, you ask, if the Comments field contains some data? In other words, what happens if that field is not Null, but instead contains text? Nothing bad happens. You merely add (concatenate) an empty string to whatever string is already in the Comments field. This process does no harm; it's like adding nothing to something.

Another suggestion: Some programmers think it's also a good idea to create a little function (name it, for example, NoNull) which accepts a variant and returns either the variant, or an empty string if the variant is null (use VB's IsNull function to test the variant).

Part VII
Working with Queries

The 5th Wave   By Rich Tennant

"I'LL BE WITH YOU AS SOON AS I EXECUTE A FEW MORE COMMANDS."

In this part . . .

It's no use having a database without asking it for information. But you don't usually just want a dump — a pile of all the information it holds. That would be about as useful as tipping over a library shelf full of hundreds of books.

No, you want to ask intelligent questions of the database, and have it give you back intelligent lists. That's where SQL comes in – the standard database query language. The chapters in Part VII show you how to get nearly any set of records your heart desires. You also work with VB's excellent Query Designer tool to design and test new SQL queries. This part also demonstrates how to get data from more than a single table (use *joins*); how to calculate with data (use functions to, for example, add all this year's sales figures to produce a total gross income figure); and how to use *action queries* to modify a database's structure, or dynamically change the data it contains.

Chapter 18

Automatic SQL: Using the Query Designer

*W*hen you open a connection to a database, you generally want to get information out of it. But in many cases, you don't want *all* the information in it, just some. That's where *queries* come into play.

A query is a request for a portion of the information in a database — for example: Show me a list of all the accounts that are past due more than three months. When you run that query, you get a recordset containing the data you requested. The data you get back in a recordset can be extracted from more than one table, grouped based on specific criteria, and sorted. These are options, but they are commonly used options when defining what you want in a recordset.

Over the years, SQL — the Structured Query Language — has become the standard way of querying databases. SQL describes queries using understandable, English-like phrases.

In most cases, you use SQL to create *recordsets* — subsets of the information stored in a database. You ask a query (question) like "Give me a list of all publishers located in California, and alphabetize the list by the publishers' names." In return, you get a recordset containing that data, arranged the way you requested. All the publishers whose State field contains PA or NY — or anything other than CA for that matter — are ignored and do not become part of the recordset.

Here's the SQL query that builds this California-publishers-only recordset:

```
SELECT * FROM Publishers WHERE State LIKE 'CA' ORDER BY
            'PubName'
```

You can use SQL in various contexts in Visual Basic database programming, including:

- ✔ The RecordSource property of a Data Control
- ✔ The Source property of an ADO Recordset object
- ✔ The Source parameter for the OpenRecordset command when using a DAO recordset object's Open method
- ✔ The Source property of an ADO Recordset object
- ✔ With a DAO QueryDef object
- ✔ With the Execute methods of DAO, ADO, and RDO

This chapter explores the uses of the *Query Designer* — a tool that makes it easy to create even complex SQL queries. This chapter focuses on the kind of SQL query that returns a set of data.

You can also use SQL to change or delete database information, and even to create new tables. SQL statements that change a database are called *action queries.* For examples of action queries, see the section "SQL Action Queries: Changing a Database," in Chapter 19.

Adding a Data Environment Designer to a Project

One of the fastest ways to create a SQL query (without having to write it yourself) is to use VB's Query Designer. But before you can use the Query Designer, you must open the Data Environment Designer and create a connection to the database that you want to query. To do that, follow these steps:

1. **Choose File⇨New Project.**

   The New Project dialog box opens.

2. **Double-click the Standard EXE icon to start a typical, traditional VB project.**

   The New Project dialog box closes, and you see a blank form.

3. **In VB's menu bar, click Project and then locate the Add Data Environment option in that menu.**

   If you don't see the Add Data Environment option on your Project menu, complete Steps 4 through 7. If you *do* see the Add Data Environment option, go to Step 8.

4. **Choose Project⇨Components.**

   The Components dialog box opens.

5. **Click the Designers tab.**

6. **Click the check box next to Data Environment.**

7. **Click OK.**

   The Components dialog box closes, and the Add Data Environment option is now available on the Project menu.

8. **Choose Project⇨Add Data Environment.**

   VB adds a new DataEnvironment to your project, and it includes a connection object named *Connection1.* The DataEnvironment is a valuable addition to VB, new in VB 6. Among other things, you use it to define a connection to a database. For a detailed explanation of its features and uses, see Chapter 4.

9. **Right-click Connection1 in the Data Environment window.**

   A context menu pops out.

10. **Choose Properties.**

    The Data Link Properties dialog box opens.

11. **On the Provider tab in the Data Link Properties dialog box, double-click Microsoft Jet 3.51 OLE DB Provider (or, if you have it, you can double-click Jet 4.0, or 3.6, or whatever other version is installed on your machine).**

    VB opens the Connection tab in the Data Link Properties dialog box.

12. **Click the button with the three dots (...) on the Connection tab.**

    A file-selection dialog box opens.

13. **Browse your hard drive until you locate the database that you want to query.**

    If you want to follow along with the examples that I describe throughout this chapter, you can connect to the BIBLIO.MDB sample database (look in the Program Files\Microsoft Visual Studio\VB98 directory).

14. **Double-click the database that you want to query.**

   To follow my example, double-click BIBLIO.MDB. The file-selection dialog box closes.

15. **Click OK.**

   The Data Link Properties dialog box closes.

   You're now connected to the selected database.

Opening the Query Designer

After you open the Data Environment Designer, you can use the Query Designer to build and test SQL queries. To see how to open the Query Designer, follow these steps:

1. **Open a DataEnvironment, and connect it to the database you want to query.**

   I show you how to open a DataEnvironment in the preceding section of this chapter. If you want to follow along with the example I describe in this section, connect a DataEnvironment to the BIBLIO.MDB sample database.

2. **Choose View⇨Data View Window.**

   The Data View window opens, with Connection1 listed.

3. **Click the small + symbol next to Connection1 in the Data View window.**

   The tree expands, revealing three folders: Tables, Views, and Stored Procedures.

4. **Drag the Tables folder from the Data View window and drop it into the Data Environment window.**

   The folders are listed in the Data Environment window beneath Connection1, as shown in Figure 18-1.

5. **In the Data Environment window, right-click the table you want to query.**

   If you're following my example, you want to query the Authors table in the BIBLIO.MDB sample database. A context menu pops out.

6. **Choose Properties.**

   A Properties dialog box opens.

7. **Click the option button next to SQL Statement in the dialog box.**

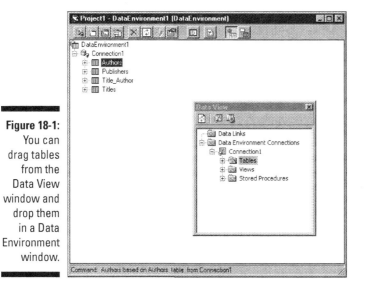

Figure 18-1:
You can
drag tables
from the
Data View
window and
drop them
in a Data
Environment
window.

8. **Click the SQL Builder button.**

The Query Designer (also known as the SQL Builder) opens, as shown in Figure 18-2.

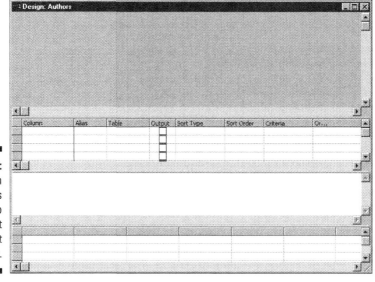

Figure 18-2:
You can
use this
designer to
construct
and test
SQL queries.

Creating an SQL Query with the Query Designer

To see how to build a SQL Query using VB's Query Designer, follow these steps:

1. **Open the Data Environment, Data View, and Query Designer windows, as I describe in the preceding section.**

2. **Drag the table you want to query from the Data View window and drop it in the top (gray) area of the Query Designer window.**

   The table's fields appear in a window, with an empty check box next to each field. Also, the Query Designer automatically starts building a SQL statement (SELECT FROM Authors), as you can see in Figure 18-3.

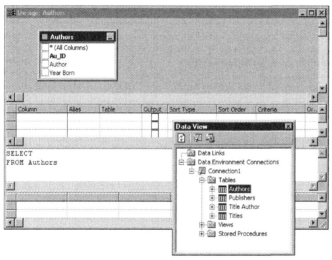

Figure 18-3: You can drag any table to use it as the target of the query you're constructing.

It's customary to put SQL commands like SELECT FROM in all caps and the rest of the SQL statement, such as Authors, in initial caps.

3. **Check the relationships between your data structures in the Query Designer window.**

As shown in Figure 18-4, the Query Designer window has four panes: Diagram, Grid, SQL, and Results. The Diagram pane shows the relationships between your data structures. The Grid pane enables you to create relationships and specify your query. In the SQL pane, you can type in (or just observe an automatically generated) SQL query. The Results pane shows you the data that results from running your query.

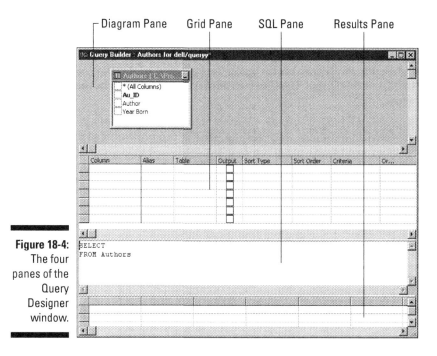

Figure 18-4:
The four panes of the Query Designer window.

4. **Click the check box next to the name of the field you want to query.**

   For example, if you want to see a list of all author names in the Authors table, click the check box next to the Author field in the Authors window, as shown in Figure 18-5.

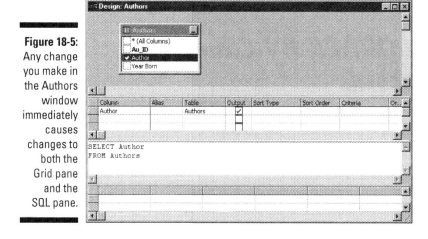

Figure 18-5:
Any change you make in the Authors window immediately causes changes to both the Grid pane and the SQL pane.

The Author field is now listed in the Grid pane, the output check box is checked, and the SQL query is automatically changed to SELECT Author FROM Authors (meaning: use the Author field from the Authors table).

5. **Right-click anywhere on the gray background of the Diagram pane (at the top of the Query Designer window) and click <u>R</u>un in the context menu.**

   Your query, SELECT Author FROM Authors, is executed against the BIBLIO.MDB database. The Results pane at the bottom of the Query Designer window displays the results of the query, as you can see in Figure 18-6. You get a complete list of all 16,000-plus authors in this database.

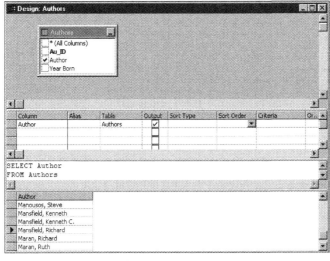

Figure 18-6: To test SQL statements, just select the Run option and then check the Results pane.

Using the ORDER BY Clause to Sort Records

A typical table in a relational database doesn't maintain its records in alphabetical (or any other) order. Consequently, a query such as SELECT Author FROM Authors doesn't automatically put its results in a useful order. However, you can adjust the output of a query in many ways by using the Grid pane to specify a sorting order and additional specifications that govern the output. In this section, I show you how to modify the Query Designer's Grid pane to sort your query results alphabetically.

As you can see in Figure 18-6, the Query Designer has several columns, including Sort Type and Sort Order. You can modify these elements in the Grid pane:

✔ **Output:** With the Output check boxes, you can specify which columns you want to display in the final result. Each column can contain a particular table, but in the examples I describe in this chapter, you're working with only one table: the Authors table.

You rarely need to show all columns in your query, but every column with a check mark in its Output check box is shown. If you choose not to display Output for a particular column, that column can nevertheless be used as a way of sorting or filtering the data displayed in other columns.

✔ **Table:** The Table column shows which table a column is attached to (so you know which tables' data are being displayed in the column).

✔ **Criteria:** These are grouping criteria, including aggregate functions that you use when generating summary reports. The SQL language is extensive and flexible, and offers many ways to filter and organize data. You can specify complicated queries, such as all authors whose first name begins with *L* and who published all their works between 1880 and 1889, for example. For additional details on SQL, see Chapter 19.

After you create some query results (like the authors query results in the example I describe in the previous section, "Creating a SQL Query with the Query Designer"), you can sort the output by following these steps:

1. **Click the Sort Type column in the Grid pane.**

   A drop-down list appears, containing three options: Ascending, Descending, and Unsorted.

2. **Choose Ascending (for an A to Z rather than a Z to A ordering).**

   The Query Designer automatically adds the appropriate line to your SQL statement (for example, `ORDER BY Author`). Note that making this change also causes the list of authors in the Results pane to turn from black to gray. The gray color tells you that changes have been made to the query that are not yet shown in the results. The result set in gray is an old set that no longer represents the SQL statement. You have to use the Run command again to create an updated result set if you want to see what the current SQL statement produces.

   You can sort by multiple fields, too. For example, sort by the City field, but if more than one company is located in the same city, then sort those companies by the CompanyName field. To see an example of sorting by multiple fields, see Chapter 19.

3. **Right-click in the top pane of the Query Designer (on the gray background).**

   A context menu pops out.

4. **Click Run in the context menu.**

   You see the sorting that you requested. The authors' names are now alphabetized.

Choosing from 73.2 Million Possible Results, Give or Take a Few

SQL enables you to create requests for information in millions of ways. SQL statements can filter and configure data in highly complicated arrangements.

Before you go too far, however, try constructing a few fairly common filters, as I describe in this section. Try the following filters by adjusting the Criteria cell in the Query Designer. This way, you get a feel for what the Criteria cell does. (The following examples build on the example query that I describe in the preceding section.)

To show authors P to Z, type > **'P'** into the Criteria cell. Then press Enter.

Immediately, you see a new line of SQL code added to the SQL statement in the SQL pane: WHERE (Author > 'P').

Choose Query⇨Run (or press Ctrl+R) to see the results of this change to your query. In the Results pane at the bottom of the Query Designer, the list starts with authors whose names start with P and ends with the Zs, just as you'd hoped, as shown in Figure 18-7.

How about seeing only Ps and Qs? Change the Criteria cell to > **'P' AND** < **'R'**. Press Enter.

The SQL statement changes to: WHERE (Author > 'P' AND Author < 'R'). Now, press Ctrl+R and see that only author names beginning with P and Q are displayed in the output.

If you want to experiment with some of the 73.2 million possible SQL filters, take a look at Chapter 19. The possibilities are not endless, but there are more ways to filter data than you'll ever use in your lifetime, dude.

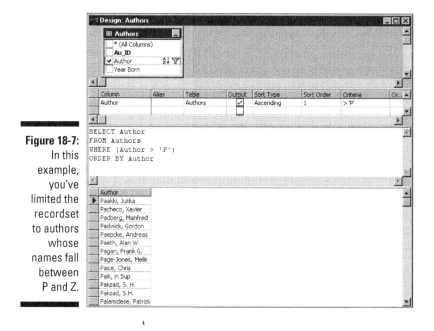

Figure 18-7:
In this
example,
you've
limited the
recordset
to authors
whose
names fall
between
P and Z.

Using Queries in Visual Basic Applications

Having queries sitting around in a Visual Basic project is fine, but how do you actually use them in a Visual Basic program? You can easily put a database command (a query) on a Visual Basic form (a window). Guess how? You drag it. After you put the data command on a form, you can then do a little programming to move among the records in the query.

To add a command to a Visual Basic program, follow these steps:

1. **Create a Visual Basic project that includes a Data Environment Designer and a Query Designer.**

   For all the details on completing this step, see the section "Creating a SQL Query with the Query Designer," earlier in this chapter.

2. **In the Project Explorer, double-click Form1 and then double-click DataEnvironment1.**

   You see the windows for Form1 and DataEnvironment1.

   Notice the SQL icon on the table in the Data Environment window, indicating that you've defined a SQL command that accesses this table.

3. **Drag the SQL command (the table with the SQL symbol) from the Data Environment window onto Form1, as shown in Figure 18-8.**

A set of labels and associated TextBoxes appear on the form. How many TextBoxes-plus-labels appear depends on how complicated your query is. For each column in the query represented by the SQL data command that you dragged and dropped, a label defines the name of that field, and a TextBox displays the actual data when you run the program. For instance, if the data command has two columns of output, you see two labels and two associated TextBoxes on the form when you drop the SQL command on it.

Figure 18-8:
You can drag SQL queries from the Data Environment window and drop them on a VB form.

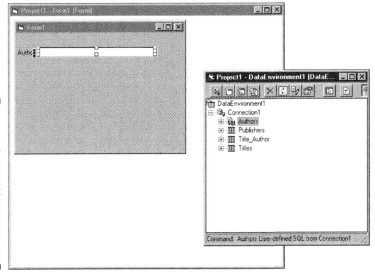

4. **Press F5 to run this program.**

The first record in the query fills the TextBoxes, as shown in Figure 18-9.

Figure 18-9:
When this Visual Basic program runs, the first record from your query appears in this TextBox.

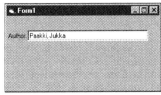

Which particular record appears when you run this program depends on the query you're using. Figure 18-9 shows the result of this SQL query:

```
SELECT Author
FROM Authors
WHERE (Author > 'P')
```

Opening the Query Designer (Part II)

Take a look at Figure 18-8. If you have an active query, one or more of the tables in the Data Environment Designer will have a SQL icon to its left (as the Authors table does in Figure 18-8). To open the Query Designer if you want to modify the query, right-click the SQL icon and choose Design from the context menu. Alternatively, you can just click the Query Designer's icon on the Data Environment Designer's toolbar (the seventh icon from the left — it looks like a paper and pencil).

From Separate Tables: Doing a Join

Sometimes, you want to get data from more than one table at a time. In the BIBLIO.MDB sample database, for instance, the Authors table includes all the names of the authors, but the Title Author table includes the ISBN numbers of the authors' books. What if you want to retrieve both the names and the ISBN numbers? You can create a *join*. (The term *join* is also known as a *relationship* — hence the phrase *relational database*.)

To join two tables, they must have a key in common. The following example shows how the SQL clause looks that represents two keys in joined tables:

```
WHERE Authors.Au_ID = `Title Author`.Au_ID
```

To see how to create a join, follow these steps:

1. **Open the Query Designer with a single table (for example, Authors) in it, as shown back in Figure 18-6.**

   Follow the steps in the section "Creating a SQL Query with the Query Designer," earlier in this chapter.

2. **From the Data View window, drag a second table (for example, Title Author) and drop it into the Diagram pane (the gray area at the top) of the Query Designer, as shown in Figure 18-10.**

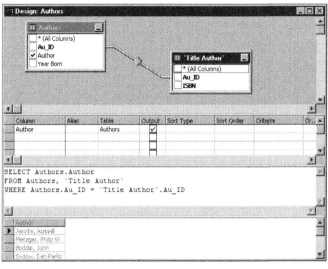

Figure18-10:
As soon as
you drop a
second
table that
has a key
in common
with the first
table, a join
is created.

Two things happen when you drop the second table into the Query Designer. First, a symbol that looks like hydraulic piping joins the two tables — a graphic illustration of their joined relationship. Notice that the pipe attaches at the location of the key fields they have in common (in the example, Au_ID). Second, the Query Designer automatically modifies the SQL statement to specify the joined fields:

```
WHERE Authors.Au_ID = `Title Author`.Au_ID
```

3. **Click the check boxes next to the fields you want to display in your query results.**

   To follow my example, you want to display the Author (name) from the Authors table and the ISBN field from the Title Author table.

4. **Right-click the Diagram pane (the gray area) in the Query Designer.**

   A context menu pops out.

5. **Choose Run in the context menu.**

   The author names and the ISBN numbers associated with them are displayed. Now your recordset displays data from two different tables.

Notice that one author name might be repeated several times in this example. That happens if an author has written more than one book. The join requires that the recordset must include each record in which the key fields (the Au_ID fields) match. Note, though, that the parent key (the primary key) and the foreign key (the key in the second table) are not required to have the same name, they simply need to be defined as a relationship in the database.

The More Joins the Merrier

You can create as many joins between tables as the tables have keys in common. The example in the preceding section of this chapter displays the author name and ISBN, but what if you want to display the book's title and year published, too? The Titles table contains that information. To see how to create a join between three tables, follow these steps:

1. **Create a join between two tables, with the result displaying two fields, as I describe in the preceding section.**

2. **From the Data View window, drag a third table (for example, Titles) and drop it into the Diagram pane (the gray area at the top) of the Query Designer.**

3. **Click the check boxes next to any additional fields that you want to display.**

   For example, click the check boxes next to Title and Year Published in the Titles window.

   The join clause in the SQL command becomes more complex:

   ```
   WHERE Authors.Au_ID = `Title Author`.Au_ID AND `Title
          Author`.ISBN = Titles.ISBN
   ```

This SQL code illustrates one good reason for using the Query Designer. SQL can get complex and it's easier if the Designer creates it for you automatically. Also, the top pane gives you a graphic display of the relationships between the tables and fields in your query.

4. **Right-click the Diagram pane (the gray area) in the Query Designer.**

   A context menu pops out.

5. **Choose Run.**

   The Query Designer displays the results of your query, as shown in Figure 18-11.

Even small database applications usually require joins. You need to understand this important feature, particularly how to work with what are called *left* or *right outer joins*. You can find that additional information and examples about joins in Chapter 19.

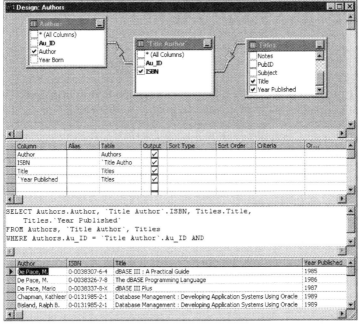

Figure 18-11:
This Query
Designer
features a
triple-join,
with four
fields
displayed
for each
record.

Creating Stored, Prewritten Queries

In addition to queries that are part of a VB database application (such as those I describe earlier in this chapter, and in Chapter 19), you can also store queries in the database itself. These kinds of queries are variously called *views, stored queries,* or *QueryDefs.* I'll stick with the term *stored queries.* (QueryDefs are specific to Microsoft Access-style .MDB databases.)

The virtue of putting a SQL query within the database itself is that the query usually executes more quickly than a query that resides in a VB database application. The stored query is already compiled, but a query in an application must be interpreted before it can be executed. (Some stored queries can be slower because they do not necessarily utilize the best possible index for the query. In general, however, stored queries are faster.)

Also, stored queries are easier to modify: Just change part of the database instead of giving everyone a new, updated version of your VB application. However, you have more flexibility when creating queries in a VB application. You can use variables, If...Then statements, and even ask the user to supply part of the query — all before the query itself is composed by your application and sent over to the database engine.

You'll want to know how to create stored queries, so follow these steps:

1. **Choose File⇨New Project.**

   The New Project dialog box opens.

2. **Double-click Standard EXE in the New Project dialog box.**

   The dialog box closes.

3. **Choose Add-Ins⇨Visual Data Manager.**

   The Visual Data Manager (VisData) opens.

4. **Choose File⇨Open Database⇨Microsoft Access in the Visual Data Manager.**

   The Open Microsoft Access Database dialog box appears.

5. **Locate the database on your hard drive in which you want to store a query, and double-click it.**

   The database is loaded into VisData. To follow my example, use the BIBLIO.MDB sample database that's located in your VB98 directory.

6. **Type a SQL query into the Visual Data Manager's SQL Statement window.**

   To follow my example, type in this query:

   ```
   SELECT * from Publishers WHERE Name = "IDG"
   ```

7. **Click the SQL Statement window's Execute button.**

   A dialog box appears, asking if this is a SQL PassThrough query (this kind of query is only used in client/server work, and is not a feature supported by Access databases).

8. **Click No.**

   The dialog box closes.

9. **You see the result of your query, as shown in Figure 18-12.**

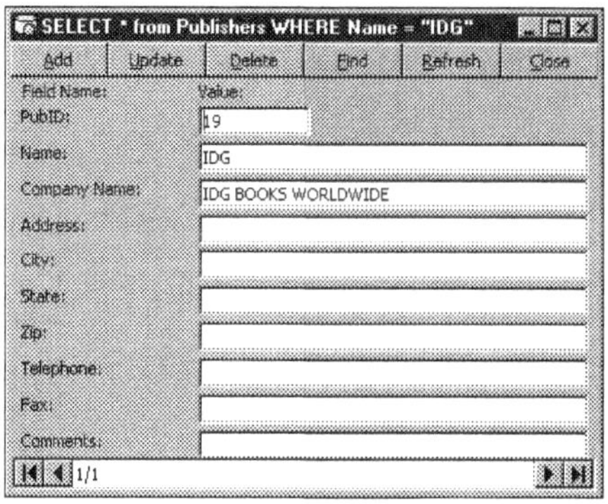

Figure 18-12: Test your query by clicking the Execute button.

10. **Close the Query window.**

11. **Click the Save button in the SLQ Statement window.**

    A VisData dialog box appears, asking you to give a name to your new QueryDef (stored query).

12. **Type in whatever name seems descriptive of your query, and, to follow convention, prefix your name with *qry*.**

    To follow my example, type **qryIDG**.

13. **Click OK.**

    That same dialog box appears, asking again if this is a SQL PassThrough query.

14. **Click No.**

    The dialog box closes. Look at the Database Window in the Visual Data Manager. There it is! Your new stored query is now part of the database.

15. **Double-click the name of your new stored query in the Database Window.**

    You're asked if you want to run the stored query as a dynaset.

16. **Click Yes.**

    You see the recordset returned by your query (the same result that's shown in Figure 18-12, if you're following my example).

Retrieving a stored query in programming

You can open a stored query (get a recordset from it) from within a VB application in much the same way as you open an ordinary table, but you use the QueryDef object, like this:

1. **Choose Project⇨References in Visual Basic, and double-click Microsoft DAO 3.x Object Library.**

2. **Put a ListBox and a CommandButton on a VB form.**

3. **In the CommandButton's Click event, type this code:**

```
Private Sub Command1_Click()
Dim db As Database
Set db = OpenDatabase("C:\Program Files\VB98\BIBLIO.MDB")

Dim rs As Recordset
Dim qd As querydef

Set qd = db.QueryDefs("qryIDG")
Set rs = qd.OpenRecordset
```

```
Do Until rs.EOF
List1.AddItem rs!Name

rs.MoveNext
Loop
End Sub
```

To customize this code to work with your own database and your own stored query, replace the path to the database in this code (`C:\Program Files\VB98\BIBLIO.MDB`) with the path to the database that you want to access. Also, replace the name of the QueryDef in this code (`qryIDG`) with the name of the stored query you are interested in seeing. Finally, replace the name(s) of the field (or fields) in the code (rs!Name) with the field(s) that are used in your stored query.

Creating a stored query in programming

You can add new stored queries to a database rather easily, using the CreateQueryDef command. Here's how:

1. **Choose Project⇨References in Visual Basic, and double-click Microsoft DAO 3.x Object Library.**

2. **Put a CommandButton on a VB form.**

3. **In the CommandButton's Click event, type this code:**

```
Private Sub Command1_Click()
Dim db As Database
Dim qd As querydef

Set db = OpenDatabase("C:\Program Files\VB98\BIBLIO.MDB")

Set qd = db.CreateQueryDef("qryIDG2", "SELECT * from
        Publishers WHERE Name = 'IDG'")
End Sub
```

To customize this code to work with your own database and your new stored query, replace the path to the database in this code (`C:\Program Files\VB98\BIBLIO.MDB`) with the path to the database in which you want to save your new stored query. Also, replace the name of the stored procedure (`qryIDG2`) with whatever name you want to give your new stored query. And finally, replace the SQL query (`"qryIDG2", "SELECT * from Publishers WHERE Name = 'IDG'"`) with your particular query.

Chapter 19

A Brief Dictionary of SQL

*T*his chapter contains concise definitions of the most important SQL terms. Use this chapter as a quick reference when you want to know how to extract particular data from a database. Each heading in the chapter names a SQL term and describes its purpose — so you can quickly scan these heads to find just the technique you need.

You can experiment with these SQL clauses by using the Run command in the Query Designer (Chapter 18 describes this handy utility). Just type in a SQL query and then run it to see what data comes out of the database.

In this chapter, I illustrate each SQL clause by using the Authors table in the BIBLIO.MDB sample database. You can find the BIBLIO.MDB database in your VB98 directory. (If the database is not there, locate it on the VB CD and copy it to your hard drive.)

Note that many flavors of SQL exist (standard ANSI SQL, Microsoft SQL Server's Transact SQL, Oracle's PL/SQL, ODBC SQL, and the version I explain here: Access SQL). These flavors of SQL are, fortunately, very similar. However, there are some differences between them. So, this chapter is not generic; it demonstrates Access SQL.

The commands in the SQL language are referred to as *clauses* (such as ORDER BY), *keywords* (such as TOP), or *operators* (such as LIKE or BETWEEN). Some people find these distinctions — an attempt at a primitive grammar — less than useful. For example, in English grammar a *clause* means a group of words containing a subject and verb. The term *clause* is used similarly in SQL (*SELECT Author*, for example, is a valid clause in both English and SQL). However, the single word *SELECT* is also sometimes called a *clause* in SQL.

In spite of these weaknesses in the terminology, when I refer to the words used in the SQL language (such as SELECT or ORDER BY), I use the common terminology *clause*, *keyword, function,* and *operator* because those terms are, by now, the conventions. I also follow the convention of capitalizing the SQL commands, which helps to distinguish them from the specific arguments (such as tables and fields).

One additional point: Some might quibble that SQL isn't actually a full computer language like VB. True enough, SQL lacks important features of a "real" computer language, and you must use SQL in conjunction with another, host language. But even though it's small and specialized, SQL is a set of words that, collectively, can be considered a language. What else would you call it?

SELECT: The Main SQL Clause to Retrieve Data

Undoubtedly one of the more important SQL clauses, the SELECT clause, appears at the start of each SQL statement that retrieves data from a database. (You can also use SQL to edit, delete, and otherwise manipulate the contents of a database.)

Here's the required format for SELECT:

```
SELECT field(s) FROM table(s)
```

And here's an example:

```
SELECT Author FROM Authors
```

Figure 19-1 shows the recordset that results from running this example.

Figure 19-1:
A simple
one-field,
one-table
recordset.

If you want to retrieve *all fields* from a table, use the * command, as in this example:

```
SELECT *
FROM Authors
```

Figure 19-2 shows the results.

Figure 19-2:
Use the
SELECT *
clause to
retrieve all
the fields in
a table.

The following example demonstrates the correct syntax for specifying two fields:

```
SELECT [Au_ID],[Author]
FROM Authors
```

You can omit the brackets if you want, but they're useful because Jet permits field names that include spaces and other special characters, and the brackets make this possible. I recommend using brackets all the time; it's simple enough, and it adds a visual cue that you're naming fields. However, even though Jet-based databases permit spaces in field names, few other kinds of databases do (and they therefore do not support the brackets, either).

SQL also includes the following optional clauses for use in a SELECT clause (I further explain each of these clauses in its own section, later in the chapter):

- ✔ **JOIN:** Specifies the key fields used to connect two tables when getting data from those tables.

- ✔ **GROUP BY:** Specifies the field you want to use to combine records with the same values when you're summarizing using aggregate functions. In plain English: You want to see a list of total sales by region, so you use `GROUP BY Region`. The new recordset lists each region *only once* and includes the tally of the number of sales in each region. The tally (which uses the SUM function described later in this chapter) is called an *aggregate function.*

- ✔ **HAVING:** Part of an aggregate function that enables you to specify criteria, such as "show me only those results in which the name of the region begins with the letter C." The HAVING clause must be used with GROUPS, described later in this chapter. It is not identical with the WHERE clause, which is not used with GROUPS.

- ✔ **ORDER BY:** Specifies how to sort the recordset.

This example alphabetizes the results, based on the data in the Author field:

```
SELECT Author
FROM Authors
ORDER BY Author
```

This example sorts on two fields, alphabetizing the last names, and if records have identical last names, ordering those records alphabetically by the first name:

```
SELECT FirstName,LastName,Phone
FROM Contacts
ORDER BY LastName,FirstName
```

WHERE: Narrowing the Field

After you specify the field(s) and table(s) by using the SELECT clause and its (required) partner, the FROM clause, you may want to further limit the data. You use the WHERE clause to provide criteria that limit (or *filter*) data, just as in English you might say, "Show me only the magazines that cost less than $1."

Here's the required format for WHERE:

```
WHERE field operator criteria
```

This example shows how you use the WHERE clause:

```
SELECT Author
FROM Authors
WHERE (Author LIKE 'Albrecht%')
```

In this example, the LIKE operator enables you to specify a pattern that must be matched. The % symbol says, "and anything else." For instance, 'Albrecht%' means "show all records that begin with *Albrecht* and end with anything in addition to those characters."

By running this example, you get the recordset shown in Figure 19-3.

Figure 19-3:
Use the
WHERE
clause to
limit data to
specific
criteria.

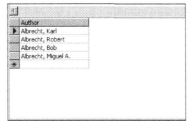

When you use the WHERE clause, you can use various operators to specify a relationship. Table 19-1 describes the meaning of each operator.

Table 19-1		Operators You Can Use with WHERE	
Operator	*Meaning*	*Example*	*Result*
<	Less than	WHERE Author< 'C%'	Shows all authors whose names begin with A or B
<=	Less than or equal to	WHERE IDNumber <= 300	Shows all IDNumbers less than or equal to 300
>	Greater than	WHERE IDNumber > 300	Shows all IDNumbers above 300
>=	Greater than or equal to	WHERE IDNumber >= 300	Shows all IDNumbers above 299
=	Equal to	WHERE IDNumber = 300	Shows IDNumber 300 only
<>	Not equal to	WHERE IDNumber <> 300	Shows all IDNumbers other than 300

(continued)

Table 19-1 *(continued)*

Operator	Meaning	Example	Result
BETWEEN	Within a range	WHERE Author BETWEEN 'A' AND 'D'	Shows all authors whose names begin with A, B, or C
LIKE	Matches a pattern	WHERE Author LIKE 'Adam%'	Shows all authors whose names begin with the characters *Adam*
IN	Matches items contained in a list	WHERE Author IN ('Andrews', 'Brown')	Shows all authors whose names are either Andrews or Brown. This syntax does not permit pattern matching (where you use the %, *, _ or ? symbols). Notice that the term *IN* here is used to mean "in this list." It is not used to mean *between*.

BETWEEN: Specifying a Range

The BETWEEN operator enables you to specify a range, such as between two dates. To try this example, you can use the Titles table in the BIBLIO.MDB database; that table contains a Year Published field.

This example shows how you use the BETWEEN operator:

```
SELECT 'Year Published'
FROM Titles
WHERE ('Year Published' BETWEEN 1993 AND 1995)
```

Figure 19-4 shows the resulting recordset when you run this example.

Figure 19-4:
The
BETWEEN
operator
enables you
to specify a
range of
text, dates,
or numbers.

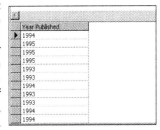

In the Titles table in the BIBLIO.MDB database, the Year Published field is Integer data type (numbers less than about 32,000). However, if it were a Date data type, you would have to surround the criteria with # symbols, like this:

```
BETWEEN #1993# AND #1995#
```

LIKE: Using a Pattern Match

The LIKE operator enables you to use wildcards when asking for data. For example, if you want to see all the records that begin with the letters *Ab*, you use this operator in your SQL query:

```
WHERE (Author LIKE 'ab%')
```

The % means "plus anything else." In other words, all author names beginning with *ab* are returned.

Here's an example that uses LIKE:

```
SELECT Author
FROM Authors
WHERE (Author LIKE 'ab%')
```

Figure 19-5 shows the result.

Figure 19-5: Use LIKE to match patterns.

You can also use an underscore character to represent a single character. For example, you can match any Author name that begins with *a* and ends in *c* by using `WHERE (Author LIKE 'a_c')`.

To match any Author name that begins with *a* and has a *c* in the third character position, use `LIKE 'a_c%'`.

Alas, you have two ways to specify wildcards in SQL. It's one of those strange factors in computer languages you just have to live with (like the fact that some lists start counting up from zero and others count up from 1).

ANSI SQL (the version of SQL used by, among other things, the Query Designer) uses % to mean *and any number of other characters.* For example, Ma% displays Max, Max Headroom, and Maximillion, among whatever other records contain text that begins with the letters *ma.* On the other hand, Jet SQL uses a * symbol rather than the %. Likewise, to specify a single character, ANSI uses an underline _ but Jet uses a ? (as in *Ma?,* which would match May, but not Mayo). If one kind of pattern-matching symbol isn't working for you, try the other.

ORDER BY: Sorting the Results

The ORDER BY clause enables you to specify how you want the data sorted: numerically or alphabetically, ascending (from a to z) or descending (from z to a). Here's an example:

```
SELECT Author
FROM Authors
ORDER BY Author
```

This example orders the Authors table, based on the contents of the Author field, alphabetically from a to z (ascending). Figure 19-6 shows the result.

Figure 19-6:
Alphabetize records with the ORDER BY clause.

To reverse the order (descending from z to a), use this clause:

```
ORDER BY Author DESC
```

You can also order by multiple fields. If a table has separate LastName and FirstName fields, for example, you could alphabetize the names first by the last names and then, within each set of last names, alphabetize by the first names, like this:

```
ORDER BY LastName, FirstName
```

To create a descending order by last name, but ascending by first name, you would use this code:

```
ORDER BY LastName DESC, FirstName
```

To sort both fields in descending order, use this code:

```
ORDER BY LastName DESC, FirstName DESC
```

TOP: Limiting a Range

If you have a large database with thousands of records, and someone wants to see the 25 best-performing products (not the entire list of products), you can use the ORDER BY DESC clause to make a list of the products in order of total sales (from most to least sales, thanks to DESC). Then, instead of stuffing the recordset with this list of all 2,000 products, you can lop off the top 25 by using the TOP keyword, like this:

```
SELECT TOP 25 *
FROM tblSales
ORDER BY TotalSales DESC
```

If any products sold exactly the same, you'll get more than 25 records when you run this example. Ties count as a single result, thereby inflating the list.

At this time, the Query Designer has a problem dealing with the TOP keyword. This SQL code, however, is correct.

You can also request a *percentage* of the total number of records, rather than a specific number of records (as in the previous example). To see the top 5 percent of the TotalSales field, use this syntax:

```
SELECT TOP 5 PERCENT *
FROM tblSales
ORDER BY TotalSales DESC
```

Using a JOIN: Getting Data from More than One Table at a Time

To create a recordset that includes data from more than a single table, you use the JOIN feature. (For a thorough description of this technique see Chapter 18.)

To create a join, you use an equals sign to connect identical fields in two different tables, as in this example:

```
SELECT Authors.Author, 'Title Author'.ISBN
FROM Authors, 'Title Author'
WHERE Authors.Au_ID = 'Title Author'.Au_ID
```

The third line is the join; it specifies that the Authors table is joined to the Title Author table. (They both share a field named Au_ID, so they can join using that field.) The first line says: Display the Author field (their names are in this field) from the Author table, and display the ISBN field from the Title Author table. Figure 19-7 shows the result of this query.

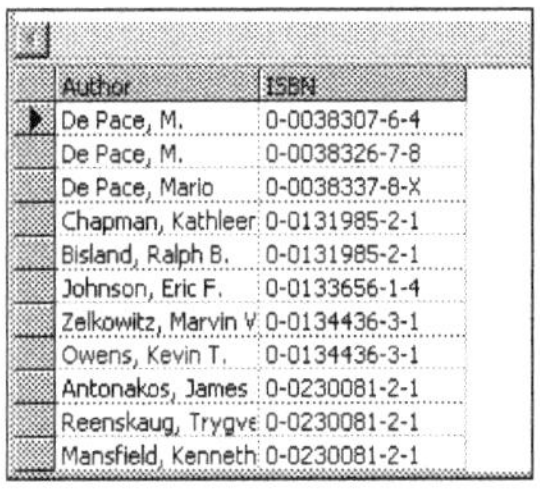

Figure 19-7:
If you want to display fields from different tables, try creating a join.

Author	ISBN
De Pace, M.	0-0038307-6-4
De Pace, M.	0-0038326-7-8
De Pace, Mario	0-0038337-8-X
Chapman, Kathleer	0-0131985-2-1
Bisland, Ralph B.	0-0131985-2-1
Johnson, Eric F.	0-0133656-1-4
Zelkowitz, Marvin V	0-0134436-3-1
Owens, Kevin T.	0-0134436-3-1
Antonakos, James	0-0230081-2-1
Reenskaug, Trygve	0-0230081-2-1
Mansfield, Kenneth	0-0230081-2-1

The previous example is called an *inner join* because a record is returned for each instance in which one table's primary key field matches a value in the key field of the other table. However, if you want to get *all* the records from one of the tables, regardless of whether you have a match between the key fields, you then use what's called an *outer join*:

```
SELECT Author, ISBN
FROM Authors LEFT JOIN
'Title Author' ON
Authors.Au_ID = 'Title Author'.Au_ID
```

The LEFT JOIN...ON clause in this example specifies that the Authors table will return all of its records (every author name will be returned), even if no comparable data (ISBN, in this example) is found in the Title Author table. You can also use a RIGHT JOIN clause, which forces a return of all ISBN numbers, whether or not they have a related Author field in the Authors table (an unlikely situation). In other words, LEFT JOIN returns the table mentioned first in the SQL query; RIGHT JOIN returns the table mentioned second.

AS: Renaming Fields (Aliasing)

In some cases, you want a field to have a different name. Perhaps the field's real name (its name in the database) is misleading or overly complicated, and it would confuse folks if displayed in a report.

Or, perhaps you're building a calculated or aggregate field, and you need to give the new field a name. (For an example showing how you use AS with an aggregate, see the section "COUNT, SUM, AVG, MAX, and MIN: Calculating with the Aggregate Functions," later in this chapter.)

The AS clause enables you to name, or rename, a field. The following example shows how you use the AS clause, if a database uses an unclear field name such as *tblAu*:

```
SELECT tblAu AS 'Author Name'
FROM Authors
```

This example renames the obscure tblAu field from the Authors table as *Author Name*. Figure 19-8 shows the result.

Figure 19-8:
With the AS clause, you can rename this database's confusing *tblAu* field, to the more descriptive *Author Name*.

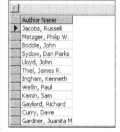

Author Name
Jacobs, Russell
Metzger, Philip W.
Boddie, John
Sydow, Dan Parks
Lloyd, John
Thiel, James R.
Ingham, Kenneth
Wellin, Paul
Kamin, Sam
Gaylord, Richard
Curry, Dave
Gardner, Juanita M

DISTINCT: Eliminating Duplicates

Sometimes, you get extraneous information when you do a query. For example, if you ask for a recordset that includes the City field in the Publishers table of the BIBLIO.MDB database, you get lots of New York entries in the recordset. To avoid duplicates, you can use the DISTINCT keyword, as in this example:

```
SELECT DISTINCT City
FROM Publishers
```

Using DISTINCT can hinder performance in a large database like BIBLIO.MDB. When I ran this example in the Query Designer, my hard drive thrashed away for several minutes, I was notified that I was running low on virtual memory, and I finally reset the computer. You've been warned.

COUNT, SUM, AVG, MAX, and MIN: Calculating with the Aggregate Functions

You can use the five aggregate functions to figure out the number of records (COUNT), the sum total of numeric records (SUM), the average value of numeric records (AVG), and the highest (MAX) or lowest (MIN) numeric record.

Only the COUNT function can be used with text records.

To try constructing an aggregate function using the Query Designer, you can create a SQL query that tells you how many author names the Authors table contains. To see how to construct an aggregate function, follow these steps:

1. **Open a Query Designer and then drop the Authors table into the Query Designer.**

   I show you how to complete this step in Chapter 18. See the section "Creating a SQL Query with the Query Designer."

2. **In the Query Designer, click the check box next to Author in the Authors window.**

   The SQL statement changes to the following code:

   ```
   SELECT Author
   FROM Authors
   ```

3. **Right-click anywhere on the gray background of the Diagram pane (at the top of the Query Builder window).**

   A context menu pops out.

4. **Choose Group By.**

   A Group By option appears in the Grid Pane of the Query Designer, as shown in Figure 19-9.

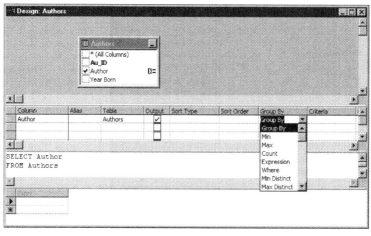

Figure 19-9:
The Group
By option
enables you
to specify
the various
aggregate
functions.

5. Click the Count option in the Group By drop-down list.

Now, the SQL Statement looks like this:

```
SELECT COUNT(Author) AS Expr1
FROM Authors
```

The AS clause has created an alias named Expr1. That's not too descriptive of what you're doing.

6. In the Grid Pane, change Expr1 **to** Total Authors.

Here's what the SQL Statement looks like:

```
SELECT COUNT(Author) AS 'Total Authors'
FROM Authors
```

Notice that because you're using two words for the alias, they've been enclosed in single quotes.

7. Right-click the gray Diagram Pane.

A context menu pops out.

8. Choose Run.

You see the total number of authors in the Author field, as shown in Figure 19-10.

Figure 19-10:
The result
of your
aggregate
function
COUNT.

GROUP BY: Summarizing

Use the GROUP BY clause if you want to collapse more than one record into a single record. For example, you can ask for a count of the number of publishers in each city. This SQL query lists each city and the total number of publishers in that city:

```
SELECT COUNT(City) AS Total, City
FROM Publishers
GROUP BY City
```

Figure 19-11 shows the result.

Figure 19-11:
You can
easily create
custom
categories
with the
GROUP BY
clause.

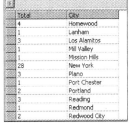

HAVING: Narrowing Criteria

The example in the preceding section shows how you can display all the cities stored in the table. If you want to narrow the number of cities, use the HAVING clause. (HAVING is quite similar to the WHERE clause, which I describe in the section "WHERE: Narrowing the Field," earlier in this chapter. However, HAVING must be used with the GROUP BY clause.) In this example, you display only cities whose names begin with the letter *s*:

```
SELECT COUNT(City) AS Total, City
FROM Publishers
GROUP BY City
HAVING (City LIKE 'S%')
```

Figure 19-12 shows the result.

Figure 19-12:
The HAVING
clause
offers yet
another
way to filter
(narrow
down)
the results
when
running a
SQL query.

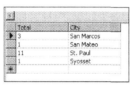

SQL Action Queries: Changing a Database

SQL returns a recordset, but you can also use SQL to change the data in a database. You can even use SQL to append new records with the INSERT clause, or add new tables with the SELECT INTO clause.

Using SQL statements to modify databases or their data is called an *action query* — but surely the word *query* isn't quite right here. Nothing is being questioned, but a great deal can be done to a database with this technique.

Using SQL this way can be a dangerous business because you can wipe out even an entire database with very little SQL code. To see what I mean, take a look at the next section.

DELETE: Removing records

The following SQL statement (don't do it!) would destroy the entire Authors table in the BIBLIO.MDB database:

```
DELETE * FROM Authors
```

If you didn't follow my advice, and you destroyed the Authors table, you can always restore the database by copying the BIBLIO.MDB sample database from your VB CD.

You can substitute the DELETE clause for SELECT in any of the examples in this chapter. When you use DELETE, instead of returning a recordset, you cause all the data that would have been returned by the SELECT clause to vanish — poof! You've been warned. Don't experiment with this clause unless you've backed up the database first.

You can use all the usual filters when defining what you want to delete. For example, this code would wipe out any author name beginning with *A*:

```
DELETE Author
FROM Authors
WHERE (Author LIKE 'A%')
```

Some versions of SQL leave out that first *Author* between the DELETE and FROM, but Access SQL uses it.

UPDATE: Changing data

If you replace the SELECT clause with UPDATE and SET clauses, instead of returning a recordset, you can change the data in a recordset. You can use the UPDATE clause with the DAO *execute* command to make the changes. For example, assume that you want to change an abbreviation for one state in the State field of the Publishers table. In place of *Pa,* you want to use the abbreviation *Pann* for Pennsylvania. Here's the SQL and source code that accomplishes this *action query*:

```
SQLAction = "UPDATE Publishers SET State = 'Pann' WHERE State
             = 'Pa'"

dbBIBI.Execute SQLAction
```

This code locates all records in the Publishers table that have *Pa* in the State field. Then, it changes each of those records, replacing *Pa* with *Pann*. To see how to create a VB program that uses an action query, follow these steps:

1. **Make a copy of the BIBLIO.MDB sample database and name it BIBI.MDB (you can find BIBLIO.MDB in your VB98 folder).**

   You can mess around with this copy, leaving the original BIBLIO.MDB as is.

2. **Start VB, and choose Standard EXE as the project type.**

3. **Double-click the ListBox icon in the Toolbox.**

   VB adds a ListBox to Form1.

4. **Double-click the CommandButton icon in the Toolbox.**

   VB adds a CommandButton to Form1.

5. **Choose Project⇨References.**

   The References dialog box opens.

6. **Click the check box next to Microsoft DAO 3.6 Object Library. (You can use Microsoft DAO versions earlier than 3.6, if you don't have the 3.6 version.)**

7. **Click OK.**

   The dialog box closes, and VB adds this library to your project.

8. **Double-click Form1.**

   You see the VB code window.

9. **Move your cursor up (press and hold the up-arrow key) until you're at the very top of the code window and then press the Enter key to create a blank line.**

   The listboxes at the top of the code window say General Declarations.

10. **Type these two variable declarations into the General Declarations section of Form1:**

    ```
    Dim dbBIBI As Database
    Dim rsState As Recordset
    ```

11. **In the Form_Load event, type this code:**

    ```
    Private Sub Form_Load()

    Dim rsState As Recordset
    Set dbBIBI = OpenDatabase("C:\PROGRAM
            FILES\VB98\BIBI.MDB")

    SQLQuery = "SELECT * FROM Publishers WHERE State LIKE
            'Pa*'"

    Set rsState = dbBIBI.OpenRecordset(SQLQuery)

    Do Until rsState.EOF = True
    ```

(continued)

(continued)

```
      List1.AddItem rsState.Fields("State")
      rsState.MoveNext
Loop

Set rsState = Nothing

End Sub
```

In place of `C:\PROGRAM FILES\VB98\BIBI.MDB` in this code, substitute the path that leads to the BIBI.MDB database file on your hard drive.

12. Into the Command1_Click event, type this code:

```
Private Sub Command1_Click()

SQLAction = "UPDATE Publishers SET State = 'Pann' WHERE
        State = 'Pa'"

dbBIBI.Execute SQLAction

dbBIBI.Close
Set dbBIBI = Nothing
End Sub
```

13. Press F5.

The program runs, and you see that six records match the criterion — that is, their State field contains *Pa*, as shown in Figure 19-13.

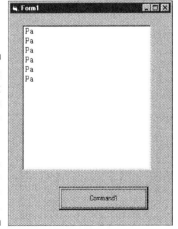

Figure 19-13:
These six *Pa* entries are about to be changed into *Pann* entries, thanks to an action query.

14. **Click the CommandButton.**

   You don't see it, but the action query is executed, and all six instances of *Pa* are changed in the database to *Pann*.

15. **Stop the program from running and then press F5 again to restart it.**

   You see that this time the ListBox contains the new *Pann* values instead. The change was made.

You can also use the UPDATE...SET clauses to perform calculations and adjust data in that way. Assume that a national surtax of 1 percent has been announced. It raises all the state taxes by 1 percent. You need to update the StateTax field in your database. Here's the code to do that:

```
Update tblOrders
SET StateTax = StateTax * 1.01
```

And if the new tax law is more complex, no problem. Assume that the 1 percent raise only applies if the state tax is less than 5 percent. With the WHERE clause, you can specify a subset on which you want to perform an action, like this:

```
Update tblOrders
SET StateTax = StateTax * 1.01
WHERE StateTax < 5
```

INSERT INTO: Adding a new record to a table

The INSERT INTO clause can copy records from one table to another table, or add a single new record to a table. The following example shows how to add a single record (with three fields) to an existing table:

```
INSERT INTO Authors(Author, [Year Born])
VALUES('Aadersen, Sven', 1899)
```

Note that the Year Born field requires brackets because it's two words, and the text value 'Aadersen, Sven' requires single quotes. The Year Born field is an ordinary numeric data type, but if it were a date data type, you'd have to surround 1899 with pound signs (#1899#).

To see a full-code example of how to add this record to the BIBLIO.MDB sample database, you can run the following code in VB. Put this code in the Form_Load event and then press F5 to run it:

```
Private Sub Form_Load()
Dim dbBIBLIO As Database
Set dbBIBLIO = OpenDatabase("C:\PROGRAM
        FILES\VB98\BIBLIO.MDB")
sqlaction = "INSERT INTO Authors(Author, [Year Born])
        VALUES('Aadersen, Sven', 1899)"
dbBIBLIO.Execute sqlaction
dbBIBLIO.Close
End Sub
```

After you run this code, delete it from the Form_Load event, and replace it
with the following code. Also, put a ListBox on Form1. When you run this
code, you'll see that the first record in your BIBLIO.MDB database is the new
one, Mr. Aadersen:

```
Private Sub Form_Load()
Dim dbBIBLIO As Database
Dim rsAuthor As Recordset

Set dbBIBLIO = OpenDatabase("C:\PROGRAM
        FILES\VB98\BIBLIO.MDB")

SQLQuery = "SELECT * FROM Authors WHERE Author LIKE 'a*'
        ORDER BY Author"

Set rsAuthor = dbBIBLIO.OpenRecordset(SQLQuery)

Do Until rsAuthor.EOF = True
    List1.AddItem rsAuthor.Fields("Author")
    rsAuthor.MoveNext
Loop

Set rsAuthor = Nothing

End Sub
```

INSERT INTO: Copying records into an existing table

To copy records from one table to another, use this syntax:

```
INSERT INTO tblNewTable
SELECT * FROM tblExistingTable
```

This code copies all the records from the ExistingTable into the NewTable. (Replace *tblNewTable* and *tblExistingTable* in the preceding example with the names of actual tables.) If you want to limit which records are copied, use the WHERE clause. In the following code, only records in which the Quantity field is greater than 2,000 are copied:

```
INSERT INTO tblNewTable
SELECT * FROM tblExistingTable
WHERE Quantity > 2000
```

For these two record-copying examples to work correctly, you must first create a table (tblNewTable) that has the same fields as the existing table from which you're copying.

SELECT INTO: Copying records into a newly-created table

To create a brand-new table and fill it with records from an existing table, use the SELECT INTO clause, which has the following syntax:

```
SELECT * INTO tblNewTable
FROM tblExistingTable
```

In this example, *tblNewTable* is created when the SQL executes.

Part VIII
The Part of Tens

In this part . . .

This part is called The Part of Tens, after a mystic ritual performed precisely once every 489 years on the island of Samnos, involving persimmons, green ribbons, three large fish, and a goat. You really don't want to know.

Actually, Part VIII is The Part of Tens because both chapters in this part have ten items in them. There are two chapters in this part. Got it?

Anyway, Chapter 20 tells you all about what I consider some of the better third-party add-ons available to extend Visual Basic's database programming capabilities. Chapter 21 truly resembles a basket of persimmons — it's a catch-all of items that I wanted to tell you about, but didn't find appropriate locations for in the rest of the book. You'll see lists of interesting Web sites, conferences you might want to attend, how to use VB's API Viewer utility, and, finally, what you can do with the mysterious *Wizard of Wizards*. As you see, everything comes back to wizards, in the end.

Chapter 20

Ten Outstanding Add-Ons

*I*n this chapter, you find what I consider some of the better products you can buy to enhance Visual Basic. Some are specialized database interfaces; others just solve general problems faced by VB programmers. In its own way, though, each can make your programming life easier.

For each described component, I include a Web site address where you'll usually find demo versions you can download, as well as the latest updates, price lists, and other products available from the same manufacturer.

 Some manufacturers of after-market, add-on commercial controls include simpler versions of their products in Visual Basic for free. For example, the MSFlexGrid control from VideoSoft is included with the Professional and Enterprise editions of Visual Basic. The commercial version, VSFlexGrid Pro, adds several enhancements to the version you get with VB.

DataDynamics' ActiveReports

ActiveReports, from DataDynamics, is a powerful, useful reporting tool. It includes an ActiveX designer that supports ODBC, OLE DB, ADO, and all the rest of the acronym soup that, collectively, make up Microsoft's database technology. It integrates smoothly into the VB IDE and permits you to include all kinds of data — even VB code and ActiveX components (a graph, for example) — in your reports. It also includes an effective Report wizard. ActiveReports is still in version 1.0 and has a few insignificant flaws, but it is well worth looking into if generating reports is part of your job description. This component is easy to use and very promising. Contact DataDynamics at www.datadynamics.com.

Leadtools Imaging

Leadtools Imaging is a feature-rich collection of imaging and graphics manipulation tools that you can add to your Visual Basic projects. Leadtools includes more than 600 functions, properties, and methods. For example, you get scanning support, color conversion, special effects, display, annotation, image processing (with more than 50 filters), image compression, extensive graphics format import/export filters, common dialogs, Internet/intranet imaging, database imaging, printing, OCR, multimedia, and FlashPix extension support. If you need to do *anything* with graphics, you'll probably find the necessary tools available in the Leadtools suite. Contact Leadtools at www.leadtools.com.

VideoSoft's VS-OCX

If you've ever written a Windows application in Visual Basic (or C++ or Delphi, for that matter), you know the nasty secret: Although these languages can make applications look great, they are *resolution dependent.* If you create a Visual Basic application in 800 x 600 resolution and then try to use it in 1,024 x 768 resolution, the forms and all the controls are tiny. Perhaps worse than that, resizing a Visual Basic application's window doesn't resize the controls on it. If you make the window smaller, the command buttons, text boxes, and other controls don't get smaller. They just get covered up. VS-OCX to the rescue. This excellent product automatically resizes all the controls on a form, makes forms resolution independent, and includes a couple of bonus components — among them a special tabs component and a parsing engine. You can contact VideoSoft at www.videosoft.com.

VSFlexGrid Pro from VideoSoft

If you connect a database to a Visual Basic project, you have plenty of uses for the VSFlexGrid Pro component. Many developers consider this component to be the best grid-style control. It behaves consistently and reliably. It's simultaneously powerful and lightweight (as well as being fast and completely dependency-free, so you won't have DLL versioning problems down the road). The component supports ADO 2.0, OLE DB, and DAO; includes data input masking; is fully data bound with read/write capability; has Outlook-style sorting and Excel-compatible tab- and comma-delimited text files; has automatic auditing to track changes in data; and has in-cell editing and many additional useful features. VSFlexGrid Pro supports up to 2 billion database rows, which should be enough. Contact VideoSoft at www.videosoft.com.

VSSpell from VideoSoft

If you want to add spell-checking or thesaurus features to your Visual Basic applications, you need VSSpell. Containing more than 50,000 entries, the VSSpell spelling engine component can generate custom dictionaries and is also compatible with dictionaries created by Microsoft Word. The thesaurus component comes with more than 30,000 entries and it permits you to create and manage custom thesaurus files. (An alternative approach — using OLE Automation to employ Microsoft Word's Spell Checker or Thesaurus — has the disadvantage of requiring that you have Microsoft Office installed.) Contact VideoSoft at www.videosoft.com.

VSData from VideoSoft

VSData is described as "a complete database engine in one ActiveX" control. Videosoft offers this engine as the best solution if you want to use databases with Internet or multimedia applications. The component includes such features as indexing on multiple fields, record locking, and the ability to save video, hyperlink, or sound files into native database fields. Contact VideoSoft at www.videosoft.com.

Desaware's ActiveX Gallimaufry Controls

Desaware calls its ActiveX Gallimaufry controls an eclectic collection of controls, which is true. For Visual Basic, these components even include their own source code so you can see how they were constructed (which can be a great way to learn how to build your own components and also enables you to modify the ActiveX Gallimaufry controls themselves). The components include an animated banner, a common dialog, a Multiple Document Interface taskbar, a cool *perspective list* component (which enables you to display text animated to look like the credits in *Star Wars*), and more. Contact Desaware at www.desaware.com.

SpyWorks from Desaware

Have you ever had C++ envy? I haven't. I've been able to do anything I want to do in Visual Basic. But if you want to go down to lower-level programming than the typical Visual Basic developer gets into, you might want to try SpyWorks. Desaware calls it the "ultimate 'you CAN do it in VB' low-level programming toolkit," and that's a good description. You can use the tools in this package to intercept Windows messages globally, create custom interfaces for your components, and use subclassing and export DLL functions. Contact Desaware at www.desaware.com.

Sheridan DataWidgets

Sheridan says, "Data Widgets 3 virtually eliminates the need for time-consuming coding when developing applications involving database operations." The DataWidgets collection includes six ActiveX controls designed to replace their namesake native VB controls: SSDBGrid, SSDataCombo, SSDBDropDown, SSDataOptSet (Option Buttons), SSDBData (the Data Control), and SSDBCommand. The latest version includes support for ADO, and you can export to HTML, print, custom format, and mask data (validate user input). Contact Sheridan at www.shersoft.com.

Crescent's QuickPak VB/J++

The QuickPak set of programming tools has been popular for many years. Visual Basic programmers have relied on its many tested functions and enhancements to the look of the user interface to amplify their own programming abilities. Now, QuickPak VB/J++ embraces J++ in addition to Visual Basic. It contains a collection of ActiveX components and features, including improved array manipulation methods, access to an undocumented API for accessing the low-level Internet Core Messaging Protocol, memory and utility productivity enhancing routines, functions that manage Microsoft's Internet Information Server and Personal/Peer Web Server, file management, and functions that can PING a TCP/IP server. Contact Crescent at crescent.progress.com.

Chapter 21

Ten Topics that Don't Fit Elsewhere in the Book (But Are Important)

○ ○

In This Chapter

▶ Keeping current via the Internet
▶ Getting the latest VB updates
▶ Finding out what's next in database technology
▶ Visiting VB Web sites
▶ Creating your own wizards
▶ Using the Application Wizard
▶ Visiting a technical conference
▶ Checking out some useful magazines
▶ Simplifying API calls with the API viewer
▶ Programming with objects

○ ○

Don't take the title of this chapter as a confession of disorganization and confusion when I planned this book. No. It merely represents some ideas and resources I think you should know about, even though they don't comfortably fit within other chapters. Take a look at all the other chapters and you'll see that the book is not chaotic or, as your grandmother might say, higgledy-piggledy. No. It's a model of method and logic.

So, glance at the headings in this chapter and see if some of these subjects interest you. I think you'll find a few topics here worthy of your inspection.

Getting All the Latest News

Microsoft maintains a Web site, and multiple newsgroups, devoted to the latest database topics. You may want to visit the Web site, at the following address: www.microsoft.com/data.

Or, try these newsgroups for Q & A:

- ✔ `Microsoft.Public.ADO`: Microsoft's Active Data Objects newsgroup

- ✔ `Microsoft.Public.VB.Database`: The main Microsoft VB database discussion group

- ✔ `Microsoft.Public.VB.Database.ODBC`: The newsgroup devoted to Open Database Connectivity issues

- ✔ `Microsoft.Public.DAO`: All about Data Access Objects

- ✔ `Microsoft.Public.RDO`: Discussion of Remote Data Objects

Keeping Visual Basic Healthy

Microsoft's Visual Basic support sites contain information and, in particular, occasional updates ("service packs") that fix bugs. You'll want to check these sites on a regular basis:

- ✔ `msdn.microsoft.com/vstudio/sp/vbfixes.asp`: Updates and bug fixes for VB and other Visual Studio components

- ✔ `msdn.microsoft.com/vbasic`: The main Microsoft VB home page

- ✔ `msdn.microsoft.com/vbasic/downloads/controls.asp`: Freebies from Microsoft you can download

- ✔ `msdn.microsoft.com/vbasic/downloads/resguide/default.asp`: Third-party add-ons you might find useful

If you haven't already, be sure to check out the first site and download Service Pack 3.

Discovering Microsoft's Plans for the Future of Database Technology

If you want to find out the latest information about ADO, OLE DB, and UDA (Microsoft's initiatives for universal data access), take a look at these sites:

- ✔ `www.microsoft.com/data/oledb/default.htm`
- ✔ `www.microsoft.com/data/ado/default.htm`
- ✔ `www.microsoft.com/data/odbc/default.htm`

Or, if you want to see some lively discussions on cutting-edge database issues, try these newsgroups:

- ✔ Microsoft.Public.VB.Database.ADO
- ✔ Microsoft.Public.OLEDB
- ✔ Microsoft.Public.ADO.RDS
- ✔ Microsoft.Public.ADO

Visiting Other Web Sites of Interest

The leading site for information of VB programming is, as you might expect, hosted by Microsoft: msdn.microsoft.com/default.asp.

One of the more active sources of useful VB information is Fawcette Publications, publisher of *Visual Basic Programmer's Journal.* Find Fawcette's latest news at www.fawcette.com.

Also, be sure to visit the following sites:

- ✔ www.devx.com: This site is also produced by Fawcette, and contains considerable information of value to Visual Basic programmers.
- ✔ www.zdjournals.com/ivb/: Inside Visual Basic, from Ziff-Davis.
- ✔ www.pinpub.com/vbd/home.htm: Visual Basic Developer, from Pinnacle.

You can also find quite a few good links to sites involving VB programming at dmoz.org/Computers/Programming/Languages/Visual_Basic.

Using the Wizard of Wizards

You've probably used some of the many wizards available in Visual Basic, and you're probably quite grateful they're there. Wizards can save lots of time and do a good deal of programming that you, otherwise, would have to do.

But what if you want to write your *own* wizard? Does a wizard exist that can help you create a new wizard? In other words, does a *MetaWizard* exist?

What? What's the point of writing a wizard? Well, perhaps you're in charge of a group of workers. They have to do some programming or designing using Visual Basic, and they have to do that task repeatedly. You want to write your own wizard to step your staff through that job to make life easier for them. Or, you may even want to create wizards to assist in tasks that you yourself frequently perform.

Does a wizard exist that helps you to create your own wizards? You bet it does! You still have to write the underlying programming to make your wizard do its thing, of course, but the Wizard wizard (Microsoft calls it the Wizard Manager) does a lot of the dirty work for you. The Wizard wizard creates the sequential forms, the Next buttons, and all the other elements that any wizard contains. In other words, your wizard looks and behaves like the wizards from Microsoft.

To start the Wizard wizard (my name for the Wizard Manager):

1. **Start Visual Basic.**

   The New Project dialog box appears. (If the New Project dialog box doesn't open, choose File⇨New Project.)

2. **Double-click the VB Wizard Manager icon in the New Project dialog box.**

   A message notifies you that a wizard form wasn't found. The message asks whether you want to create a new wizard project.

3. **Click Yes.**

   The Wizard Manager message box closes, and a Save New Wizard As dialog box opens.

4. **Click Save.**

   The dialog box closes, and VB saves your wizard project to the hard drive using the default filename: MyWizard.Vbp. The Wizard Manager window appears, and the wizard template files are listed in the Project Explorer.

5. **Now you can compose the various pages of your wizard to lead others through a task step-by-step.**

Creating Instant Windows Programs

Visual Basic includes a special wizard that helps you get a Windows application quickly sketched in (and then you later fill in the programming that makes it do some useful job). This wizard, called the VB Application wizard, helps you create applications that have a family resemblance — that share the traditional Windows user-interface design, such as gunmetal gray backgrounds. The wizard also jump-starts beginners, giving them a useful template to customize.

To try the VB Application wizard, follow these steps:

1. **Start Visual Basic by clicking its icon on your desktop.**

   The New Project dialog box opens. If it doesn't open, choose File⇨ New Project.

2. **Double-click the VB Application Wizard icon in the New Project dialog box.**

   The first page of the wizard appears.

3. **Click Next.**

   Visual Basic asks what kind of interface you want — Multiple (like a word processor window that can hold smaller windows) or Single (only one window, with no child windows inside it). A third option is the Explorer-style window (like Windows Explorer and Internet Explorer).

4. **Click Single Document Interface (SDI).**

5. **Click Next.**

   The menus page appears. Choose whatever menus you want to include in your application.

6. **Click Next.**

   The Toolbar page appears. Here, you specify which standard Toolbar options you want to make available to your application's users. Usually, these options include such commands as Save, Copy, Bold, and Italic — the contents of the Standard toolbar in most Microsoft applications.

7. **Click Next twice.**

   You've skipped the Resources page (for foreign language applications) and are at the Internet Connectivity page. The Internet Connectivity page enables users of your applications to easily go online. Offering this gateway is wise. People today like to be able to access the Internet from practically *anywhere* in their computer, including your application.

8. **Click Next.**

   You can choose to add a template or four traditional features to your application on this page:

   - **Splash Screen:** A graphic or logo that is displayed when your application is first started.

   - **ID and password window:** Filters who gets into your application.

   - **Options dialog box:** Enables users to customize your application.

   - **Standard Windows About message box:** The box that's displayed if users choose Help➪About.

9. **Click Next.**

   You're now offered the option of attaching a database to your application.

10. **Click Next, and then click Finish.**

    A warning message box appears, telling you that creating your new application could take a few minutes.

11. **Click OK.**

    Visual Basic rapidly builds your application template to your specifications.

    Another message box appears, telling you that Visual Basic has created the application. This is fairly redundant information, so you might want to click the check box labeled Don't Show This Dialog In The Future.

12. **Click OK.**

    You see your template, in all its glory, ready for you to add the programming that will make the buttons, menus, and other features actually do their jobs.

Attending Technical Conferences

Usually held annually, Microsoft's Professional Developers Conference (PDC) and TechEd are excellent conferences if you want to learn how to build the latest applications using the latest tools and technologies. Find out about them at microsoft.com/events.

Check out this site for information on VBITS, the Visual Basic Insiders' Technical Summit: www.windx.com. The conference sponsors describe it as "the leading international conference for professional Windows programmers. You'll join the core of the Visual Basic development community as we discover new and better ways to use VB and related technologies."

If you work more with VBA and Microsoft Office programming, consider Microsoft Office and VBA Solutions (MOVS) Conference & Expo. It's described as "nearly 600 software developers, speakers, and third-party independent software vendors. . . .The features in Office 2000 as well as the latest in VBA technology were just some of the highlights of MOVS '99." For more on these conferences, see the Web site at this address: www.informant.com/mod.

Checking Out Journals and Periodicals

Several publishers put out journals covering the applications and technologies in Visual Studio 6. These magazines and newsletters provide up-to-date advice, source code examples, tutorials, and other aids for the harried developer:

  ✔ The Cobb Group (www.zdjournals.com/publicat.htm) publishes a variety of monthlies.

✔ Pinnacle Publishing (www.pinpub.com/home.htm) is another good source of monthlies.

✔ Fawcette Technical Publications(www.windx.com) has a particularly useful site that is updated frequently.

Using the New API Viewer

If you use API calls in your VB programs, you'll be happy to know that Visual Basic 6 includes a handy little utility. API, Application Programmers Interface, is a collection of all the procedures that drive Windows. You can do many things with the API that you can't in plain VB, but you can use the API from within VB. Books exist on this subject, if you're interested. Take a look at *Windows 98 API Programming For Dummies Quick Reference* (IDG Books Worldwide) or *Visual Basic Programmer's Guide to the Windows API* (Ziff-Davis).

New in VB6 is the API Viewer, which prevents the single biggest source of problems when making an API call: typos. It's sooooo easy to goof up the procedure declarations, yet they must be exactly correct or the API call won't work. Here's how to bring up the API Viewer:

1. **Choose Add-Ins⇨Add-In Manager.**

   The Add-In Manager dialog box appears.

2. **Double-click VB 6 API Viewer.**

   The Viewer is loaded.

3. **Click OK.**

   The dialog box closes.

4. **Choose Add-Ins⇨API Viewer.**

   The API Viewer opens.

5. **In the API Viewer, choose File⇨Load Text File.**

   A file browser dialog box appears, displaying the Winapi folder.

6. **Double-click WIN32API.TXT in the dialog box.**

   The dialog box closes, and the 32-bit version of the API is loaded into the Viewer.

    If WIN32API.TXT isn't visible in the dialog box, use Start⇨Find to locate it.

7. **Type in the first few letters of the API call you're interested in.**

   The API call appears in the Available Items list, as shown in Figure 21-1.

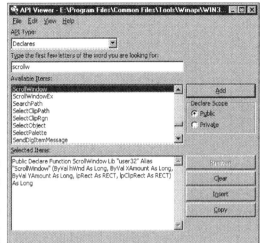

Figure 21-1:
Use this API
viewer to
avoid typos.

8. **Double-click the API call you want to use.**

   Its entire parameter list is added to the Selected Items list.

9. **Click Insert.**

   A message box appears, asking you if you want to add this code to Form1.

10. **Click Yes.**

    The message box closes, and the code is inserted into Form1.

Figuring Out Syntax When Using Objects

Have you ever had problems trying to deal with the exact, correct syntax when working with an object?

Is it `object.fields(0).value` or is it `object.fields("named").value`?

The *Component Object Model* (COM) is a Microsoft implementation of object-oriented programming. If you've worked with Visual Basic, you've already used objects (the Toolbox is full of objects, such as the TextBox). Perhaps you've even created some objects of your own in the form of UserControls, or you may have done some programming involving creating classes. The database libraries such as DAO or ADO are also filled with objects, like the *recordset* object.

To whatever extent you're acquainted with objects in a general sense, each new object presents you with a new challenge: You must learn its particulars. When you work with an object, you have to figure out what *members* it has. Members are the events, methods, and properties of an object (also called the object's *interface*).

What properties does it have (color, fontsize)? What events are triggered in it (click, keypress)? What methods can it perform (addition, moving itself to a new position on-screen)? And, most important, *what is the syntax for using those members?*

The members are called the *interface* because you, the programmer, are allowed to mess around with them. They are exposed to you, for your use.

But what is the *syntax*? Many, many programmers have wasted many, many hours trying out variations on the syntax of objects' members to see if they can get the darn things working. Documentation and examples should be a required component of every object. All too often, it's hard to figure out what, precisely, the interface requires in an actual program.

Assume that you're trying to figure out how to work with the Count property of the Fields object. Your first step can be to press F2. This action brings up the VB Object Browser. Then, you click one of the items in the left pane titled *Classes*. The members of the object you clicked are then displayed in the right pane. Click one of them, and you see some information in the bottom pane, as shown in Figure 21-2.

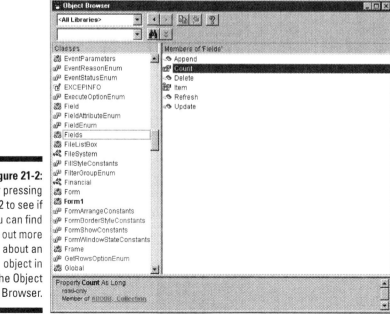

Figure 21-2:
Try pressing
F2 to see if
you can find
out more
about an
object in
the Object
Browser.

TIP

If you don't see the Fields object in the Classes list, choose Project⇨References and then double-click the Microsoft ActiveX Data Objects 2.0 (or 2.5) Object Library.

Unfortunately, the Object Browser is rarely of much real programming help. You want to see an example of an object's programming syntax. Perhaps as time goes by, this browser will offer more information. However, the Object Browser is a good way to quickly see all the members available for any given object. Anyway, your next step is to click the ? icon at the top of the Object Browser.

VB's Help engine fires up, and you get more information, sometimes including an example hyperlink at the top of the window, as shown in Figure 21-3.

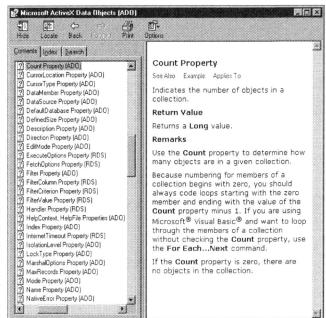

Figure 21-3:
This help is fairly helpful, but you'll want to click the Example hyperlink at the top of the window.

After you get a help screen like the one shown in Figure 21-3, you're almost home. The Example hyperlink takes you, at long last, to the syntax you need to work with the Count property of the Fields object:

```
rstEmployees.Fields.Count
```

Index

• V •

• W •

FOR DUMMIES®

A world of resources to help you grow

HOME, GARDEN & HOBBIES

0-7645-5295-3

0-7645-5130-2

0-7645-5106-X

Also available:

Auto Repair For Dummies
(0-7645-5089-6)

Chess For Dummies
(0-7645-5003-9)

Home Maintenance For
Dummies
(0-7645-5215-5)

Organizing For Dummies
(0-7645-5300-3)

Piano For Dummies
(0-7645-5105-1)

Poker For Dummies
(0-7645-5232-5)

Quilting For Dummies
(0-7645-5118-3)

Rock Guitar For Dummies
(0-7645-5356-9)

Roses For Dummies
(0-7645-5202-3)

Sewing For Dummies
(0-7645-5137-X)

FOOD & WINE

0-7645-5250-3

0-7645-5390-9

0-7645-5114-0

Also available:

Bartending For Dummies
(0-7645-5051-9)

Chinese Cooking For
Dummies
(0-7645-5247-3)

Christmas Cooking For
Dummies
(0-7645-5407-7)

Diabetes Cookbook For
Dummies
(0-7645-5230-9)

Grilling For Dummies
(0-7645-5076-4)

Low-Fat Cooking For
Dummies
(0-7645-5035-7)

Slow Cookers For Dummies
(0-7645-5240-6)

TRAVEL

0-7645-5453-0

0-7645-5438-7

0-7645-5448-4

Also available:

America's National Parks For
Dummies
(0-7645-6204-5)

Caribbean For Dummies
(0-7645-5445-X)

Cruise Vacations For
Dummies 2003
(0-7645-5459-X)

Europe For Dummies
(0-7645-5456-5)

Ireland For Dummies
(0-7645-6199-5)

France For Dummies
(0-7645-6292-4)

London For Dummies
(0-7645-5416-6)

Mexico's Beach Resorts For
Dummies
(0-7645-6262-2)

Paris For Dummies
(0-7645-5494-8)

RV Vacations For Dummies
(0-7645-5443-3)

Walt Disney World & Orlando
For Dummies
(0-7645-5444-1)

Available wherever books are sold. Go to www.dummies.com or call 1-877-762-2974 to order direct.

FOR DUMMIES®

Helping you expand your horizons and realize your potential

INTERNET

0-7645-0894-6

0-7645-1659-0

0-7645-1642-6

DIGITAL MEDIA

0-7645-1664-7

0-7645-1675-2

0-7645-0806-7

GRAPHICS

0-7645-0817-2

0-7645-1651-5

0-7645-0895-4

FOR DUMMIES®

The advice and explanations you need to succeed

FOR DUMMIES®

We take the mystery out of complicated subjects

WEB DEVELOPMENT

0-7645-1643-4

0-7645-0723-0

0-7645-1630-2

Also available:

ASP.NET For Dummies
(0-7645-0866-0)

Building a Web Site For
Dummies
(0-7645-0720-6)

ColdFusion "MX" For
Dummies (0-7645-1672-8)

Creating Web Pages
All-in-One Desk Reference For
Dummies
(0-7645-1542-X)

FrontPage 2002 For Dummies
(0-7645-0821-0)

HTML 4 For Dummies Quick
Reference
(0-7645-0721-4)

Macromedia Studio "MX"
All-in-One Desk Reference For
Dummies
(0-7645-1799-6)

Web Design For Dummies
(0-7645-0823-7)

PROGRAMMING & DATABASES

0-7645-0746-X

0-7645-1657-4

0-7645-0818-0

Also available:

Beginning Programming For
Dummies
(0-7645-0835-0)

Crystal Reports "X"
For Dummies
(0-7645-1641-8)

Java & XML For Dummies
(0-7645-1658-2)

Java 2 For Dummies
(0-7645-0765-6)

JavaScript For Dummies
(0-7645-0633-1)

Oracle9i For Dummies
(0-7645-0880-6)

Perl For Dummies
(0-7645-0776-1)

PHP and MySQL For
Dummies
(0-7645-1650-7)

SQL For Dummies
(0-7645-0737-0)

VisualBasic .NET For Dummies
(0-7645-0867-9)

Visual Studio .NET All-in-One
Desk Reference For Dummies
(0-7645-1626-4)

LINUX, NETWORKING & CERTIFICATION

0-7645-1545-4

0-7645-0772-9

0-7645-0812-1

Also available:

CCNP All-in-One Certification
For Dummies
(0-7645-1648-5)

Cisco Networking For
Dummies
(0-7645-1668-X)

CISSP For Dummies
(0-7645-1670-1)

CIW Foundations For
Dummies with CD-ROM
(0-7645-1635-3)

Firewalls For Dummies
(0-7645-0884-9)

Home Networking For
Dummies
(0-7645-0857-1)

Red Hat Linux All-in-One
Desk Reference For Dummies
(0-7645-2442-9)

TCP/IP For Dummies
(0-7645-1760-0)

UNIX For Dummies
(0-7645-0419-3)

Available wherever books are sold.

Go to www.dummies.com or call 1-877-762-2974 to order direct.

Notes

Notes

Notes

Notes

Notes

Notes